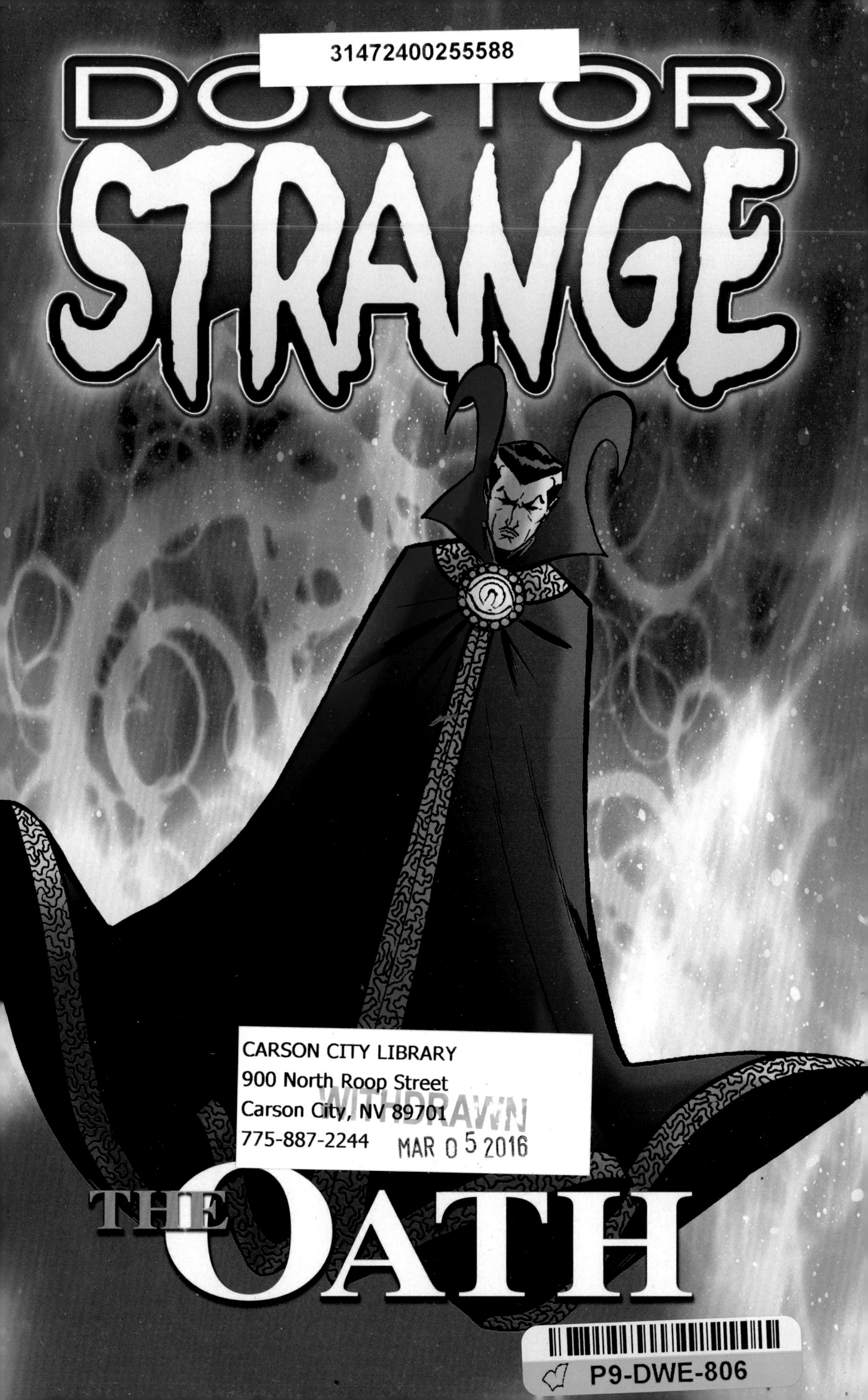
DOCTOR STRANGE
THE OATH

DOCTOR STRANGE

THE OATH

WRITER: BRIAN K. VAUGHAN
ART: MARCOS MARTIN

INKS, ISSUE #1: ALVARO LOPEZ
COLORS: JAVIER RODRIGUEZ
LETTERS: WILLIE SCHUBERT
ASSISTANT EDITORS: MOLLY LAZER & AUBREY SITTERSON
EDITOR: TOM BREVOORT

COLLECTION EDITOR: JENNIFER GRÜNWALD
ASSISTANT EDITOR: SARAH BRUNSTAD
ASSOCIATE MANAGING EDITOR: ALEX STARBUCK
EDITOR, SPECIAL PROJECTS: MARK D. BEAZLEY
SENIOR EDITOR, SPECIAL PROJECTS: JEFF YOUNGQUIST
SVP PRINT, SALES & MARKETING: DAVID GABRIEL
BOOK DESIGNER: PATRICK MCGRATH

EDITOR IN CHIEF: AXEL ALONSO
CHIEF CREATIVE OFFICER: JOE QUESADA
PUBLISHER: DAN BUCKLEY
EXECUTIVE PRODUCER: ALAN FINE

DOCTOR STRANGE: THE OATH. Contains material originally published in magazine form as DOCTOR STRANGE: THE OATH #1-5. Second edition. Second printing 2014. ISBN# 978-0-7851-8786-8. Published by MARVEL WORLDWIDE, INC., a subsidiary of MARVEL ENTERTAINMENT, LLC. OFFICE OF PUBLICATION: 135 West 50th Street, New York, NY 10020. **Printed in Canada.** ALAN FINE, EVP - Office of the President, Marvel Worldwide, Inc. and EVP & CMO Marvel Characters B.V.; DAN BUCKLEY, Publisher & President - Print, Animation & Digital Divisions; JOE QUESADA, Chief Creative Officer; TOM BREVOORT, SVP of Publishing; DAVID BOGART, SVP of Operations & Procurement, Publishing; C.B. CEBULSKI, SVP of Creator & Content Development; DAVID GABRIEL, SVP Print, Sales & Marketing; JIM O'KEEFE, VP of Operations & Logistics; DAN CARR, Executive Director of Publishing Technology; SUSAN CRESPI, Editorial Operations Manager; ALEX MORALES, Publishing Operations Manager; STAN LEE, Chairman Emeritus. For information regarding advertising in Marvel Comics or on Marvel.com, please contact Niza Disla, Director of Marvel Partnerships, at ndisla@marvel.com. For Marvel subscription inquiries, please call 800-217-9158. **Manufactured between 1/21/2015 and 2/23/15 by SOLISCO PRINTERS, SCOTT, QC, CANADA.**

10 9 8 7 6 5 4 3 2

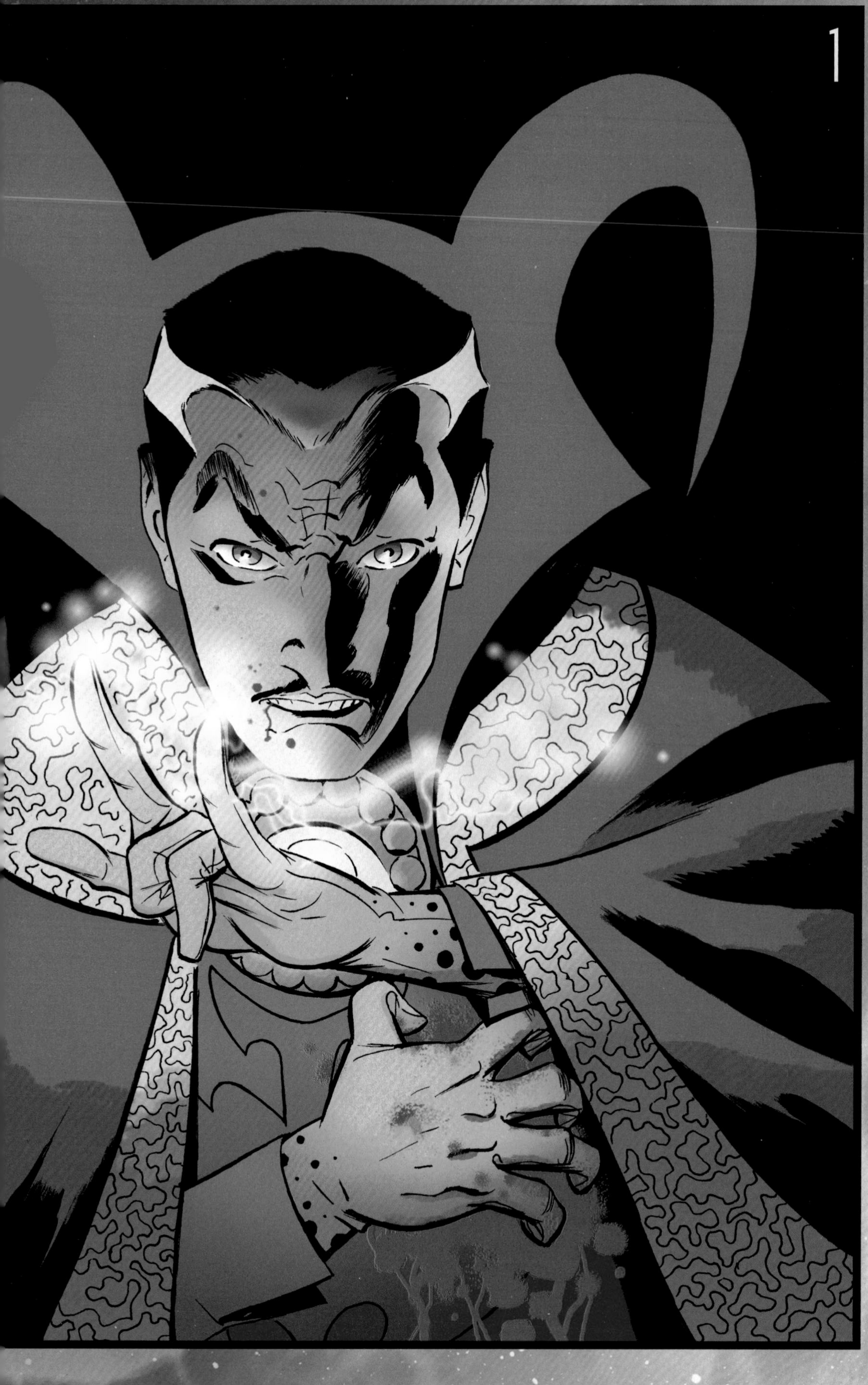
1

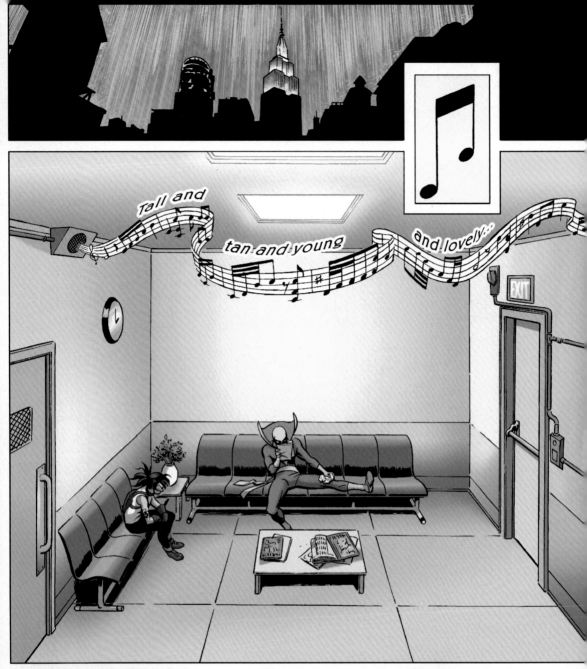

Tall and tan and young and lovely...

UM...

YES, I'M IRON FIST. NO, I DON'T KNOW WHERE POWER MAN IS.

WE'RE PARTNERS, NOT A *COUPLE.*

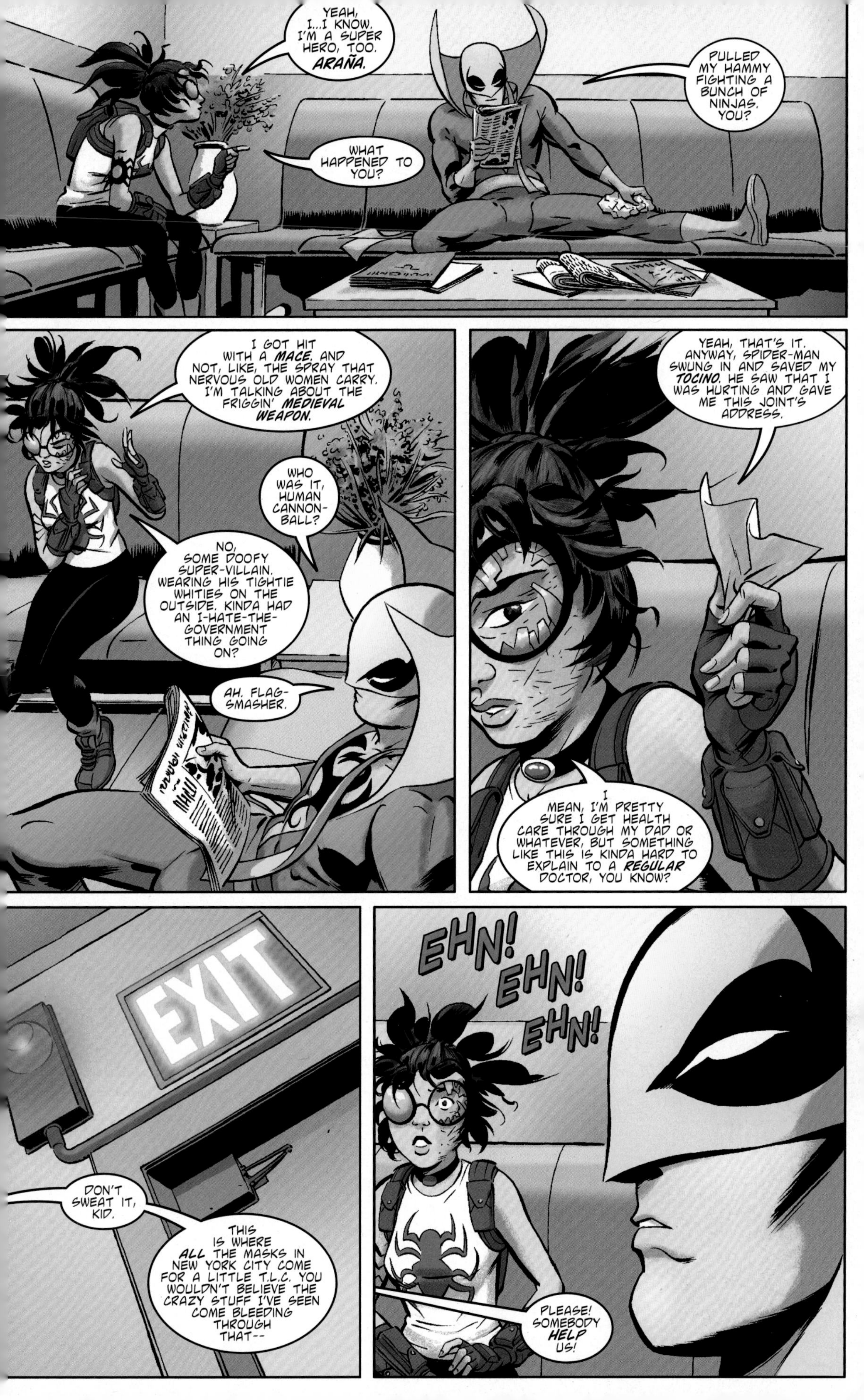
YEAH, I...I KNOW. I'M A SUPER HERO, TOO. ARAÑA.
PULLED MY HAMMY FIGHTING A BUNCH OF NINJAS. YOU?
WHAT HAPPENED TO YOU?
I GOT HIT WITH A MACE. AND NOT, LIKE, THE SPRAY THAT NERVOUS OLD WOMEN CARRY. I'M TALKING ABOUT THE FRIGGIN' MEDIEVAL WEAPON.
WHO WAS IT, HUMAN CANNON-BALL?
NO, SOME DOOFY SUPER-VILLAIN. WEARING HIS TIGHTIE WHITIES ON THE OUTSIDE. KINDA HAD AN I-HATE-THE-GOVERNMENT THING GOING ON?
AH. FLAG-SMASHER.
YEAH, THAT'S IT. ANYWAY, SPIDER-MAN SWUNG IN AND SAVED MY TOCINO. HE SAW THAT I WAS HURTING AND GAVE ME THIS JOINT'S ADDRESS.
I MEAN, I'M PRETTY SURE I GET HEALTH CARE THROUGH MY DAD OR WHATEVER, BUT SOMETHING LIKE THIS IS KINDA HARD TO EXPLAIN TO A REGULAR DOCTOR, YOU KNOW?
EXIT
DON'T SWEAT IT, KID.
THIS IS WHERE ALL THE MASKS IN NEW YORK CITY COME FOR A LITTLE T.L.C. YOU WOULDN'T BELIEVE THE CRAZY STUFF I'VE SEEN COME BLEEDING THROUGH THAT--
EHN! EHN! EHN!
PLEASE! SOMEBODY HELP US!

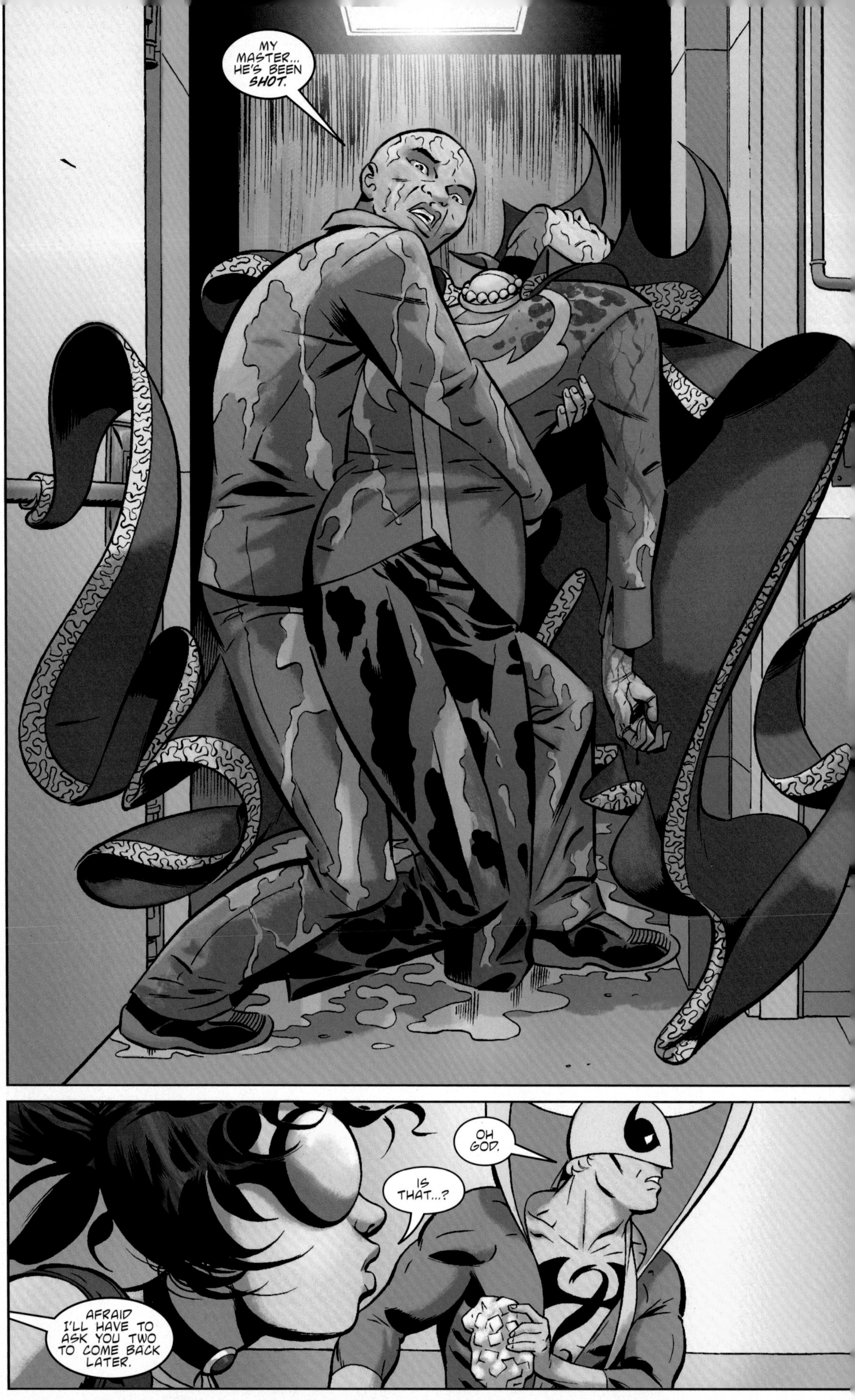
MY MASTER... HE'S BEEN SHOT.
OH GOD.
IS THAT...?
AFRAID I'LL HAVE TO ASK YOU TWO TO COME BACK LATER.

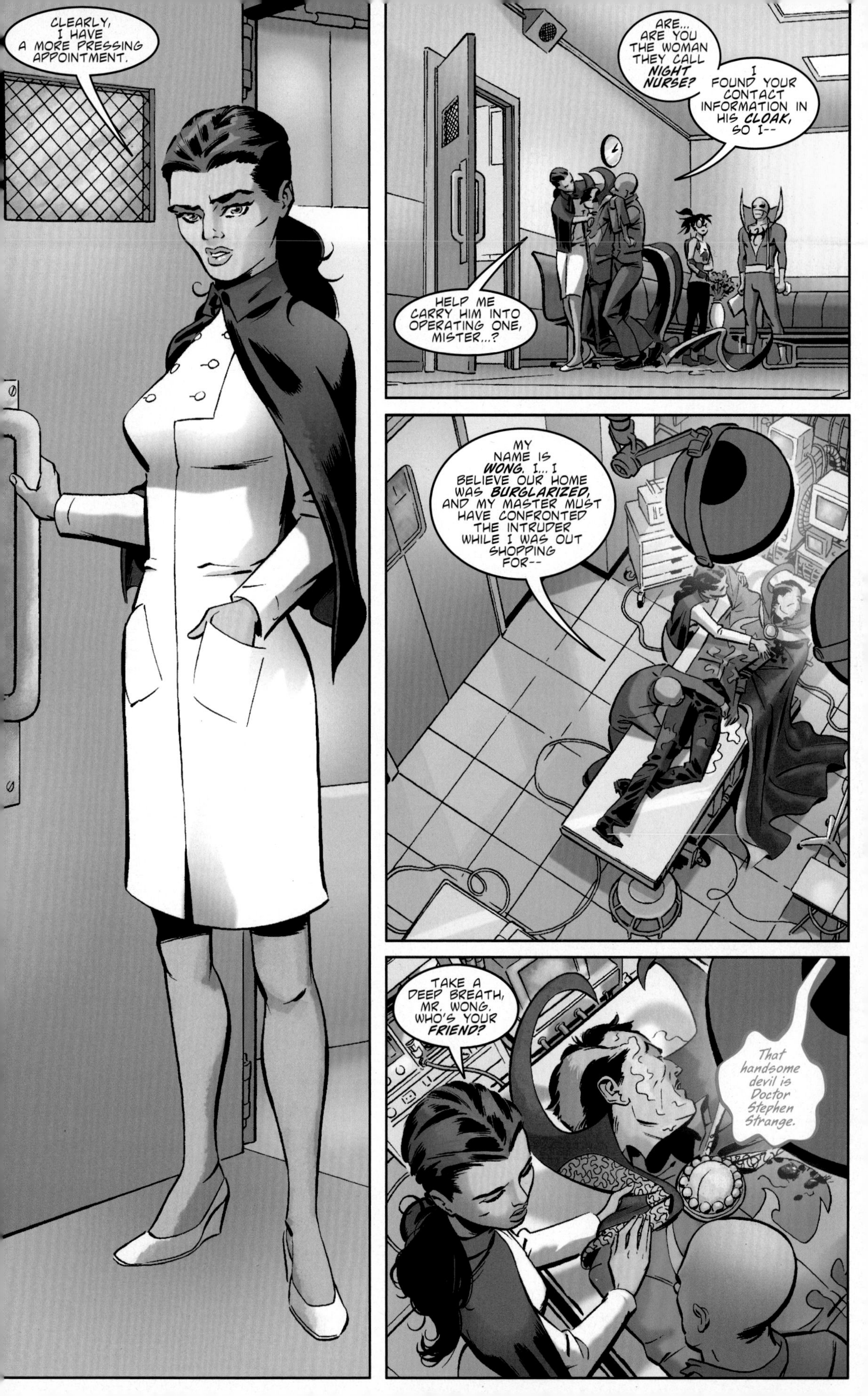
CLEARLY, I HAVE A MORE PRESSING APPOINTMENT.
ARE... ARE YOU THE WOMAN THEY CALL NIGHT NURSE?
I FOUND YOUR CONTACT INFORMATION IN HIS CLOAK, SO I--
HELP ME CARRY HIM INTO OPERATING ONE, MISTER...?
MY NAME IS WONG. I... I BELIEVE OUR HOME WAS BURGLARIZED, AND MY MASTER MUST HAVE CONFRONTED THE INTRUDER WHILE I WAS OUT SHOPPING FOR--
TAKE A DEEP BREATH, MR. WONG. WHO'S YOUR FRIEND?
That handsome devil is Doctor Stephen Strange.

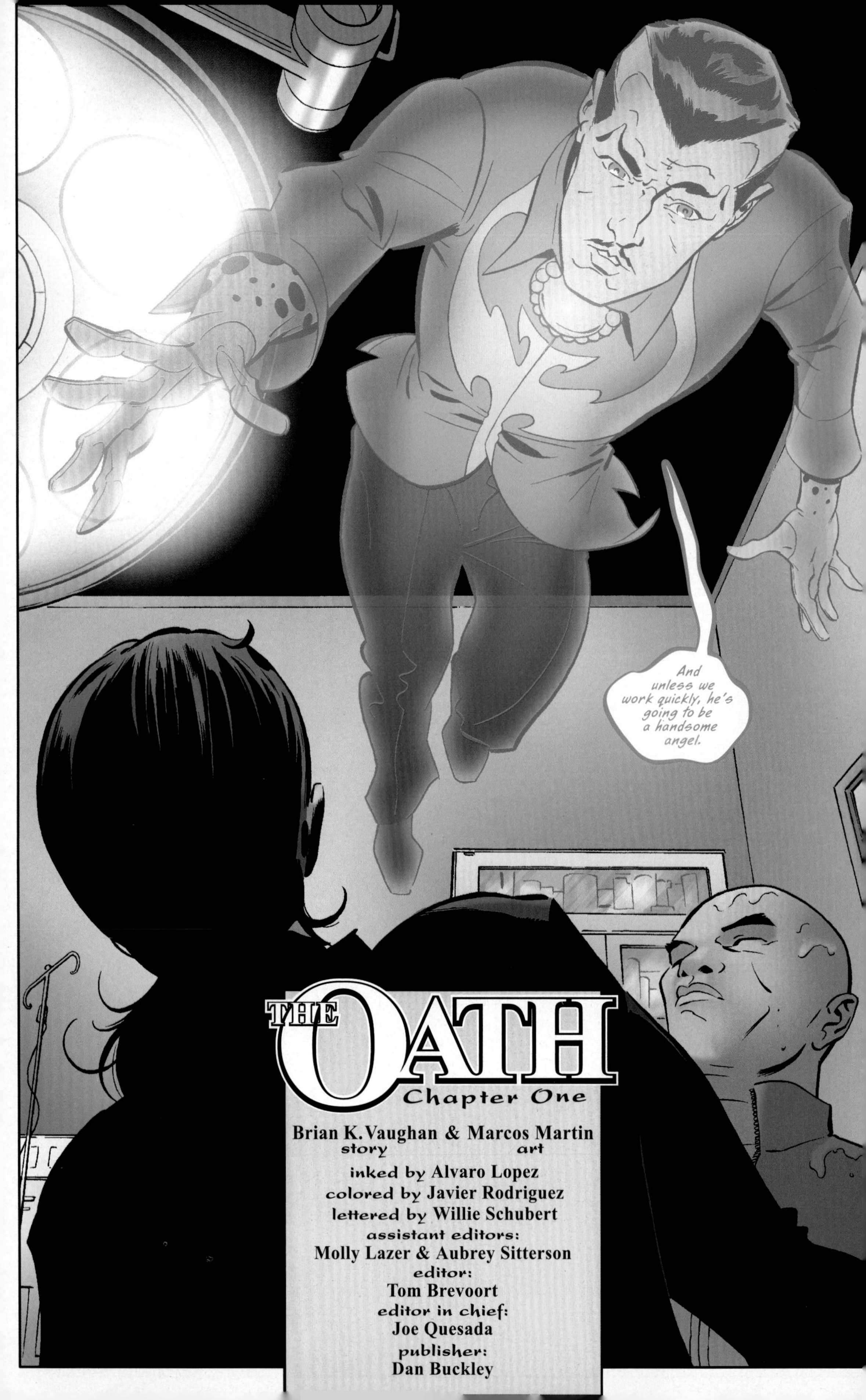
And unless we work quickly, he's going to be a handsome angel.
THE OATH
Chapter One
Brian K. Vaughan & Marcos Martin
story art
inked by Alvaro Lopez
colored by Javier Rodriguez
lettered by Willie Schubert
assistant editors:
Molly Lazer & Aubrey Sitterson
editor:
Tom Brevoort
editor in chief:
Joe Quesada
publisher:
Dan Buckley

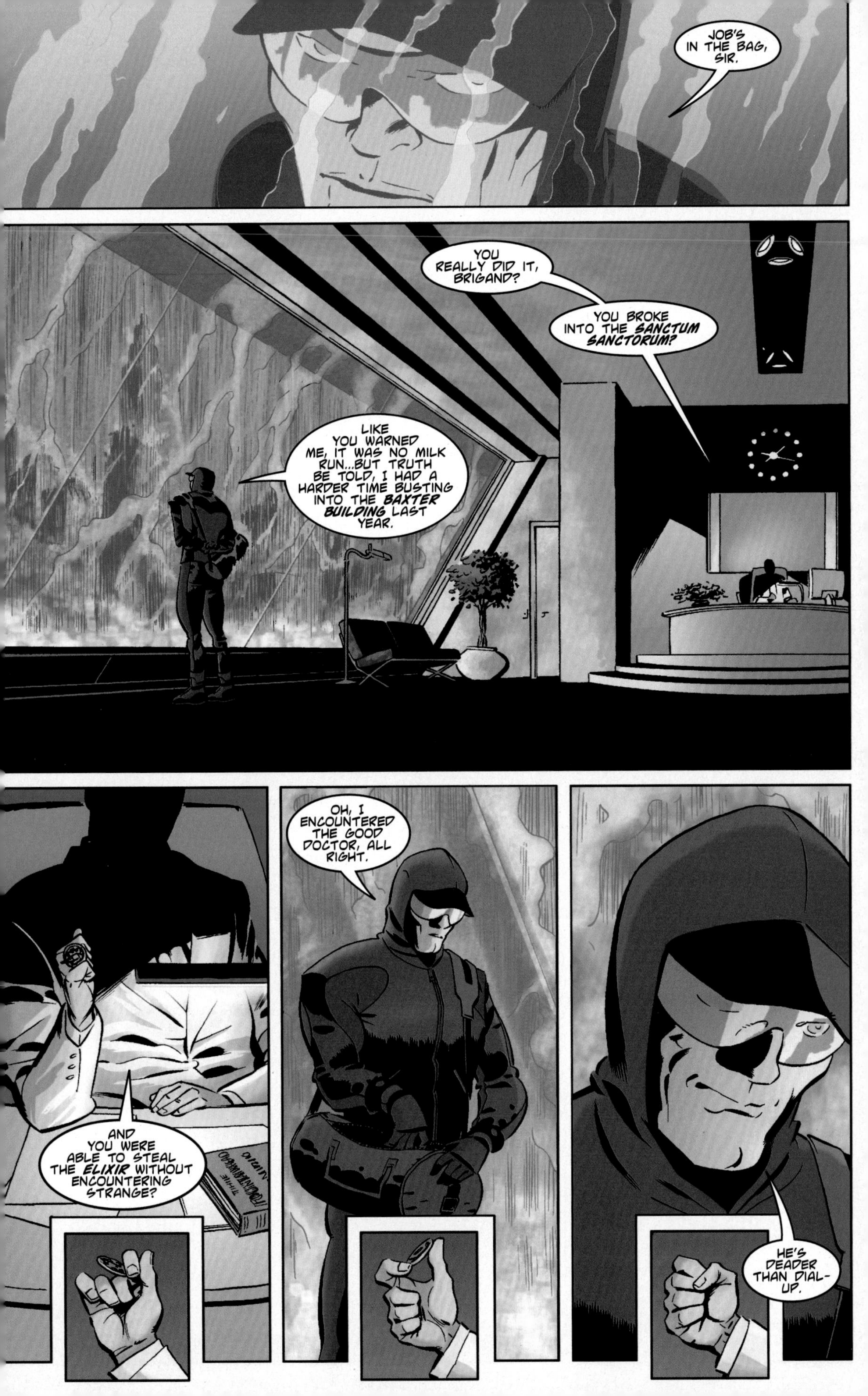
JOB'S IN THE BAG, SIR.
YOU REALLY DID IT, BRIGAND?
YOU BROKE INTO THE SANCTUM SANCTORUM?
LIKE YOU WARNED ME, IT WAS NO MILK RUN...BUT TRUTH BE TOLD, I HAD A HARDER TIME BUSTING INTO THE BAXTER BUILDING LAST YEAR.
AND YOU WERE ABLE TO STEAL THE ELIXIR WITHOUT ENCOUNTERING STRANGE?
OH, I ENCOUNTERED THE GOOD DOCTOR, ALL RIGHT.
HE'S DEADER THAN DIAL-UP.

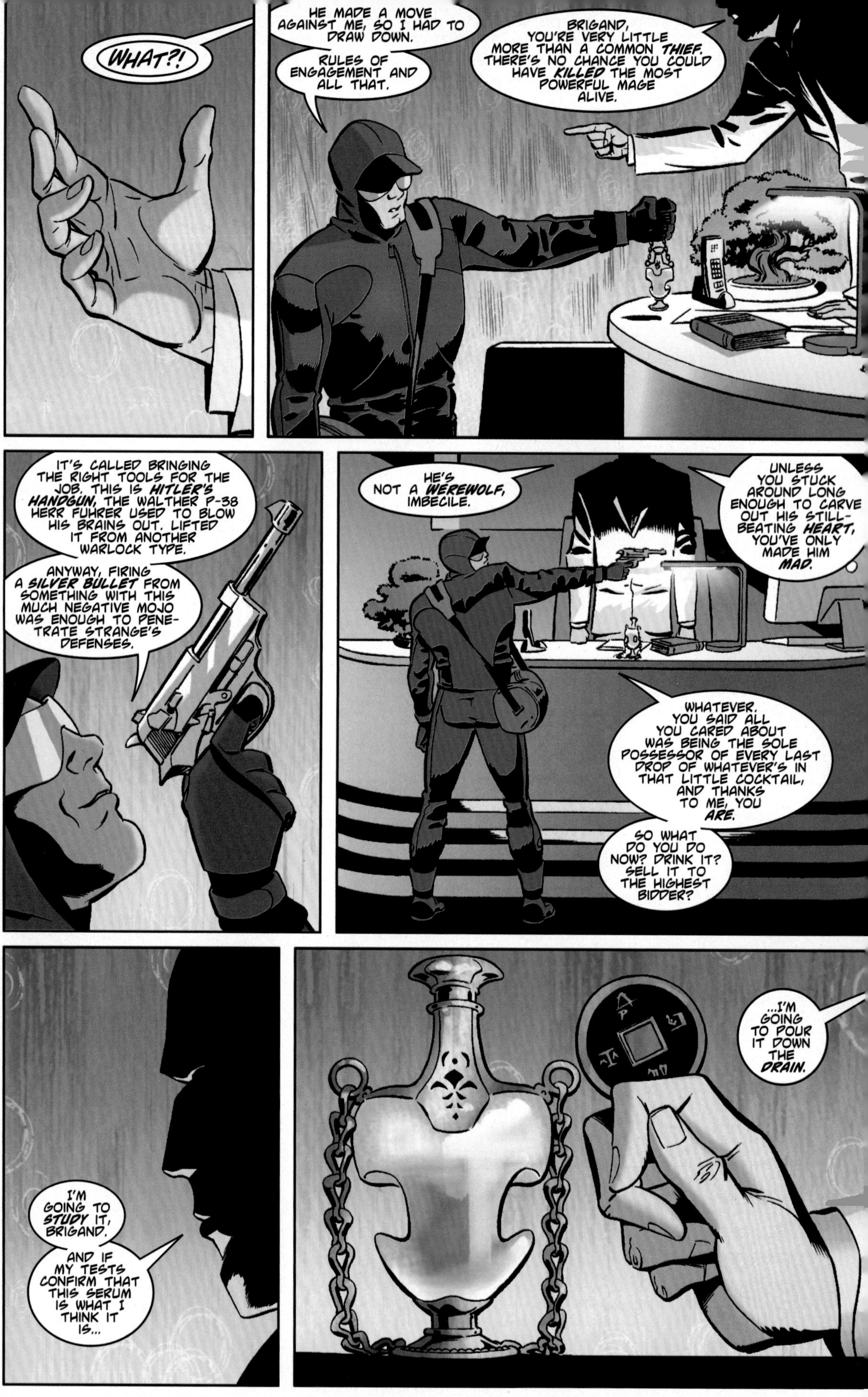
WHAT?!
HE MADE A MOVE AGAINST ME, SO I HAD TO DRAW DOWN.
RULES OF ENGAGEMENT AND ALL THAT.
BRIGAND, YOU'RE VERY LITTLE MORE THAN A COMMON THIEF. THERE'S NO CHANCE YOU COULD HAVE KILLED THE MOST POWERFUL MAGE ALIVE.
IT'S CALLED BRINGING THE RIGHT TOOLS FOR THE JOB. THIS IS HITLER'S HANDGUN, THE WALTHER P-38 HERR FUHRER USED TO BLOW HIS BRAINS OUT. LIFTED IT FROM ANOTHER WARLOCK TYPE.
ANYWAY, FIRING A SILVER BULLET FROM SOMETHING WITH THIS MUCH NEGATIVE MOJO WAS ENOUGH TO PENETRATE STRANGE'S DEFENSES.
HE'S NOT A WEREWOLF, IMBECILE.
UNLESS YOU STUCK AROUND LONG ENOUGH TO CARVE OUT HIS STILL-BEATING HEART, YOU'VE ONLY MADE HIM MAD.
WHATEVER. YOU SAID ALL YOU CARED ABOUT WAS BEING THE SOLE POSSESSOR OF EVERY LAST DROP OF WHATEVER'S IN THAT LITTLE COCKTAIL, AND THANKS TO ME, YOU ARE.
SO WHAT DO YOU DO NOW? DRINK IT? SELL IT TO THE HIGHEST BIDDER?
I'M GOING TO STUDY IT, BRIGAND.
AND IF MY TESTS CONFIRM THAT THIS SERUM IS WHAT I THINK IT IS...
...I'M GOING TO POUR IT DOWN THE DRAIN.

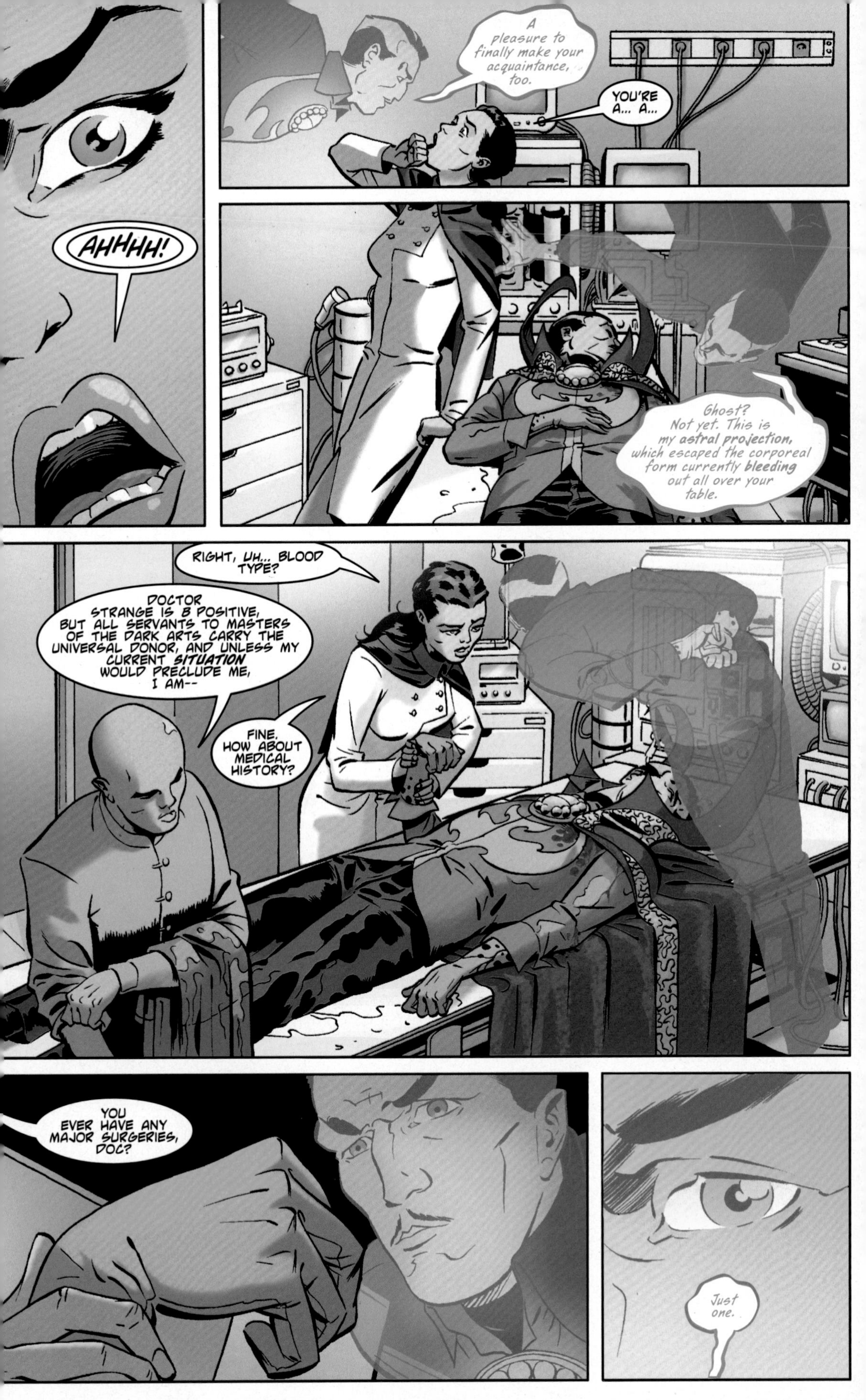
AHHHH!
A pleasure to finally make your acquaintance, too.
YOU'RE A... A...
Ghost? Not yet. This is my **astral projection**, which escaped the corporeal form currently **bleeding** out all over your table.
RIGHT, UH... BLOOD TYPE?
DOCTOR STRANGE IS B POSITIVE, BUT ALL SERVANTS TO MASTERS OF THE DARK ARTS CARRY THE UNIVERSAL DONOR, AND UNLESS MY CURRENT ***SITUATION*** WOULD PRECLUDE ME, I AM--
FINE. HOW ABOUT MEDICAL HISTORY?
YOU EVER HAVE ANY MAJOR SURGERIES, DOC?
Just one.

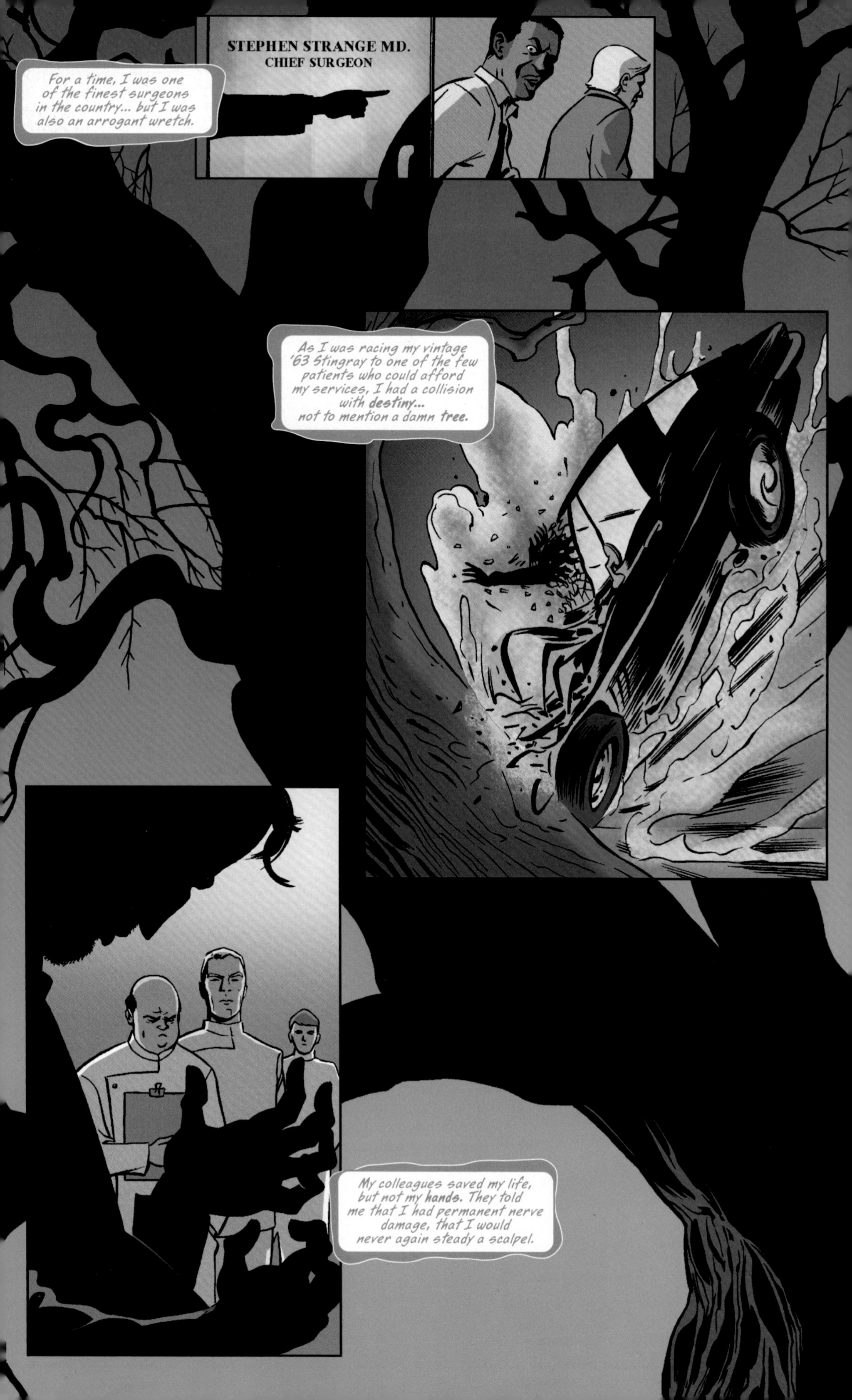

For a time, I was one of the finest surgeons in the country... but I was also an arrogant wretch.
STEPHEN STRANGE MD.
CHIEF SURGEON
As I was racing my vintage '63 Stingray to one of the few patients who could afford my services, I had a collision with **destiny**... not to mention a damn **tree**.
My colleagues saved my life, but not my **hands**. They told me that I had permanent nerve damage, that I would never again steady a scalpel.

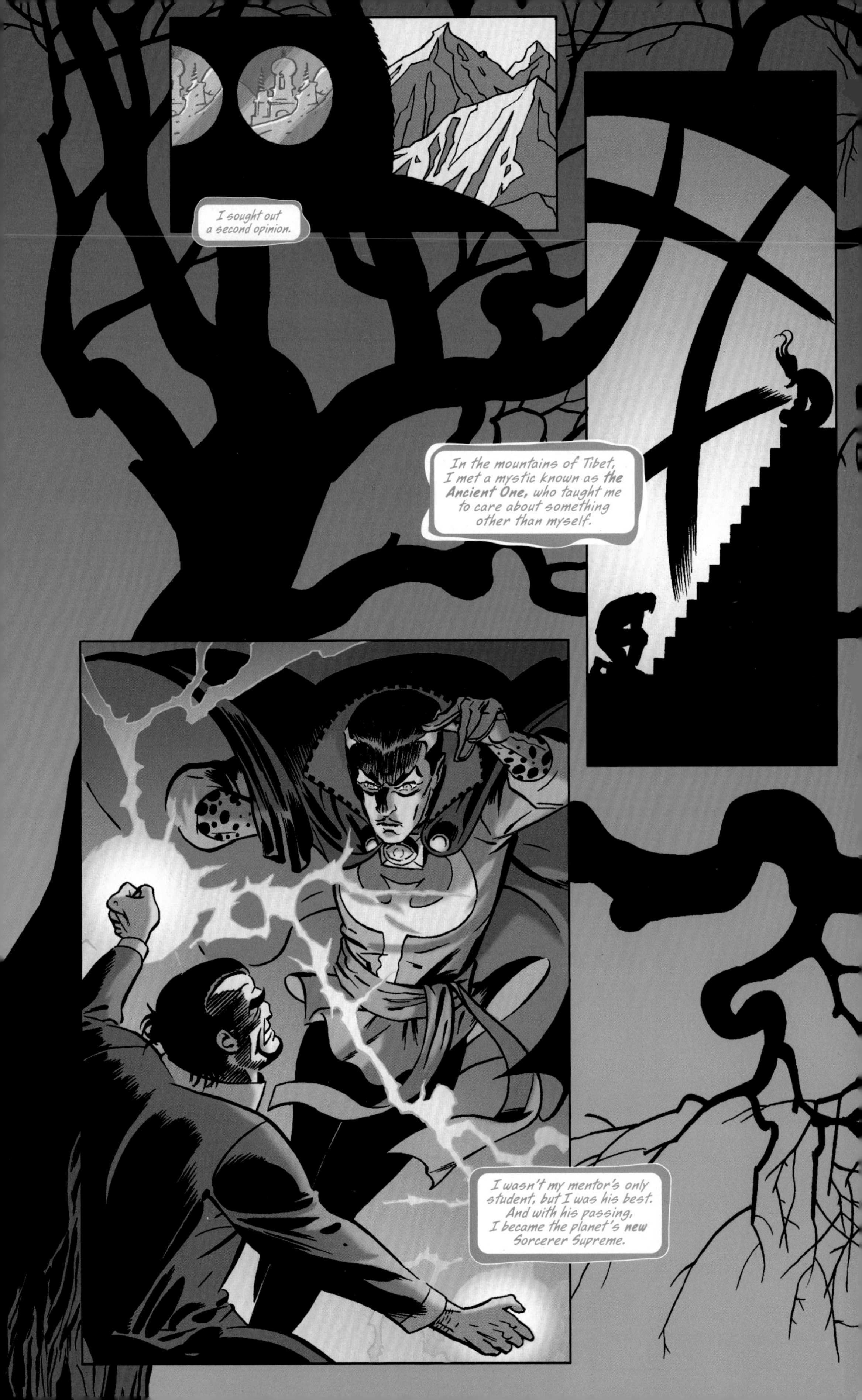
I sought out a second opinion.
In the mountains of Tibet, I met a mystic known as the Ancient One, who taught me to care about something other than myself.
I wasn't my mentor's only student, but I was his best. And with his passing, I became the planet's new Sorcerer Supreme.

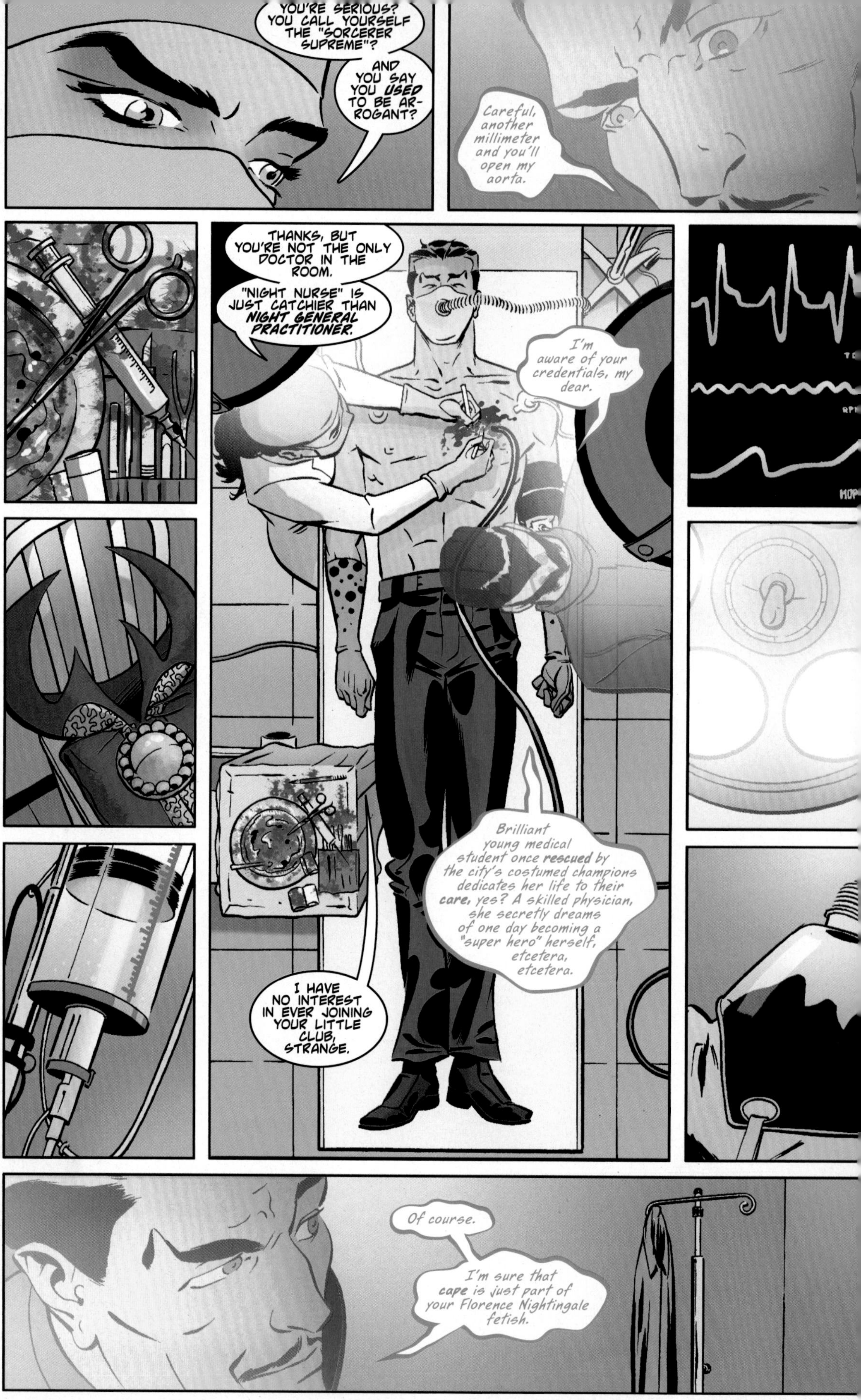
YOU'RE SERIOUS? YOU CALL YOURSELF THE "SORCERER SUPREME"?
AND YOU SAY YOU USED TO BE AR-ROGANT?
Careful, another millimeter and you'll open my aorta.
THANKS, BUT YOU'RE NOT THE ONLY DOCTOR IN THE ROOM.
"NIGHT NURSE" IS JUST CATCHIER THAN NIGHT GENERAL PRACTITIONER.
I'm aware of your credentials, my dear.
Brilliant young medical student once rescued by the city's costumed champions dedicates her life to their care, yes? A skilled physician, she secretly dreams of one day becoming a "super hero" herself, etcetera, etcetera.
I HAVE NO INTEREST IN EVER JOINING YOUR LITTLE CLUB, STRANGE.
Of course.
I'm sure that cape is just part of your Florence Nightingale fetish.

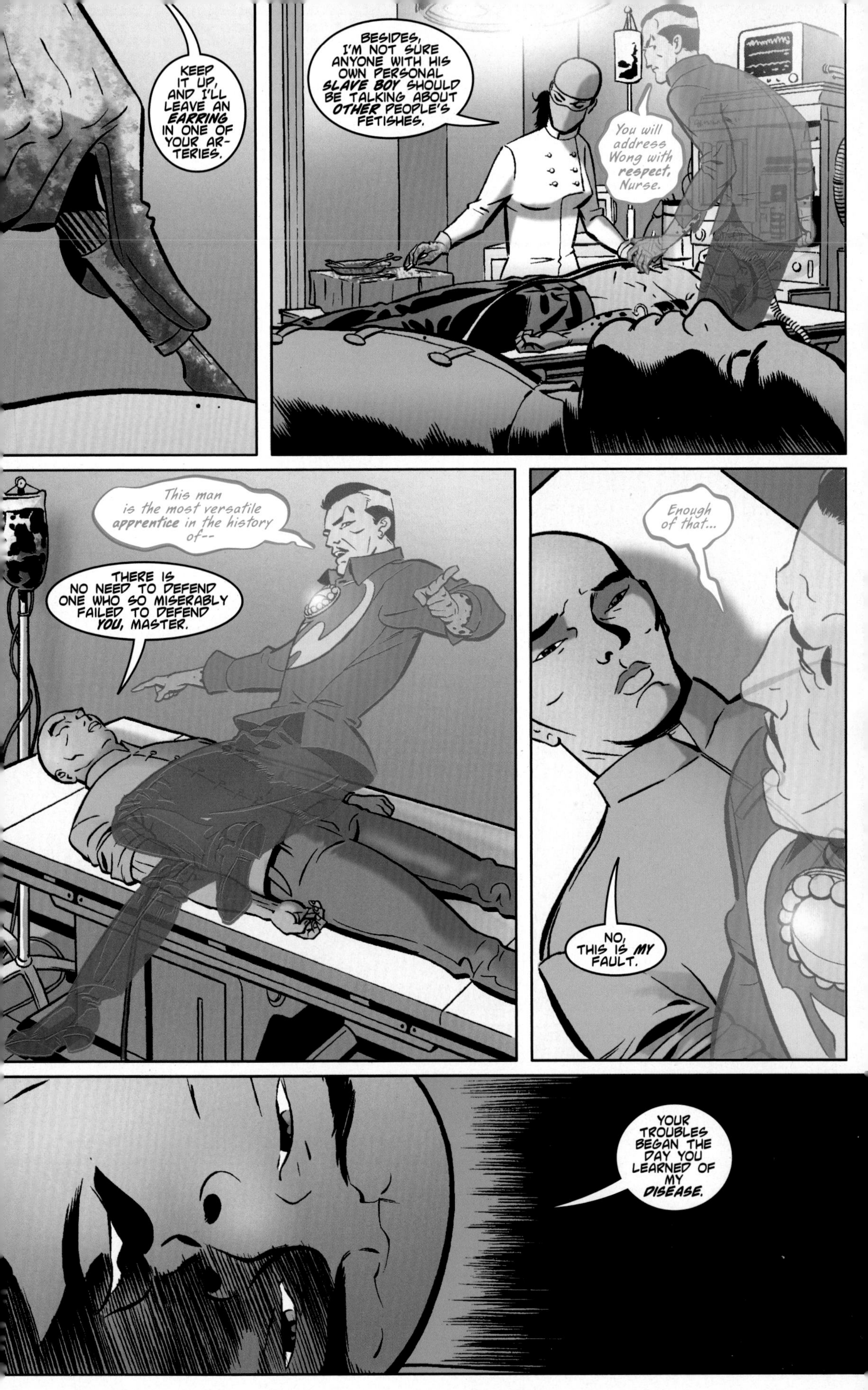

KEEP IT UP, AND I'LL LEAVE AN EARRING IN ONE OF YOUR ARTERIES.
BESIDES, I'M NOT SURE ANYONE WITH HIS OWN PERSONAL SLAVE BOY SHOULD BE TALKING ABOUT OTHER PEOPLE'S FETISHES.
You will address Wong with respect, Nurse.
This man is the most versatile apprentice in the history of--
THERE IS NO NEED TO DEFEND ONE WHO SO MISERABLY FAILED TO DEFEND YOU, MASTER.
Enough of that...
NO, THIS IS MY FAULT.
YOUR TROUBLES BEGAN THE DAY YOU LEARNED OF MY DISEASE.

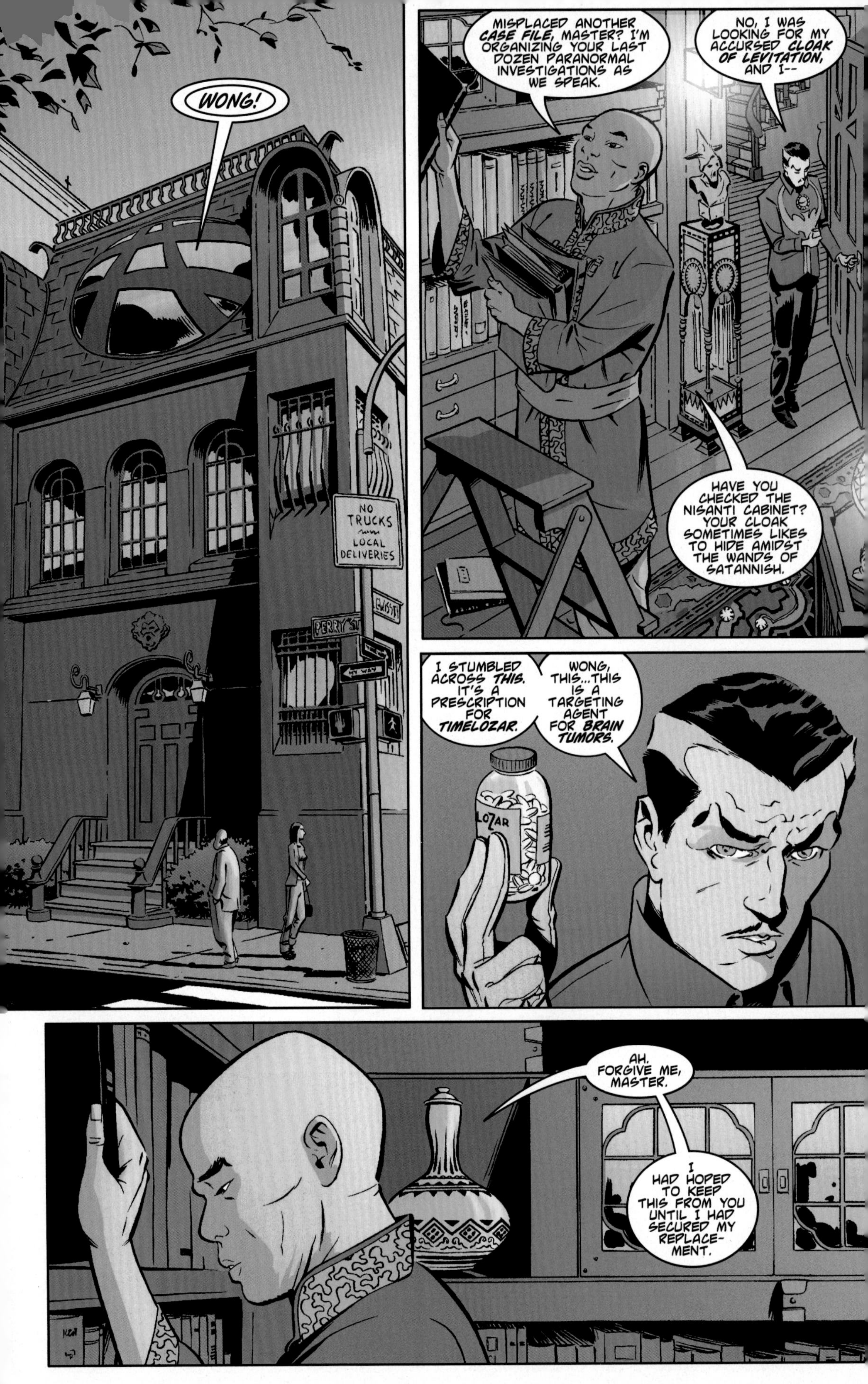
WONG!
NO TRUCKS
LOCAL DELIVERIES
PERRY ST
MISPLACED ANOTHER CASE FILE, MASTER? I'M ORGANIZING YOUR LAST DOZEN PARANORMAL INVESTIGATIONS AS WE SPEAK.
NO, I WAS LOOKING FOR MY ACCURSED CLOAK OF LEVITATION, AND I--
HAVE YOU CHECKED THE NISANTI CABINET? YOUR CLOAK SOMETIMES LIKES TO HIDE AMIDST THE WANDS OF SATANNISH.
I STUMBLED ACROSS THIS. IT'S A PRESCRIPTION FOR TIMELOZAR.
WONG, THIS...THIS IS A TARGETING AGENT FOR BRAIN TUMORS.
LOZAR
AH. FORGIVE ME, MASTER.
I HAD HOPED TO KEEP THIS FROM YOU UNTIL I HAD SECURED MY REPLACE-MENT.

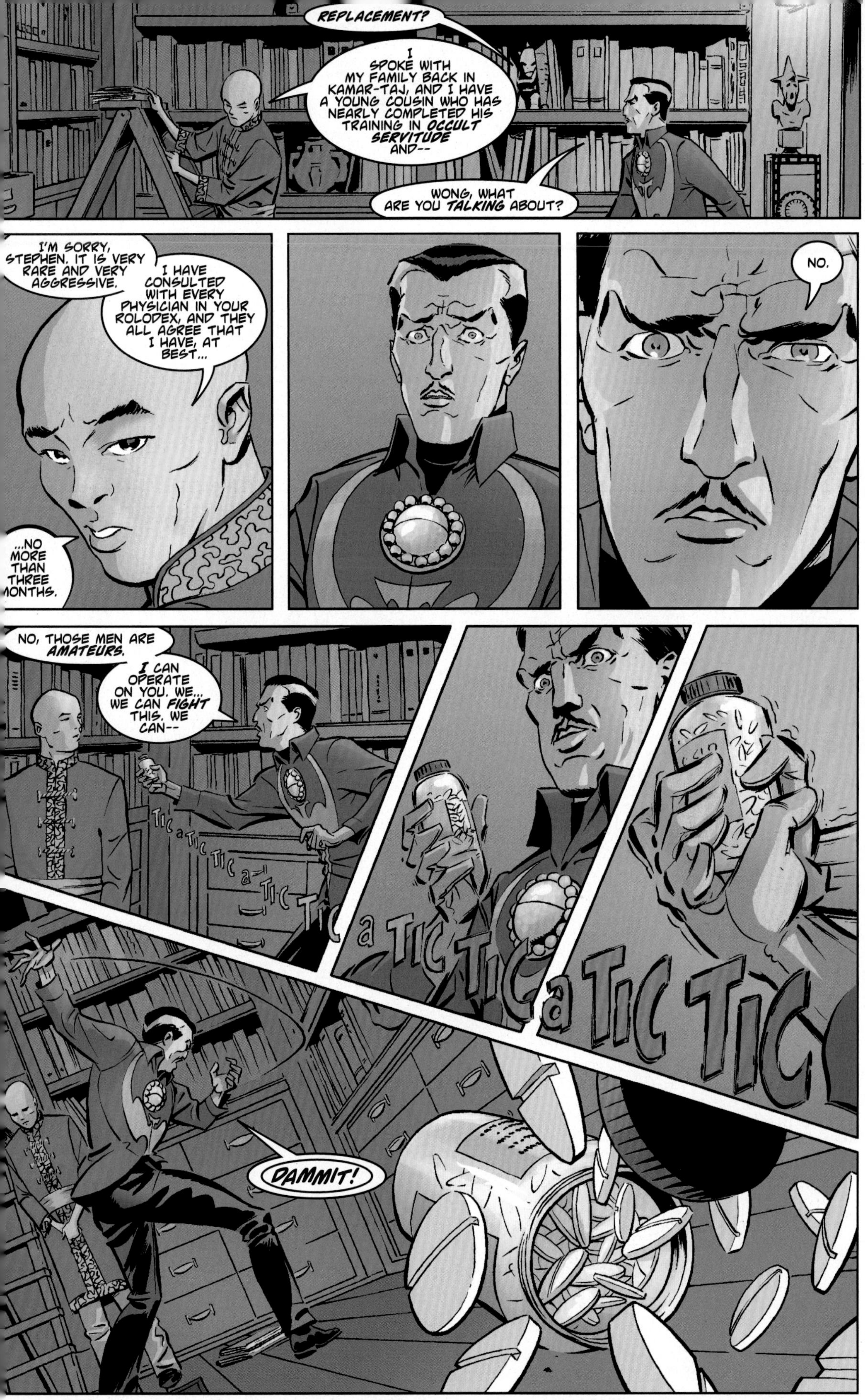
REPLACEMENT?
I SPOKE WITH MY FAMILY BACK IN KAMAR-TAJ, AND I HAVE A YOUNG COUSIN WHO HAS NEARLY COMPLETED HIS TRAINING IN OCCULT SERVITUDE AND--
WONG, WHAT ARE YOU TALKING ABOUT?
I'M SORRY, STEPHEN. IT IS VERY RARE AND VERY AGGRESSIVE.
I HAVE CONSULTED WITH EVERY PHYSICIAN IN YOUR ROLODEX, AND THEY ALL AGREE THAT I HAVE, AT BEST...
...NO MORE THAN THREE MONTHS.
NO.
NO, THOSE MEN ARE AMATEURS.
I CAN OPERATE ON YOU. WE... WE CAN FIGHT THIS. WE CAN--
TICaTIC TICaTIC TIC
TICaTIC TICaTIC TIC
DAMMIT!

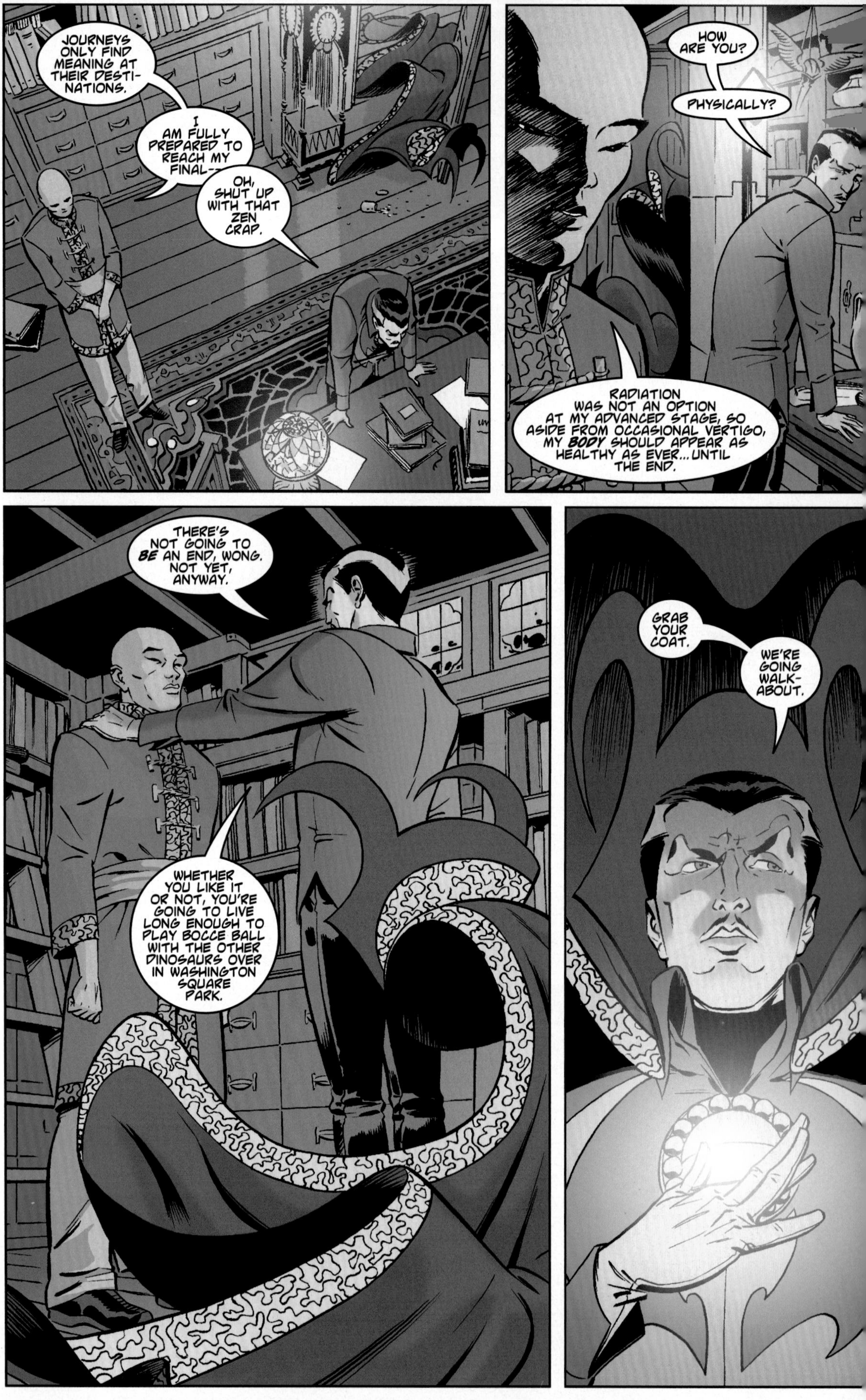
JOURNEYS ONLY FIND MEANING AT THEIR DESTINATIONS.
I AM FULLY PREPARED TO REACH MY FINAL--
OH, SHUT UP WITH THAT ZEN CRAP.
HOW ARE YOU?
PHYSICALLY?
RADIATION WAS NOT AN OPTION AT MY ADVANCED STAGE, SO ASIDE FROM OCCASIONAL VERTIGO, MY BODY SHOULD APPEAR AS HEALTHY AS EVER... UNTIL THE END.
THERE'S NOT GOING TO BE AN END, WONG. NOT YET, ANYWAY.
WHETHER YOU LIKE IT OR NOT, YOU'RE GOING TO LIVE LONG ENOUGH TO PLAY BOCCE BALL WITH THE OTHER DINOSAURS OVER IN WASHINGTON SQUARE PARK.
GRAB YOUR COAT.
WE'RE GOING WALK-ABOUT.

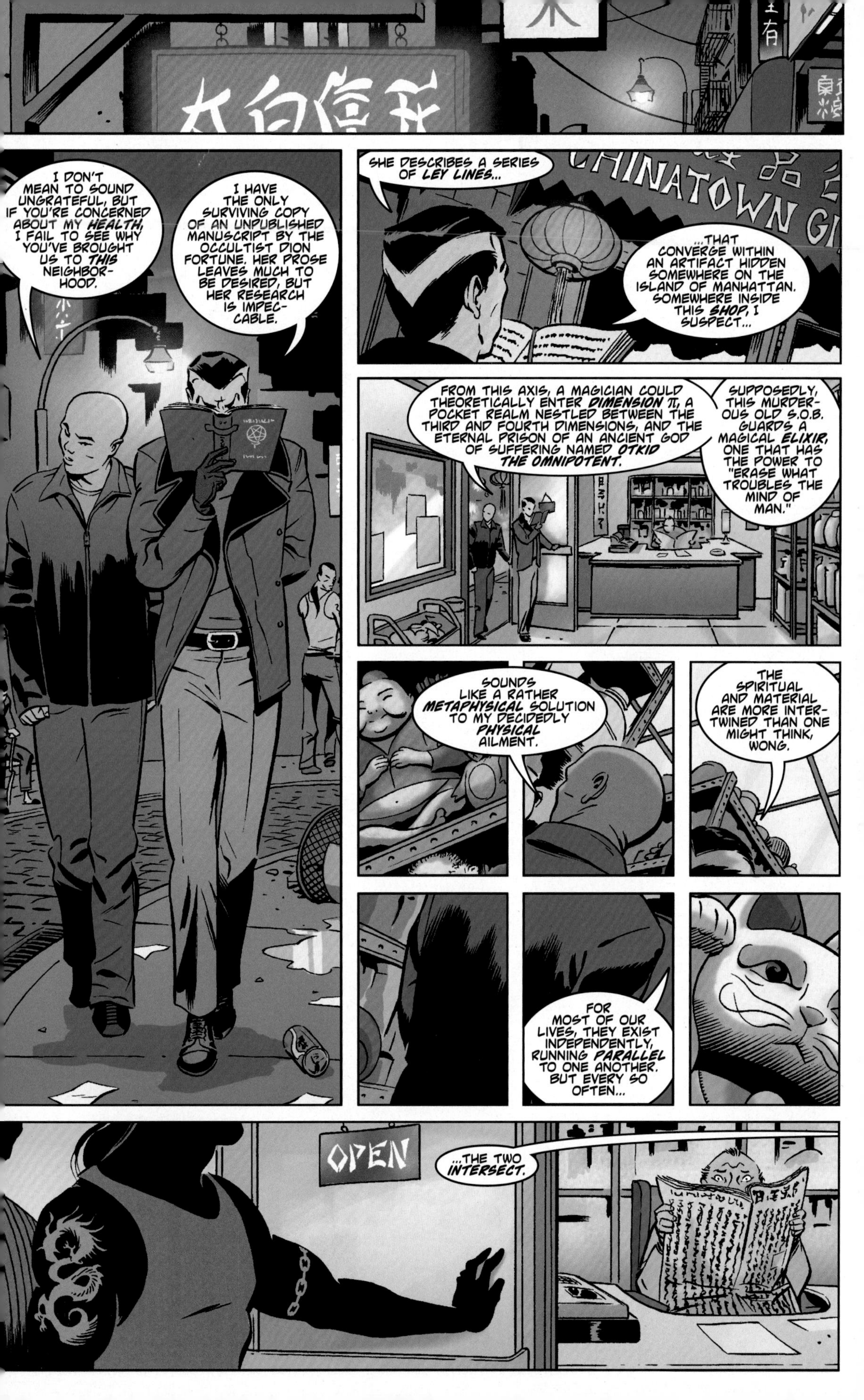
I DON'T MEAN TO SOUND UNGRATEFUL, BUT IF YOU'RE CONCERNED ABOUT MY *HEALTH*, I FAIL TO SEE WHY YOU'VE BROUGHT US TO *THIS* NEIGHBOR-HOOD.
I HAVE THE ONLY SURVIVING COPY OF AN UNPUBLISHED MANUSCRIPT BY THE OCCULTIST DION FORTUNE. HER PROSE LEAVES MUCH TO BE DESIRED, BUT HER RESEARCH IS IMPEC-CABLE.
SHE DESCRIBES A SERIES OF *LEY LINES*...
CHINATOWN GI
...THAT CONVERGE WITHIN AN ARTIFACT HIDDEN SOMEWHERE ON THE ISLAND OF MANHATTAN. SOMEWHERE INSIDE THIS *SHOP*, I SUSPECT...
FROM THIS AXIS, A MAGICIAN COULD THEORETICALLY ENTER *DIMENSION π*, A POCKET REALM NESTLED BETWEEN THE THIRD AND FOURTH DIMENSIONS, AND THE ETERNAL PRISON OF AN ANCIENT GOD OF SUFFERING NAMED *OTKID THE OMNIPOTENT*.
SUPPOSEDLY, THIS MURDER-OUS OLD S.O.B. GUARDS A MAGICAL *ELIXIR*, ONE THAT HAS THE POWER TO "ERASE WHAT TROUBLES THE MIND OF MAN."
SOUNDS LIKE A RATHER *METAPHYSICAL* SOLUTION TO MY DECIDEDLY *PHYSICAL* AILMENT.
THE SPIRITUAL AND MATERIAL ARE MORE INTER-TWINED THAN ONE MIGHT THINK, WONG.
FOR MOST OF OUR LIVES, THEY EXIST INDEPENDENTLY, RUNNING *PARALLEL* TO ONE ANOTHER. BUT EVERY SO OFTEN...
OPEN
...THE TWO *INTERSECT*.

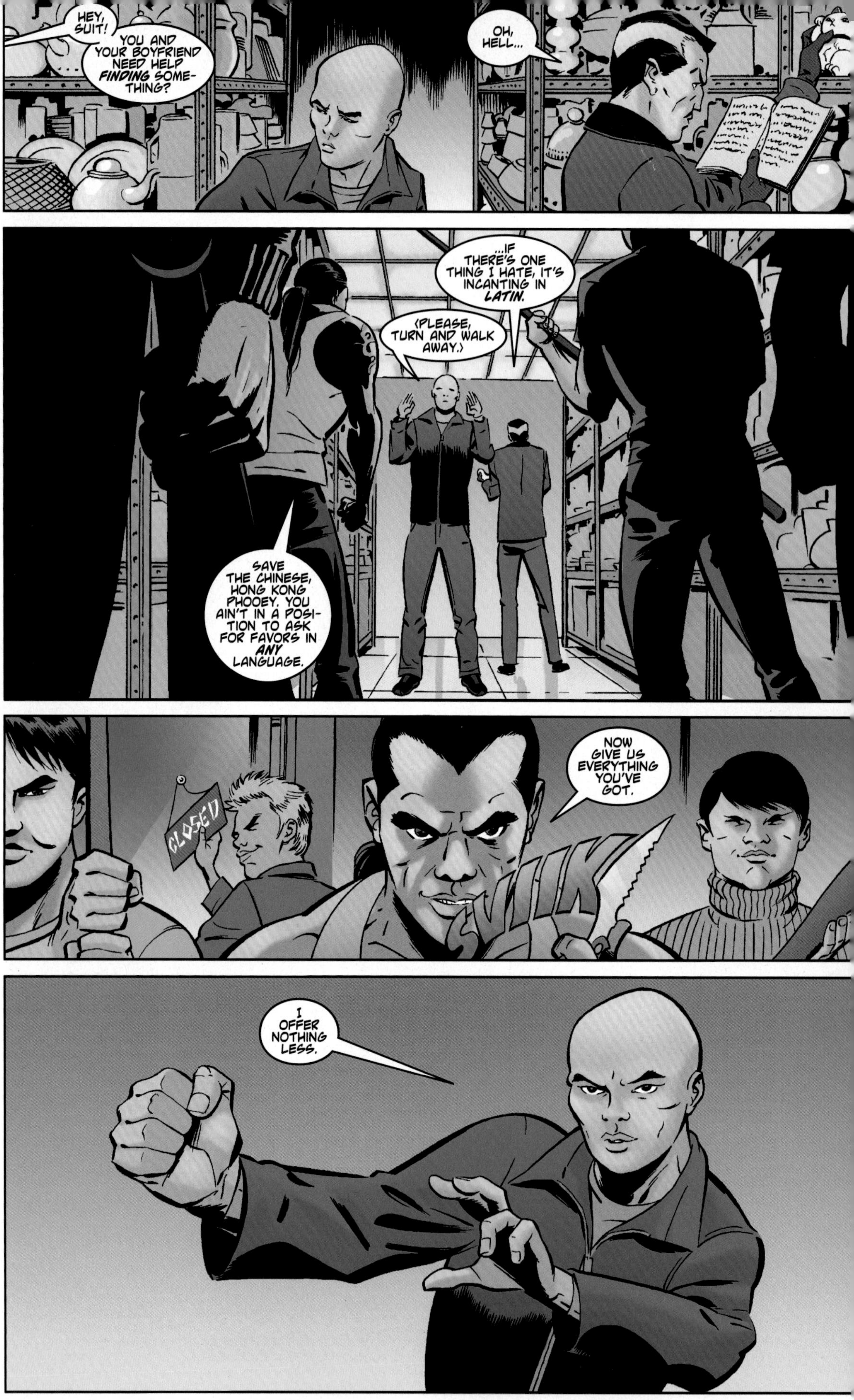
HEY, SUIT!
YOU AND YOUR BOYFRIEND NEED HELP FINDING SOME-THING?
OH, HELL...
...IF THERE'S ONE THING I HATE, IT'S INCANTING IN LATIN.
(PLEASE, TURN AND WALK AWAY.)
SAVE THE CHINESE, HONG KONG PHOOEY. YOU AIN'T IN A POSI-TION TO ASK FOR FAVORS IN ANY LANGUAGE.
CLOSED
NOW GIVE US EVERYTHING YOU'VE GOT.
SVIIK
I OFFER NOTHING LESS.

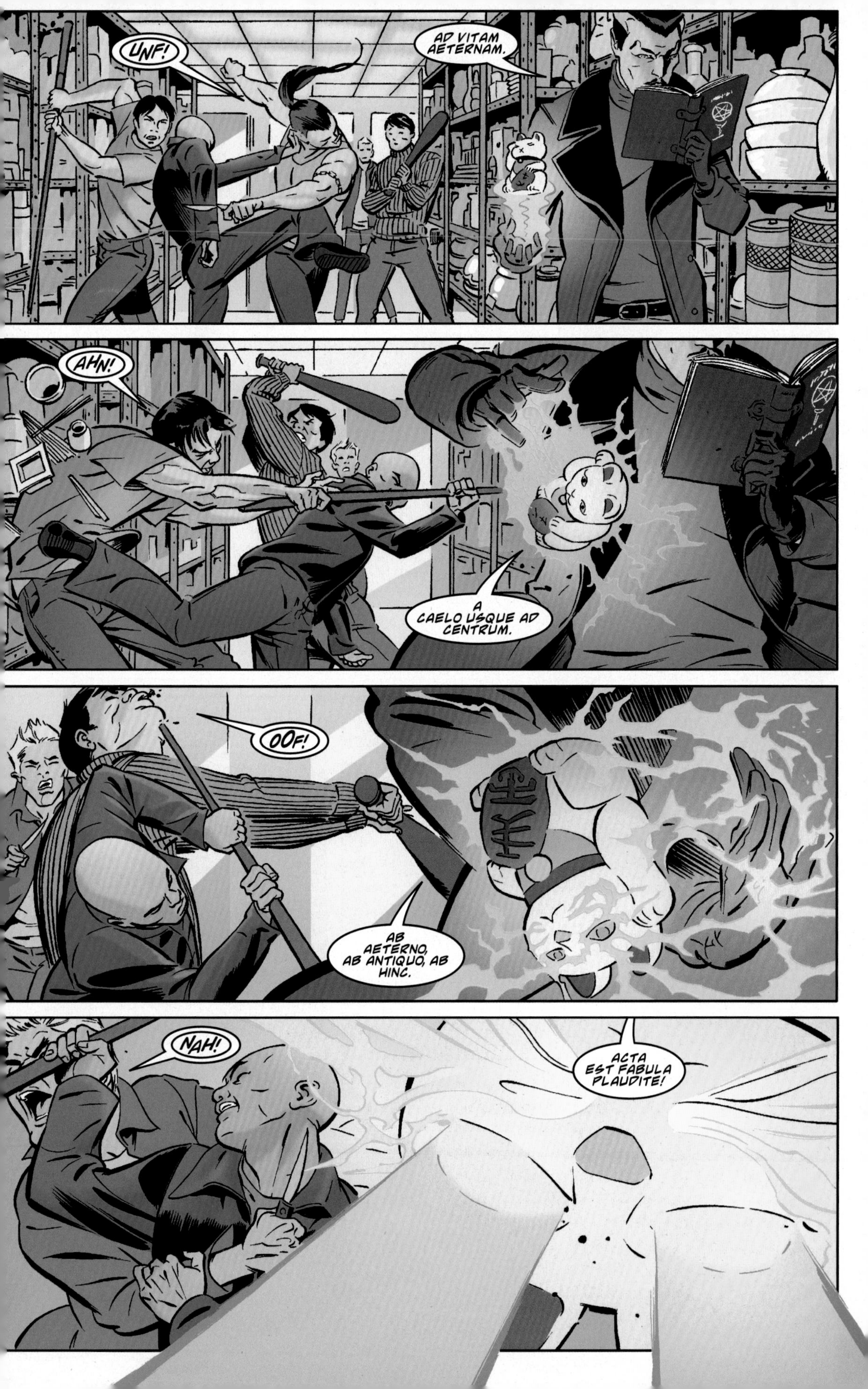
UNF!
AD VITAM AETERNAM.
AHN!
A CAELO USQUE AD CENTRUM.
OOF!
AB AETERNO, AB ANTIQUO, AB HINC.
NAH!
ACTA EST FABULA PLAUDITE!

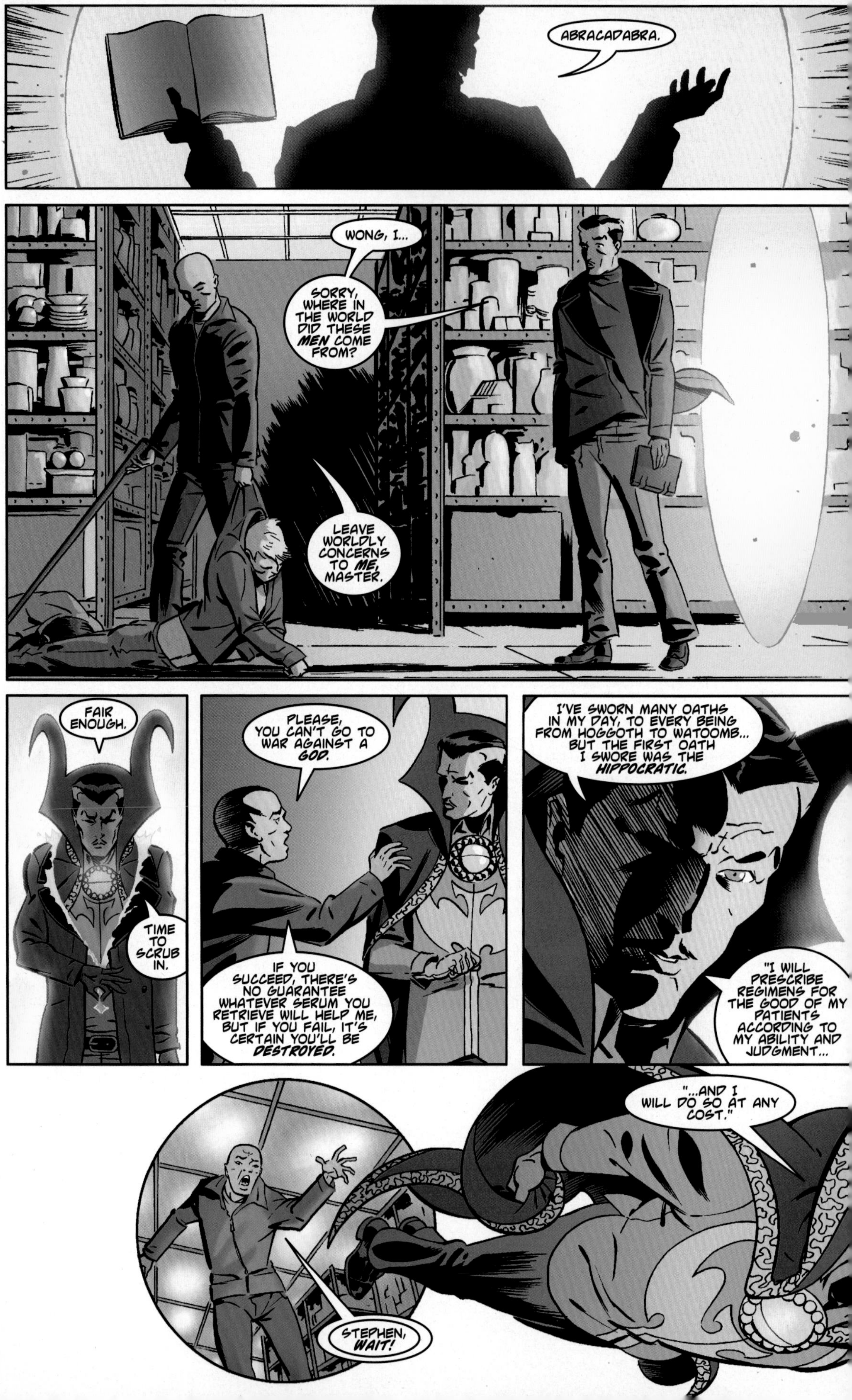
ABRACADABRA.
WONG, I...
SORRY, WHERE IN THE WORLD DID THESE MEN COME FROM?
LEAVE WORLDLY CONCERNS TO ME, MASTER.
FAIR ENOUGH.
TIME TO SCRUB IN.
PLEASE, YOU CAN'T GO TO WAR AGAINST A GOD.
IF YOU SUCCEED, THERE'S NO GUARANTEE WHATEVER SERUM YOU RETRIEVE WILL HELP ME, BUT IF YOU FAIL, IT'S CERTAIN YOU'LL BE DESTROYED.
I'VE SWORN MANY OATHS IN MY DAY, TO EVERY BEING FROM HOGGOTH TO WATOOMB... BUT THE FIRST OATH I SWORE WAS THE HIPPOCRATIC.
"I WILL PRESCRIBE REGIMENS FOR THE GOOD OF MY PATIENTS ACCORDING TO MY ABILITY AND JUDGMENT...
"...AND I WILL DO SO AT ANY COST."
STEPHEN, WAIT!

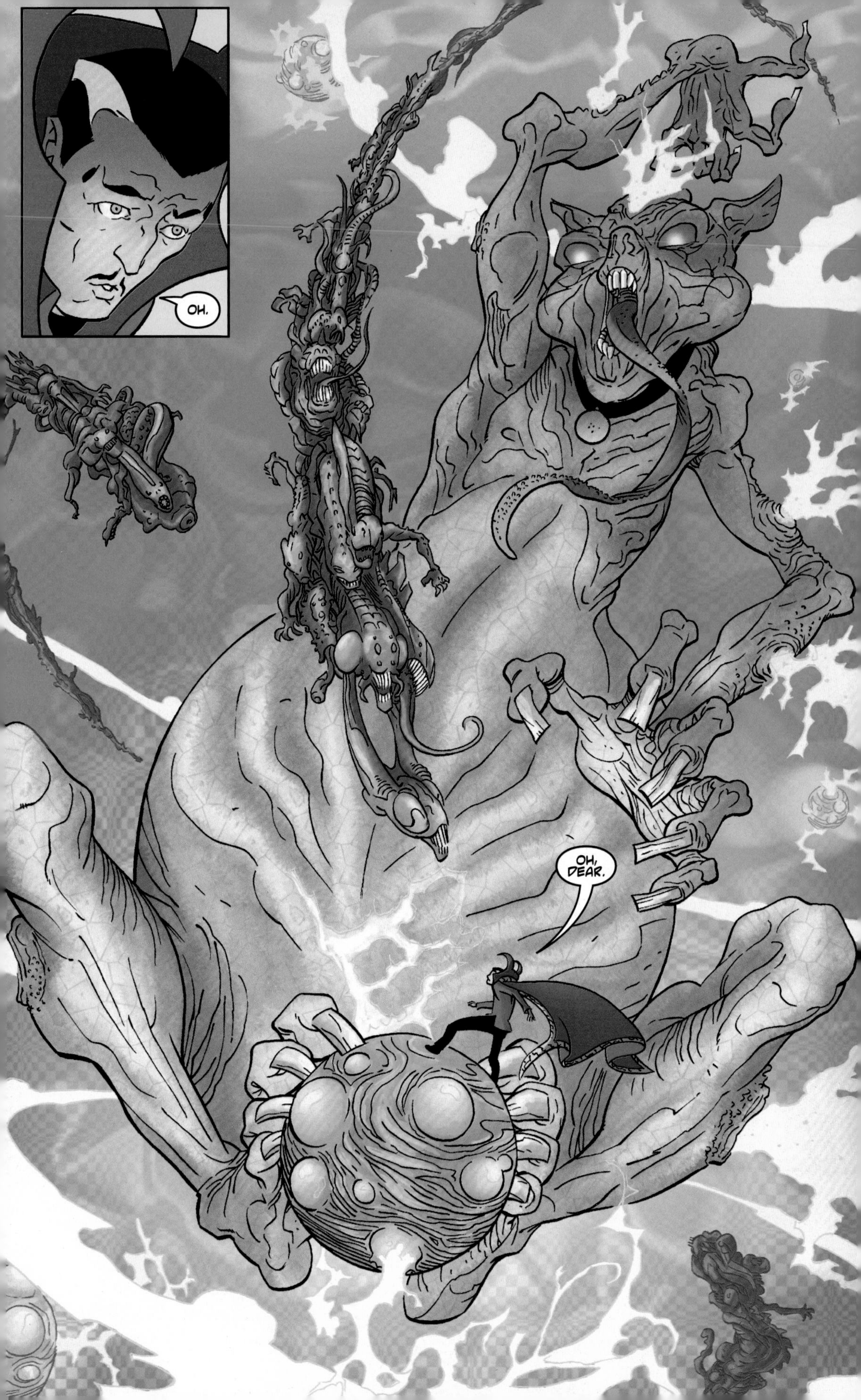
OH.
OH, DEAR.

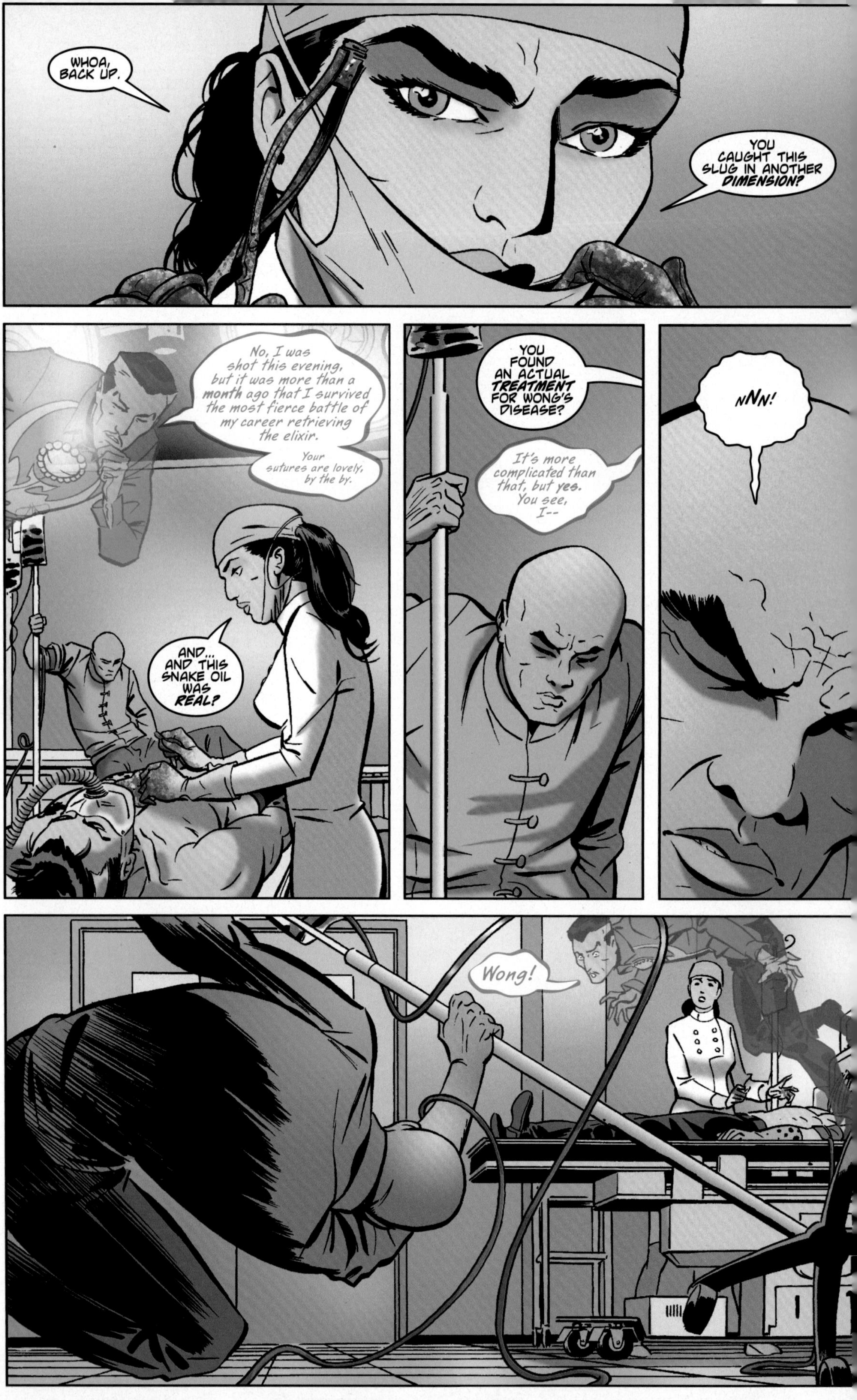

WHOA, BACK UP.
YOU CAUGHT THIS SLUG IN ANOTHER DIMENSION?
No, I was shot this evening, but it was more than a month ago that I survived the most fierce battle of my career retrieving the elixir.
Your sutures are lovely, by the by.
AND... AND THIS SNAKE OIL WAS REAL?
YOU FOUND AN ACTUAL TREATMENT FOR WONG'S DISEASE?
It's more complicated than that, but yes. You see, I--
NNN!
Wong!

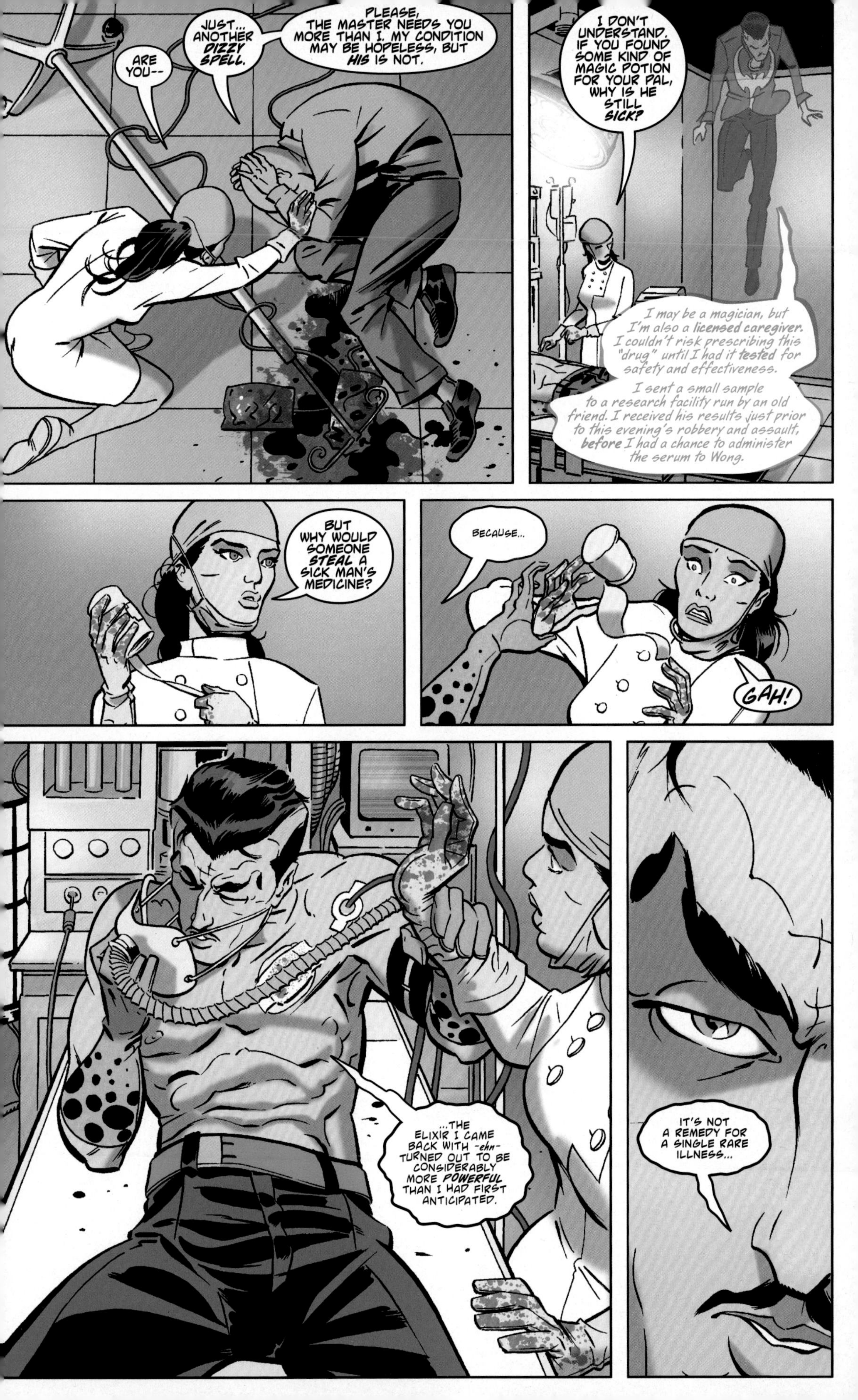
ARE YOU--
JUST... ANOTHER DIZZY SPELL.
PLEASE, THE MASTER NEEDS YOU MORE THAN I. MY CONDITION MAY BE HOPELESS, BUT HIS IS NOT.
I DON'T UNDERSTAND. IF YOU FOUND SOME KIND OF MAGIC POTION FOR YOUR PAL, WHY IS HE STILL SICK?
I may be a magician, but I'm also a licensed caregiver. I couldn't risk prescribing this "drug" until I had it tested for safety and effectiveness.
I sent a small sample to a research facility run by an old friend. I received his results just prior to this evening's robbery and assault, before I had a chance to administer the serum to Wong.
BUT WHY WOULD SOMEONE STEAL A SICK MAN'S MEDICINE?
BECAUSE...
GAH!
...THE ELIXIR I CAME BACK WITH -ehn- TURNED OUT TO BE CONSIDERABLY MORE POWERFUL THAN I HAD FIRST ANTICIPATED.
IT'S NOT A REMEDY FOR A SINGLE RARE ILLNESS...

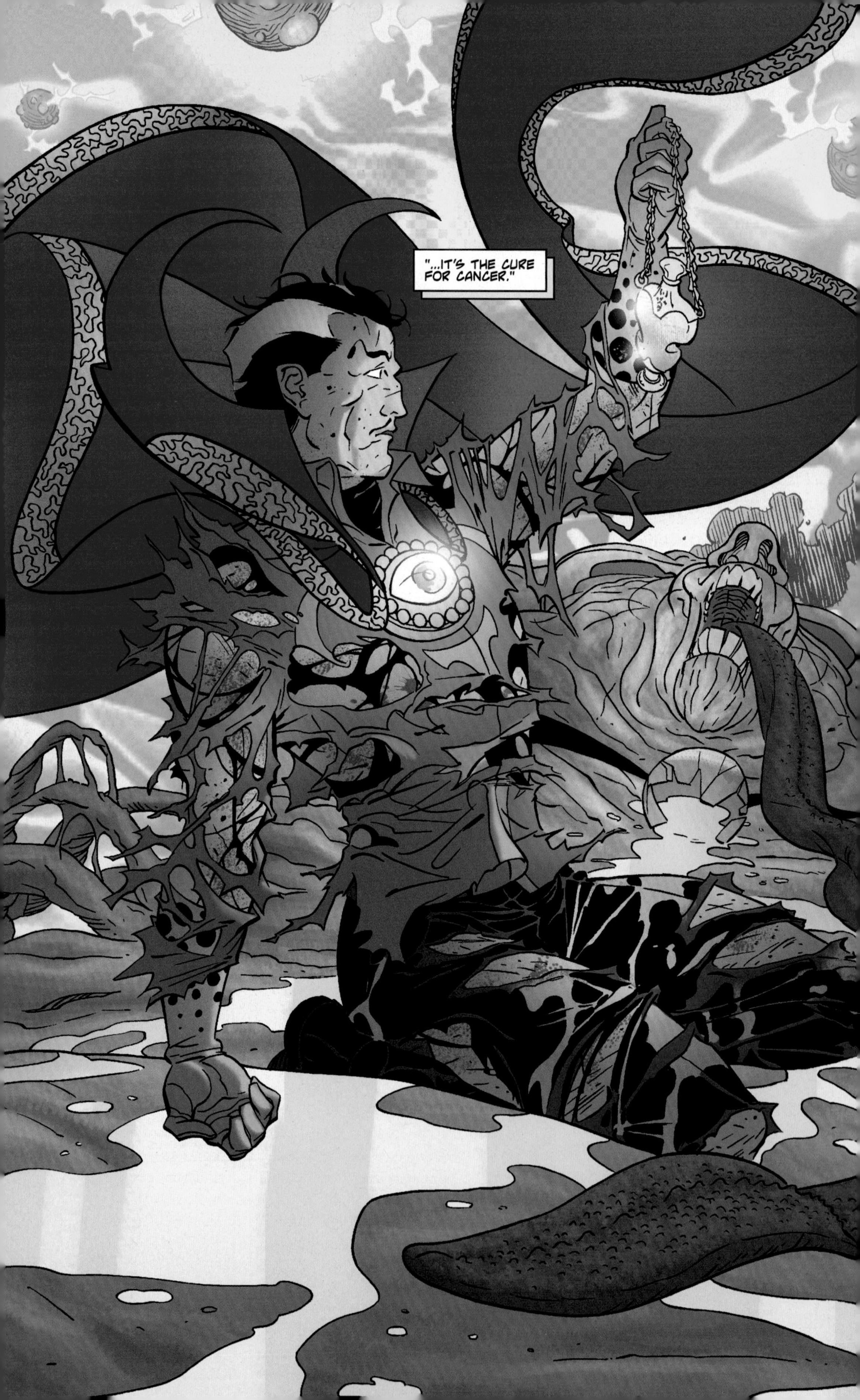
"...IT'S THE CURE FOR CANCER."

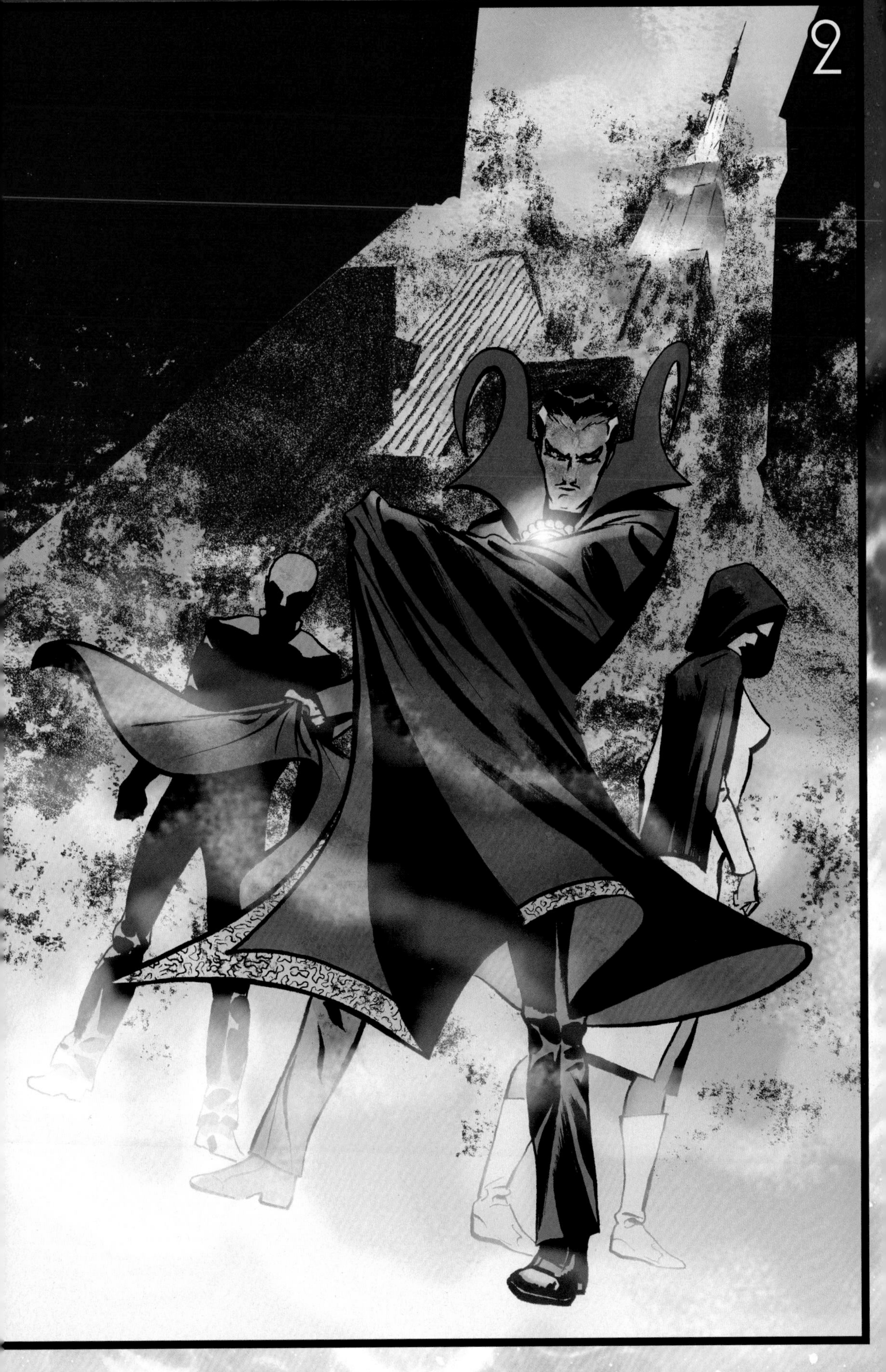
2

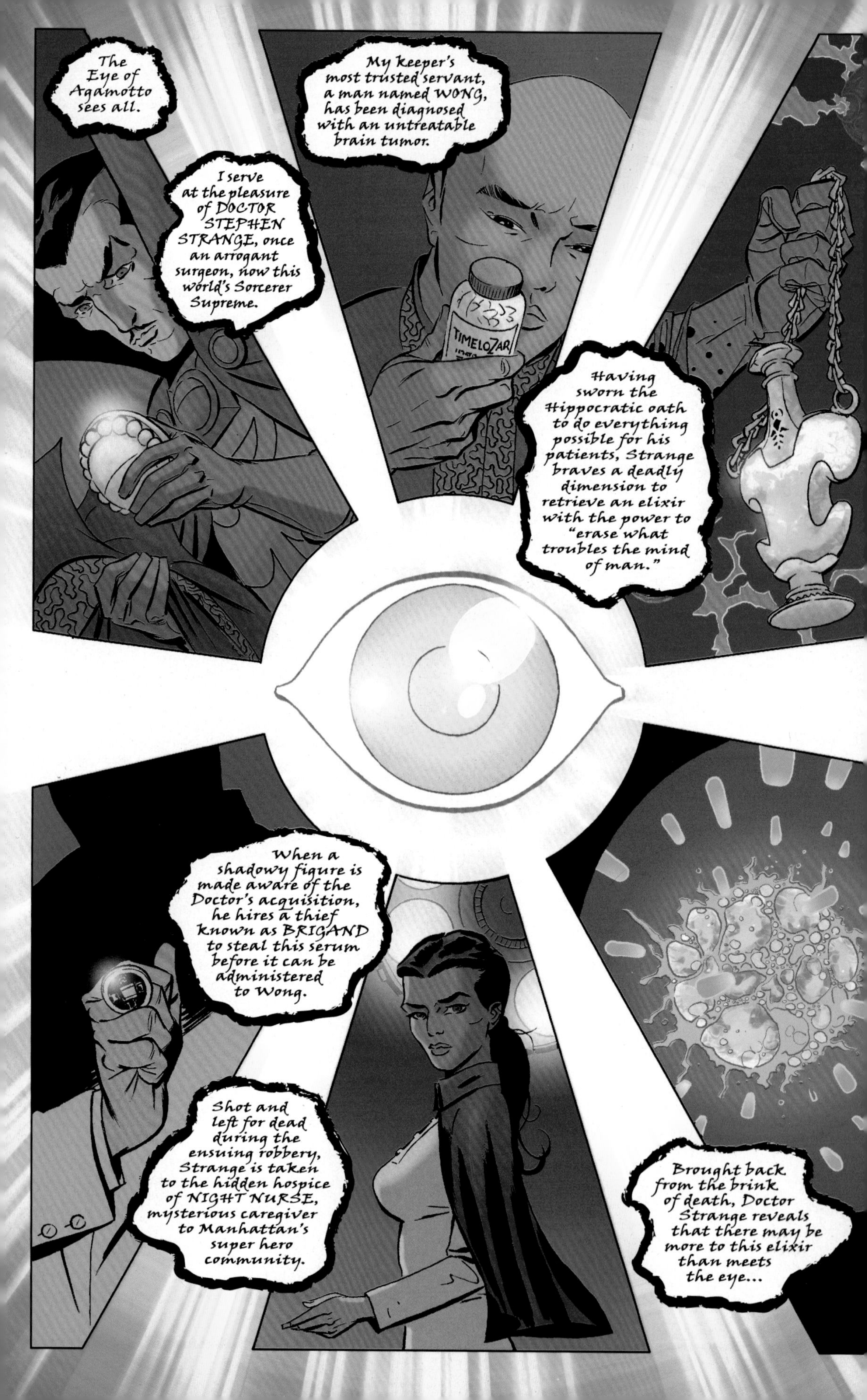
The Eye of Agamotto sees all.
My keeper's most trusted servant, a man named WONG, has been diagnosed with an untreatable brain tumor.
I serve at the pleasure of DOCTOR STEPHEN STRANGE, once an arrogant surgeon, now this world's Sorcerer Supreme.
TIMELOZAR
Having sworn the Hippocratic oath to do everything possible for his patients, Strange braves a deadly dimension to retrieve an elixir with the power to "erase what troubles the mind of man."
When a shadowy figure is made aware of the Doctor's acquisition, he hires a thief known as BRIGAND to steal this serum before it can be administered to Wong.
Shot and left for dead during the ensuing robbery, Strange is taken to the hidden hospice of NIGHT NURSE, mysterious caregiver to Manhattan's super hero community.
Brought back from the brink of death, Doctor Strange reveals that there may be more to this elixir than meets the eye...

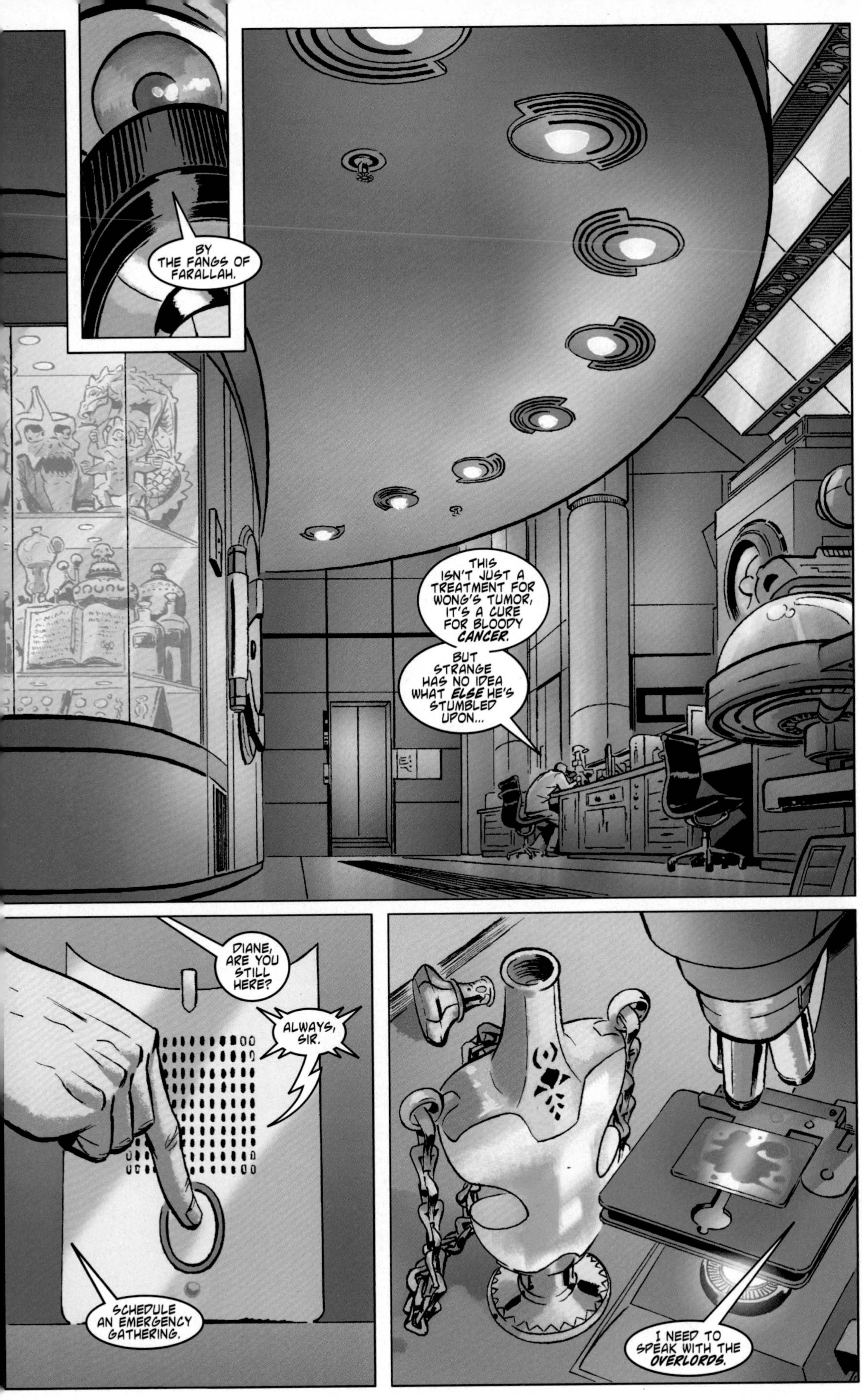
BY THE FANGS OF FARALLAH.
THIS ISN'T JUST A TREATMENT FOR WONG'S TUMOR, IT'S A CURE FOR BLOODY CANCER.
BUT STRANGE HAS NO IDEA WHAT ELSE HE'S STUMBLED UPON...
DIANE, ARE YOU STILL HERE?
ALWAYS, SIR.
SCHEDULE AN EMERGENCY GATHERING.
I NEED TO SPEAK WITH THE OVERLORDS.

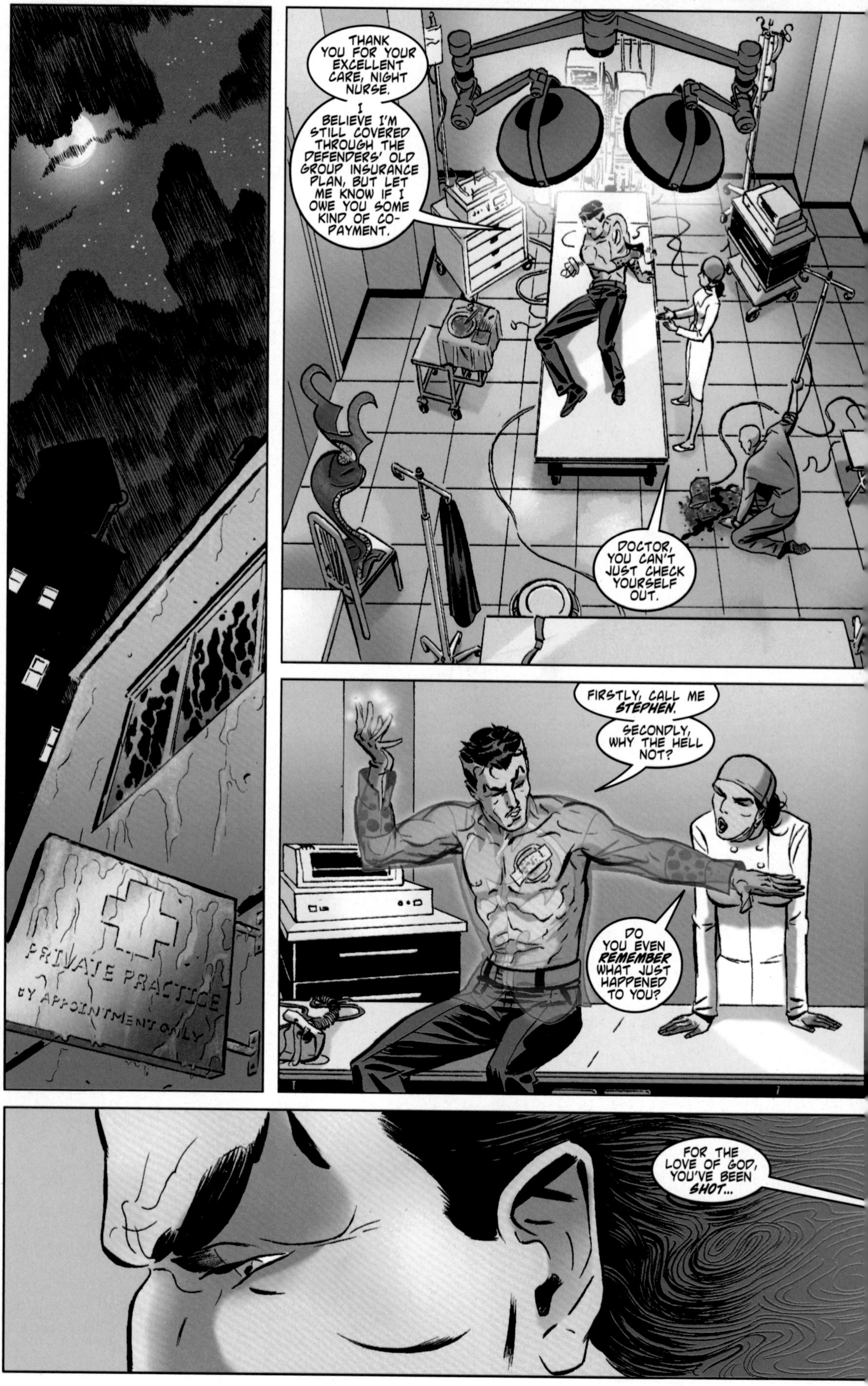
PRIVATE PRACTICE
BY APPOINTMENT ONLY
THANK YOU FOR YOUR EXCELLENT CARE, NIGHT NURSE.
I BELIEVE I'M STILL COVERED THROUGH THE DEFENDERS' OLD GROUP INSURANCE PLAN, BUT LET ME KNOW IF I OWE YOU SOME KIND OF CO-PAYMENT.
DOCTOR, YOU CAN'T JUST CHECK YOURSELF OUT.
FIRSTLY, CALL ME STEPHEN.
SECONDLY, WHY THE HELL NOT?
DO YOU EVEN REMEMBER WHAT JUST HAPPENED TO YOU?
FOR THE LOVE OF GOD, YOU'VE BEEN SHOT...

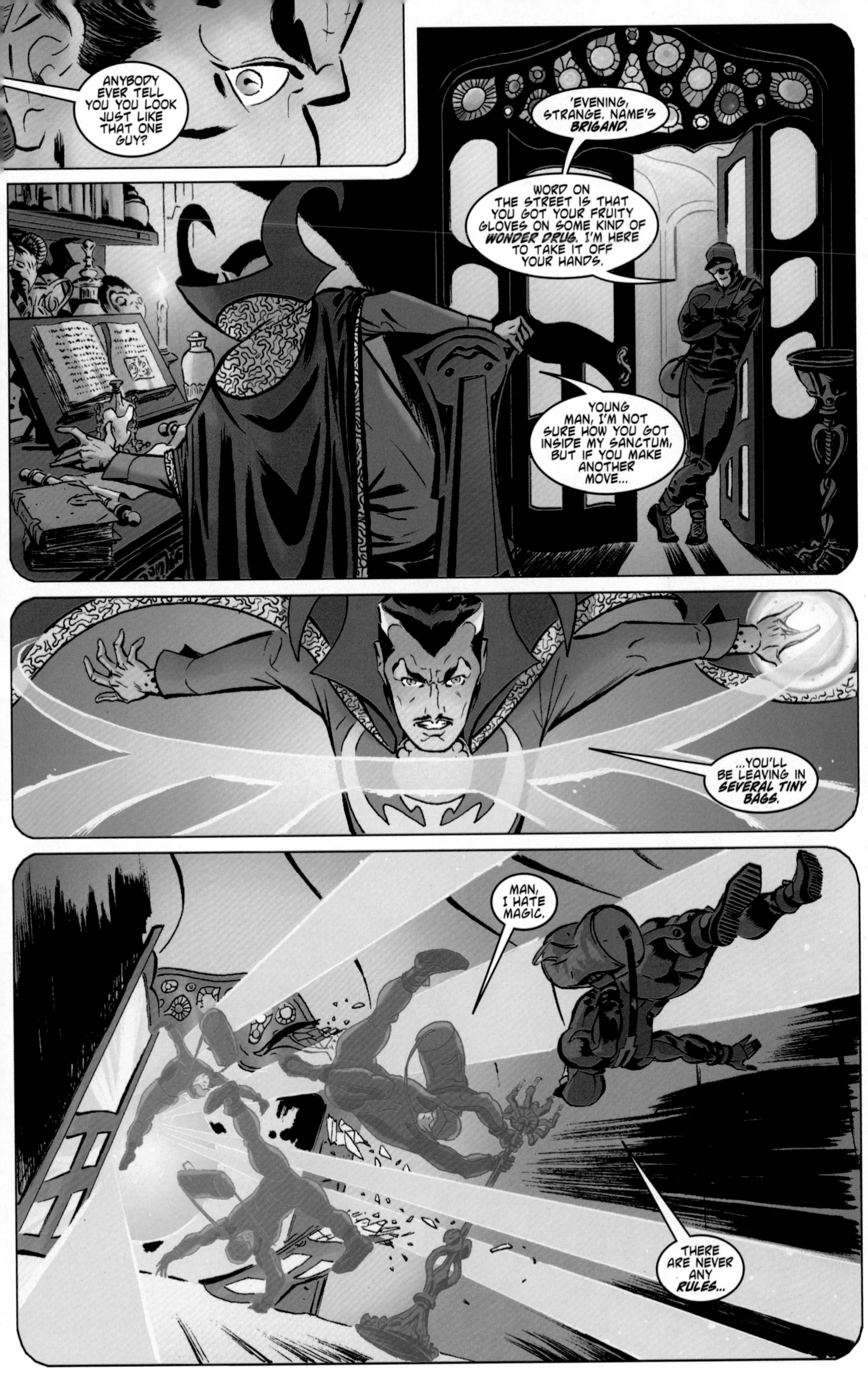
ANYBODY EVER TELL YOU YOU LOOK JUST LIKE THAT ONE GUY?
'EVENING, STRANGE. NAME'S BRIGAND.
WORD ON THE STREET IS THAT YOU GOT YOUR FRUITY GLOVES ON SOME KIND OF WONDER DRUG. I'M HERE TO TAKE IT OFF YOUR HANDS.
YOUNG MAN, I'M NOT SURE HOW YOU GOT INSIDE MY SANCTUM, BUT IF YOU MAKE ANOTHER MOVE...
...YOU'LL BE LEAVING IN SEVERAL TINY BAGS.
MAN, I HATE MAGIC.
THERE ARE NEVER ANY RULES...

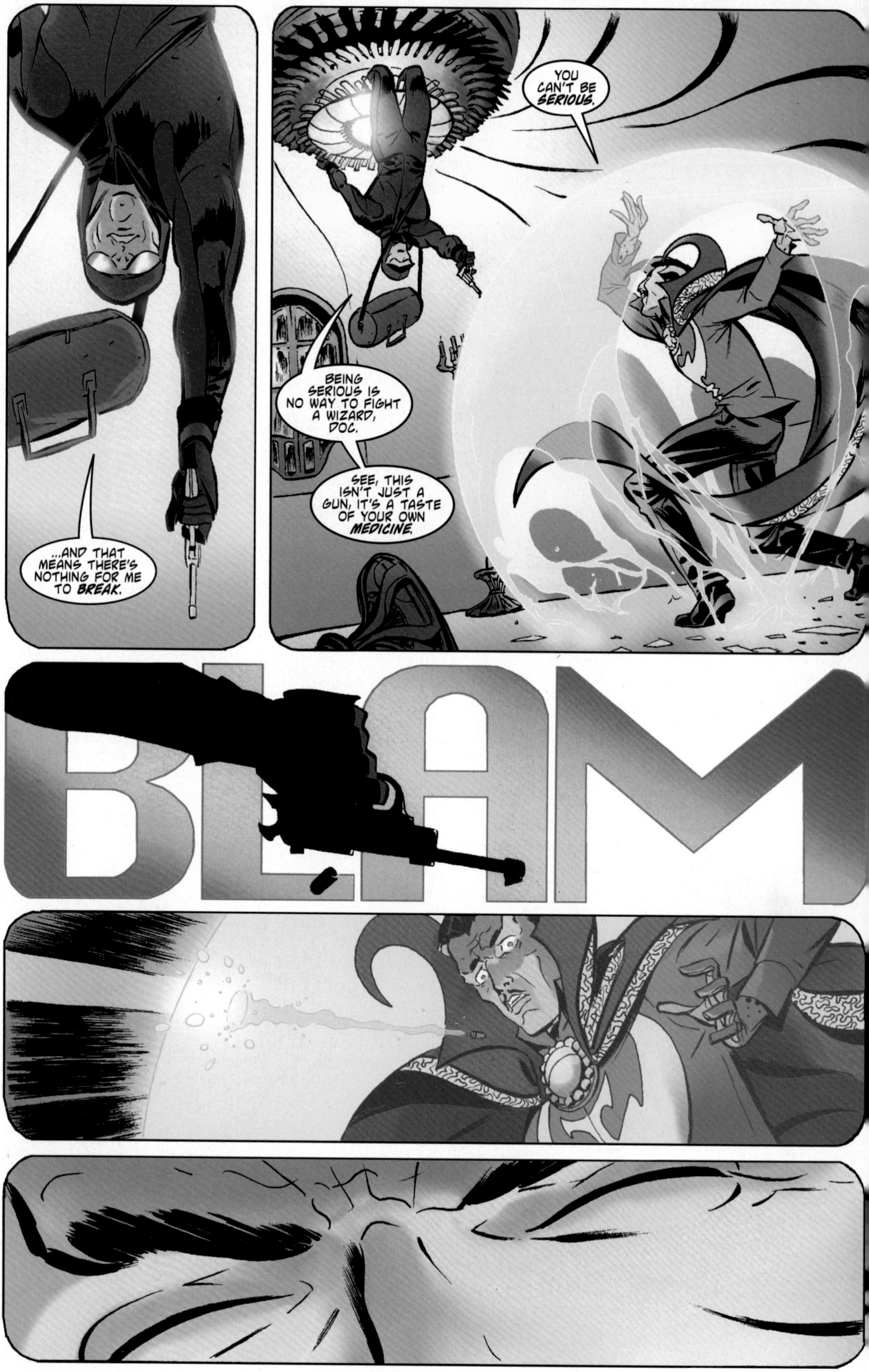

...AND THAT MEANS THERE'S NOTHING FOR ME TO BREAK.
YOU CAN'T BE SERIOUS.
BEING SERIOUS IS NO WAY TO FIGHT A WIZARD, DOC.
SEE, THIS ISN'T JUST A GUN, IT'S A TASTE OF YOUR OWN MEDICINE.
BLAM

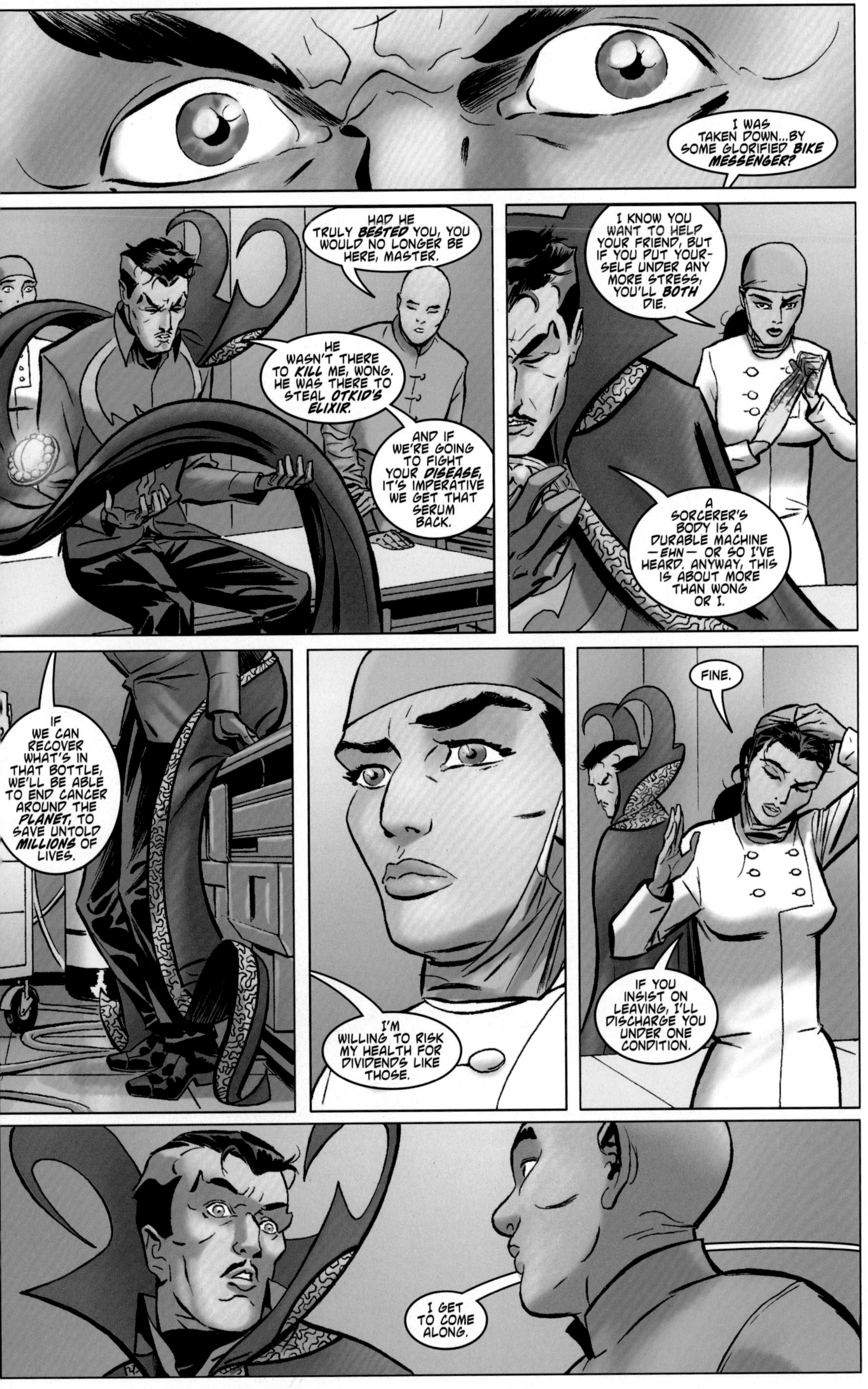
I WAS TAKEN DOWN...BY SOME GLORIFIED BIKE MESSENGER?
HAD HE TRULY BESTED YOU, YOU WOULD NO LONGER BE HERE, MASTER.
HE WASN'T THERE TO KILL ME, WONG. HE WAS THERE TO STEAL OTKID'S ELIXIR.
AND IF WE'RE GOING TO FIGHT YOUR DISEASE, IT'S IMPERATIVE WE GET THAT SERUM BACK.
I KNOW YOU WANT TO HELP YOUR FRIEND, BUT IF YOU PUT YOURSELF UNDER ANY MORE STRESS, YOU'LL BOTH DIE.
A SORCERER'S BODY IS A DURABLE MACHINE —EHN— OR SO I'VE HEARD. ANYWAY, THIS IS ABOUT MORE THAN WONG OR I.
IF WE CAN RECOVER WHAT'S IN THAT BOTTLE, WE'LL BE ABLE TO END CANCER AROUND THE PLANET, TO SAVE UNTOLD MILLIONS OF LIVES.
I'M WILLING TO RISK MY HEALTH FOR DIVIDENDS LIKE THOSE.
FINE.
IF YOU INSIST ON LEAVING, I'LL DISCHARGE YOU UNDER ONE CONDITION.
I GET TO COME ALONG.

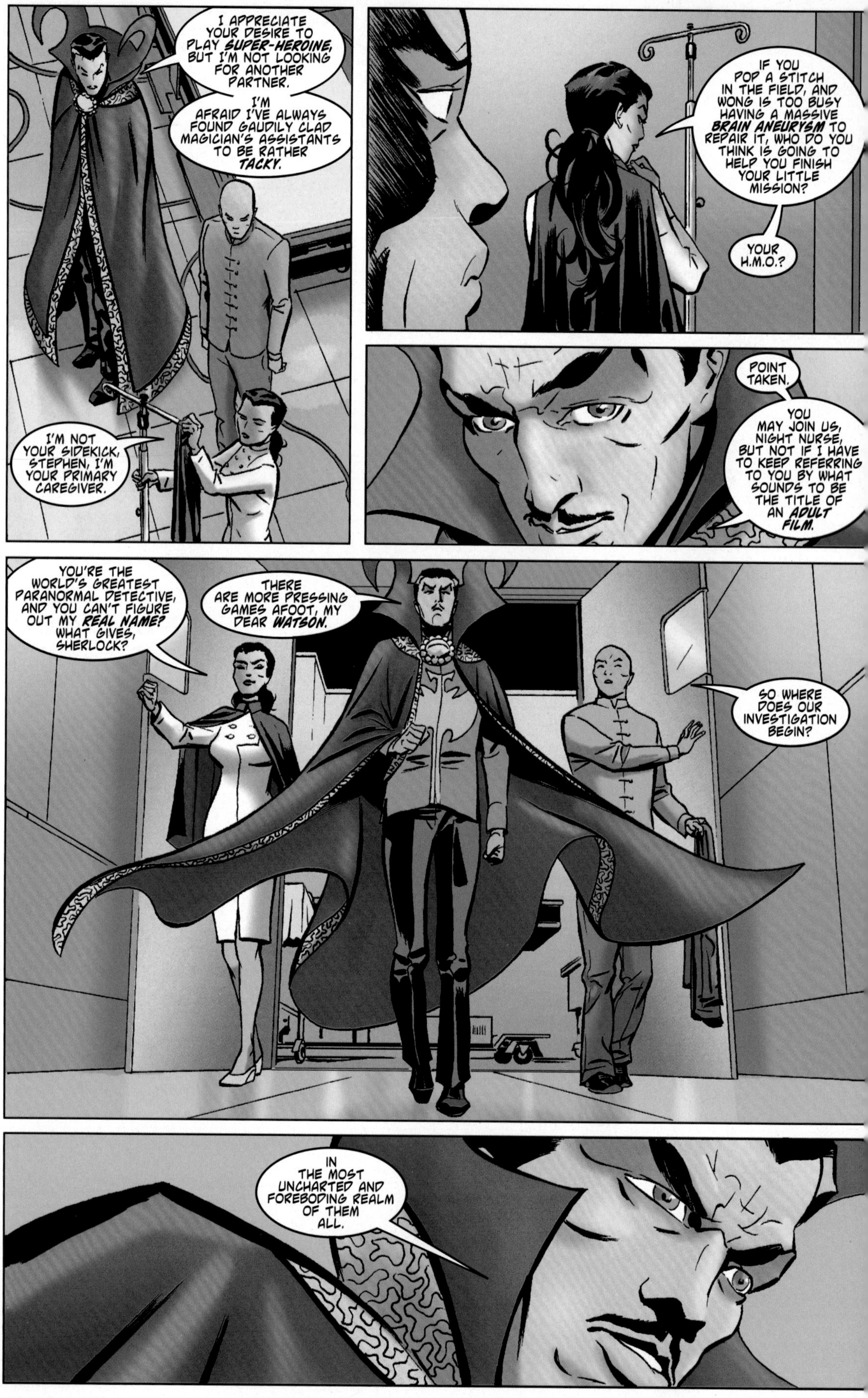
I APPRECIATE YOUR DESIRE TO PLAY SUPER-HEROINE, BUT I'M NOT LOOKING FOR ANOTHER PARTNER.
I'M AFRAID I'VE ALWAYS FOUND GAUDILY CLAD MAGICIAN'S ASSISTANTS TO BE RATHER TACKY.
I'M NOT YOUR SIDEKICK, STEPHEN, I'M YOUR PRIMARY CAREGIVER.
IF YOU POP A STITCH IN THE FIELD, AND WONG IS TOO BUSY HAVING A MASSIVE BRAIN ANEURYSM TO REPAIR IT, WHO DO YOU THINK IS GOING TO HELP YOU FINISH YOUR LITTLE MISSION?
YOUR H.M.O.?
POINT TAKEN.
YOU MAY JOIN US, NIGHT NURSE, BUT NOT IF I HAVE TO KEEP REFERRING TO YOU BY WHAT SOUNDS TO BE THE TITLE OF AN ADULT FILM.
YOU'RE THE WORLD'S GREATEST PARANORMAL DETECTIVE, AND YOU CAN'T FIGURE OUT MY REAL NAME? WHAT GIVES, SHERLOCK?
THERE ARE MORE PRESSING GAMES AFOOT, MY DEAR WATSON.
SO WHERE DOES OUR INVESTIGATION BEGIN?
IN THE MOST UNCHARTED AND FOREBODING REALM OF THEM ALL.

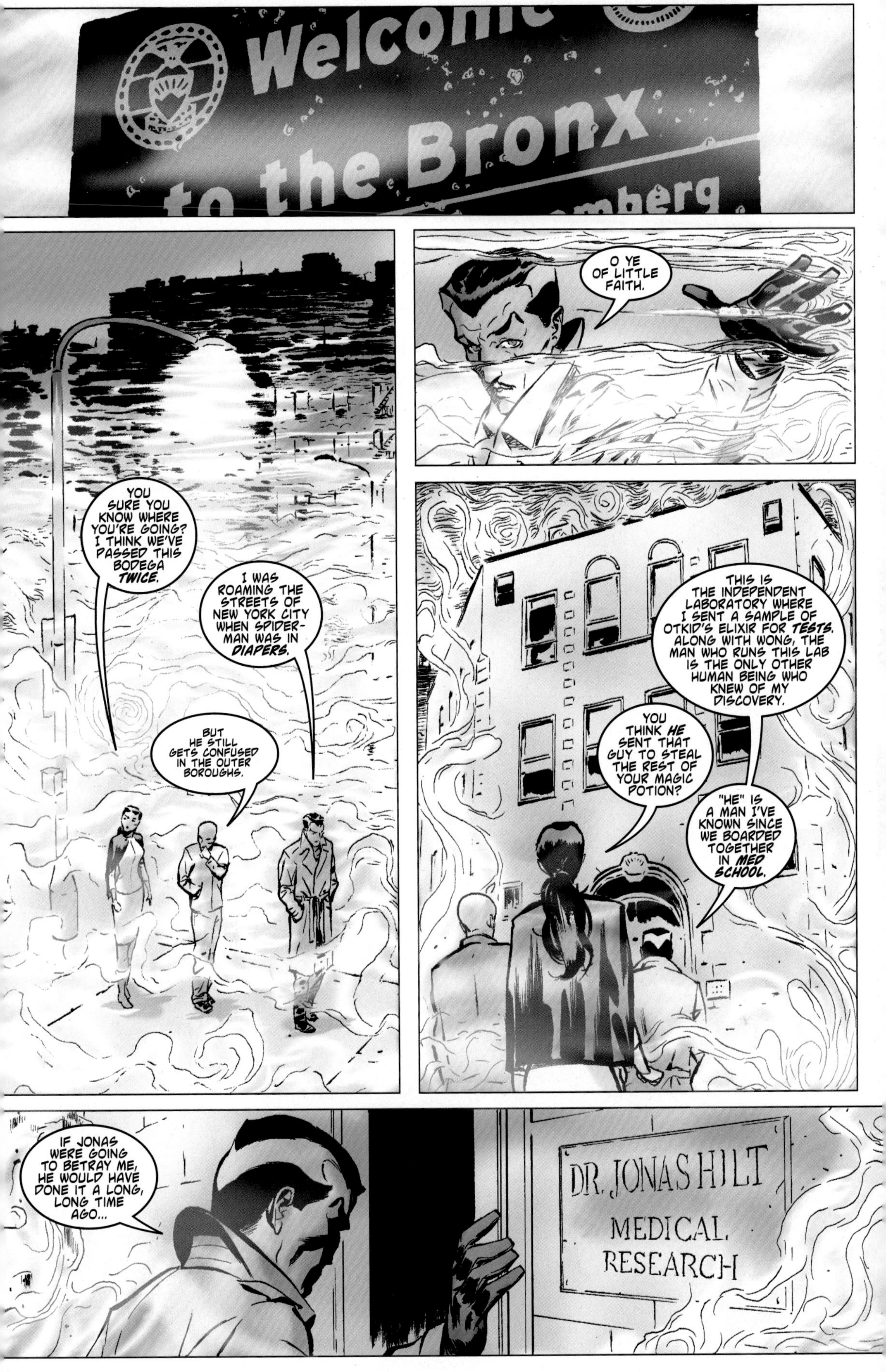
Welcome
to the Bronx
O YE OF LITTLE FAITH.
YOU SURE YOU KNOW WHERE YOU'RE GOING? I THINK WE'VE PASSED THIS BODEGA TWICE.
I WAS ROAMING THE STREETS OF NEW YORK CITY WHEN SPIDER-MAN WAS IN DIAPERS.
BUT HE STILL GETS CONFUSED IN THE OUTER BOROUGHS.
THIS IS THE INDEPENDENT LABORATORY WHERE I SENT A SAMPLE OF OTKID'S ELIXIR FOR TESTS. ALONG WITH WONG, THE MAN WHO RUNS THIS LAB IS THE ONLY OTHER HUMAN BEING WHO KNEW OF MY DISCOVERY.
YOU THINK HE SENT THAT GUY TO STEAL THE REST OF YOUR MAGIC POTION?
"HE" IS A MAN I'VE KNOWN SINCE WE BOARDED TOGETHER IN MED SCHOOL.
IF JONAS WERE GOING TO BETRAY ME, HE WOULD HAVE DONE IT A LONG, LONG TIME AGO...
DR. JONAS HILT
MEDICAL
RESEARCH

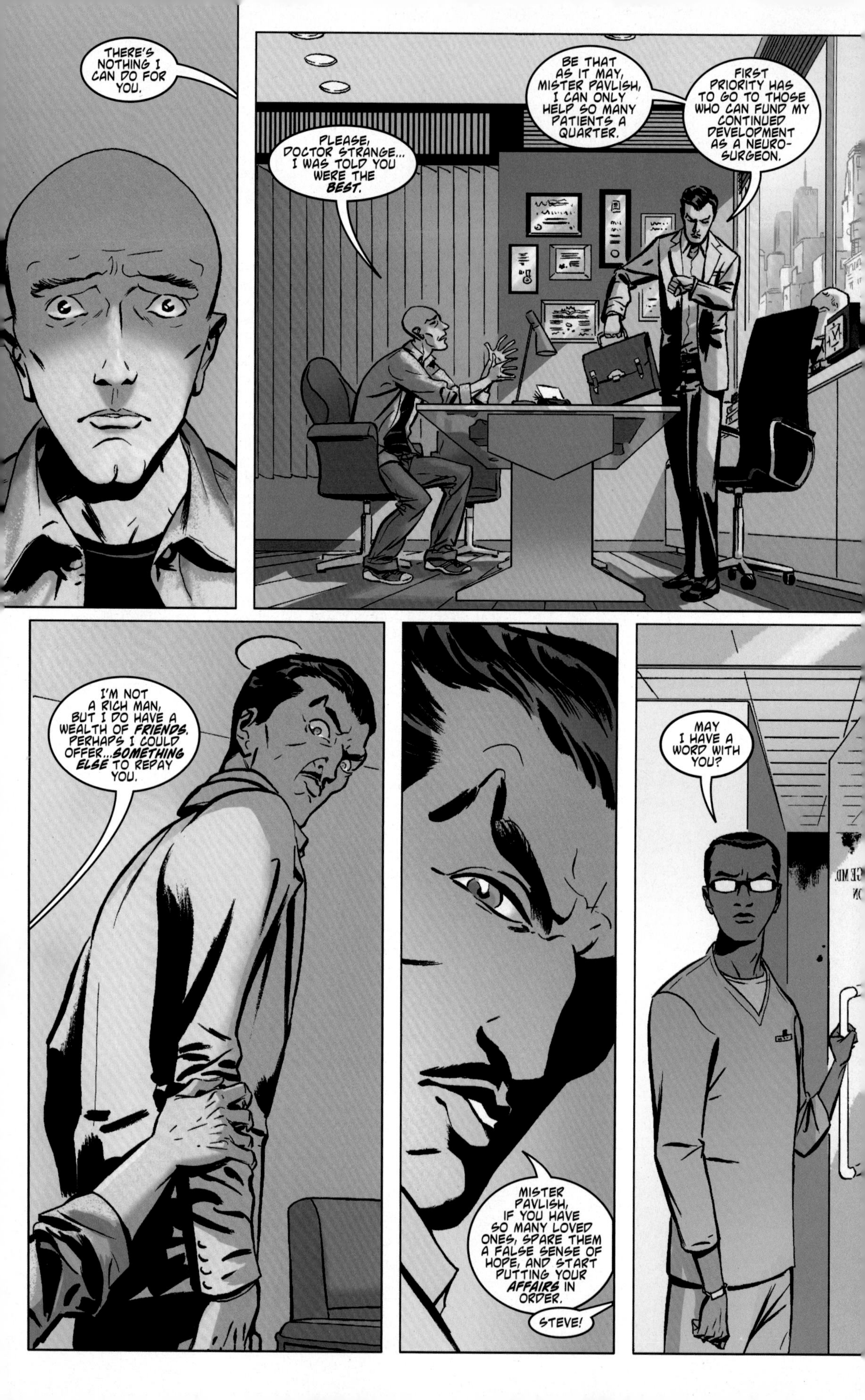
THERE'S NOTHING I CAN DO FOR YOU.
PLEASE, DOCTOR STRANGE... I WAS TOLD YOU WERE THE BEST.
BE THAT AS IT MAY, MISTER PAVLISH, I CAN ONLY HELP SO MANY PATIENTS A QUARTER.
FIRST PRIORITY HAS TO GO TO THOSE WHO CAN FUND MY CONTINUED DEVELOPMENT AS A NEURO-SURGEON.
I'M NOT A RICH MAN, BUT I DO HAVE A WEALTH OF FRIENDS. PERHAPS I COULD OFFER...SOMETHING ELSE TO REPAY YOU.
MISTER PAVLISH, IF YOU HAVE SO MANY LOVED ONES, SPARE THEM A FALSE SENSE OF HOPE, AND START PUTTING YOUR AFFAIRS IN ORDER.
STEVE!
MAY I HAVE A WORD WITH YOU?

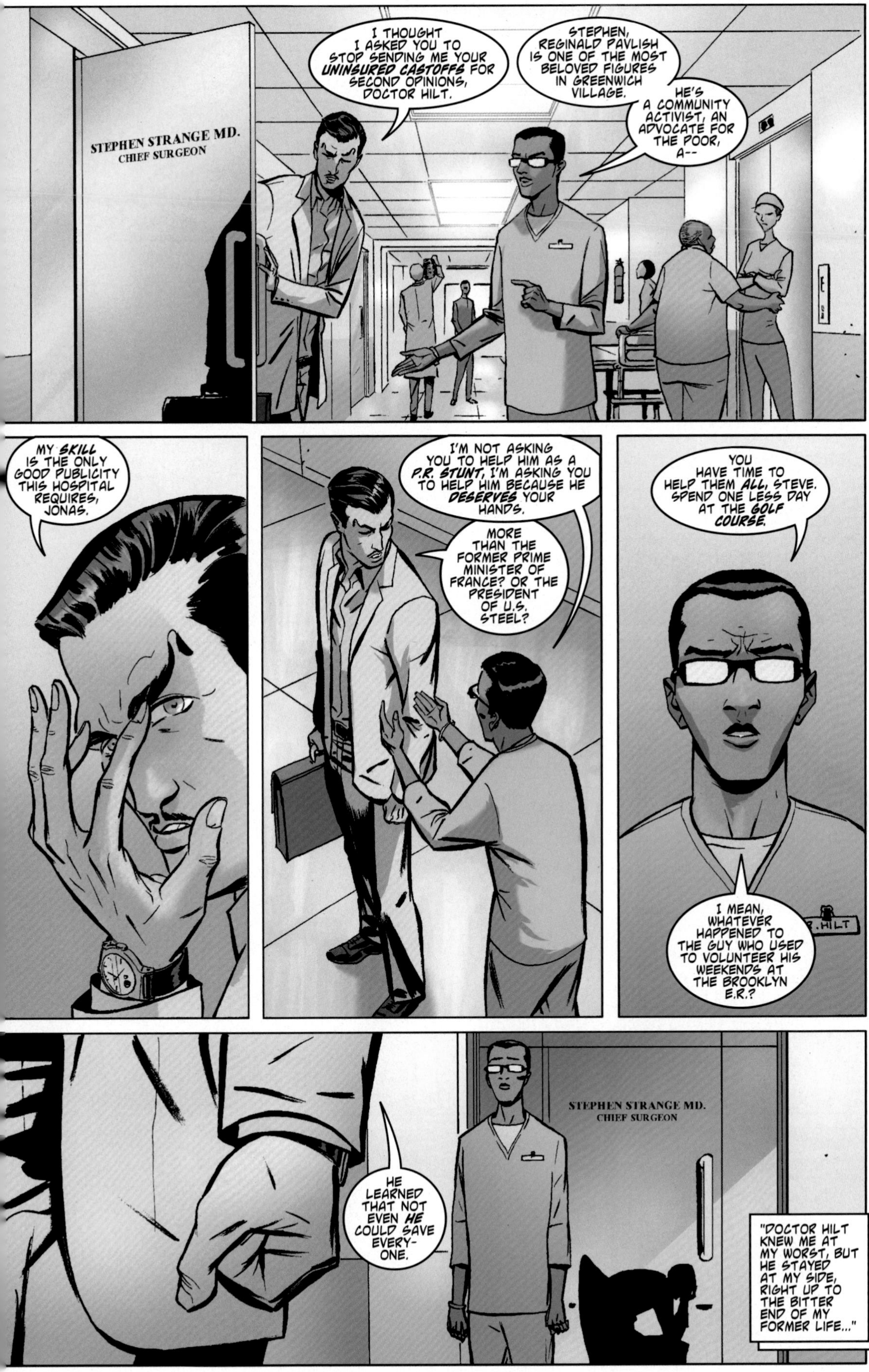
STEPHEN STRANGE MD.
CHIEF SURGEON
I THOUGHT I ASKED YOU TO STOP SENDING ME YOUR UNINSURED CASTOFFS FOR SECOND OPINIONS, DOCTOR HILT.
STEPHEN, REGINALD PAVLISH IS ONE OF THE MOST BELOVED FIGURES IN GREENWICH VILLAGE.
HE'S A COMMUNITY ACTIVIST, AN ADVOCATE FOR THE POOR, A--
MY SKILL IS THE ONLY GOOD PUBLICITY THIS HOSPITAL REQUIRES, JONAS.
I'M NOT ASKING YOU TO HELP HIM AS A P.R. STUNT, I'M ASKING YOU TO HELP HIM BECAUSE HE DESERVES YOUR HANDS.
MORE THAN THE FORMER PRIME MINISTER OF FRANCE? OR THE PRESIDENT OF U.S. STEEL?
YOU HAVE TIME TO HELP THEM ALL, STEVE. SPEND ONE LESS DAY AT THE GOLF COURSE.
I MEAN, WHATEVER HAPPENED TO THE GUY WHO USED TO VOLUNTEER HIS WEEKENDS AT THE BROOKLYN E.R.?
HE LEARNED THAT NOT EVEN HE COULD SAVE EVERY-ONE.
STEPHEN STRANGE MD.
CHIEF SURGEON
"DOCTOR HILT KNEW ME AT MY WORST, BUT HE STAYED AT MY SIDE, RIGHT UP TO THE BITTER END OF MY FORMER LIFE..."

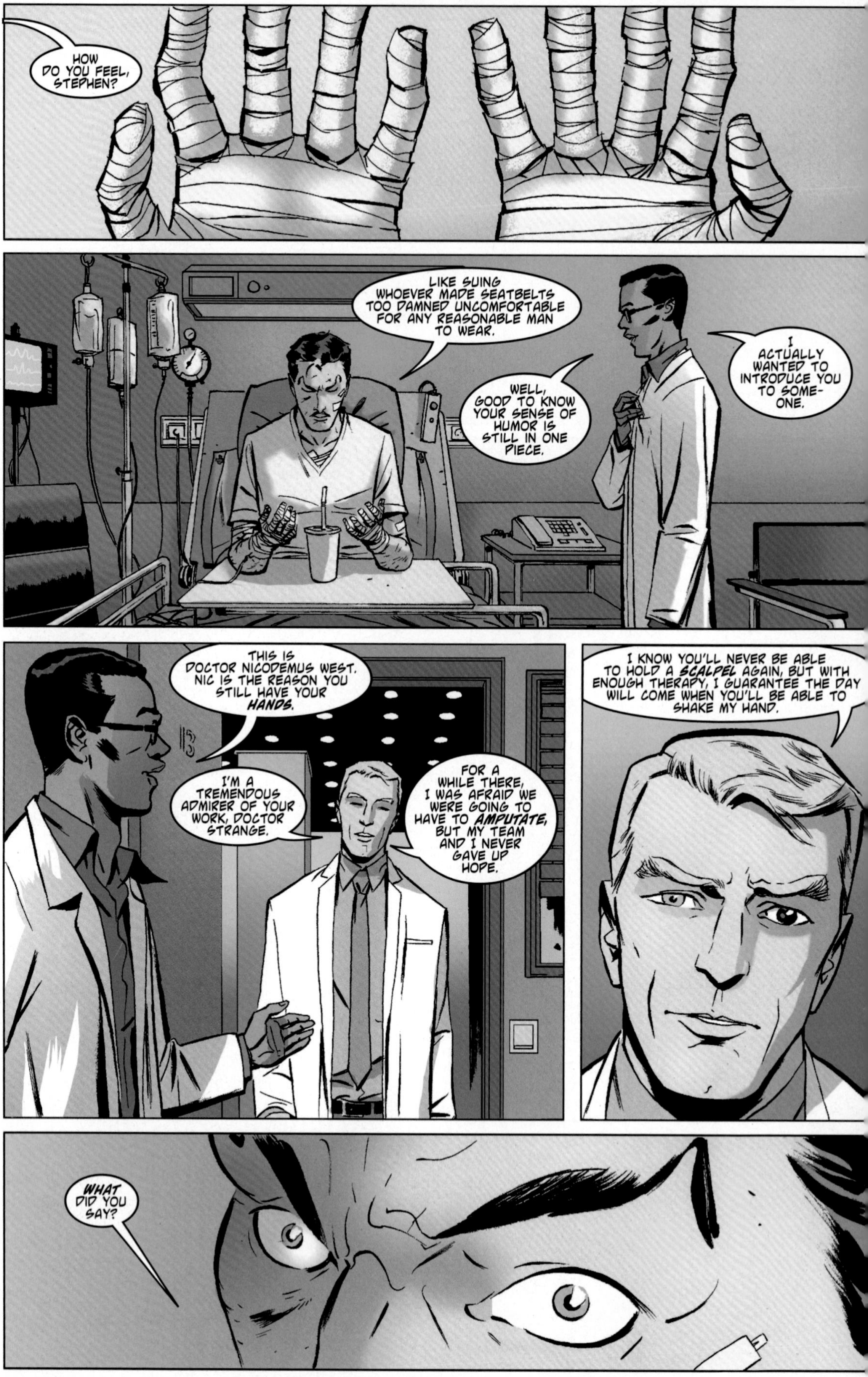
HOW DO YOU FEEL, STEPHEN?
LIKE SUING WHOEVER MADE SEATBELTS TOO DAMNED UNCOMFORTABLE FOR ANY REASONABLE MAN TO WEAR.
WELL, GOOD TO KNOW YOUR SENSE OF HUMOR IS STILL IN ONE PIECE.
I ACTUALLY WANTED TO INTRODUCE YOU TO SOME-ONE.
THIS IS DOCTOR NICODEMUS WEST. NIC IS THE REASON YOU STILL HAVE YOUR HANDS.
I'M A TREMENDOUS ADMIRER OF YOUR WORK, DOCTOR STRANGE.
FOR A WHILE THERE, I WAS AFRAID WE WERE GOING TO HAVE TO AMPUTATE, BUT MY TEAM AND I NEVER GAVE UP HOPE.
I KNOW YOU'LL NEVER BE ABLE TO HOLD A SCALPEL AGAIN, BUT WITH ENOUGH THERAPY, I GUARANTEE THE DAY WILL COME WHEN YOU'LL BE ABLE TO SHAKE MY HAND.
WHAT DID YOU SAY?

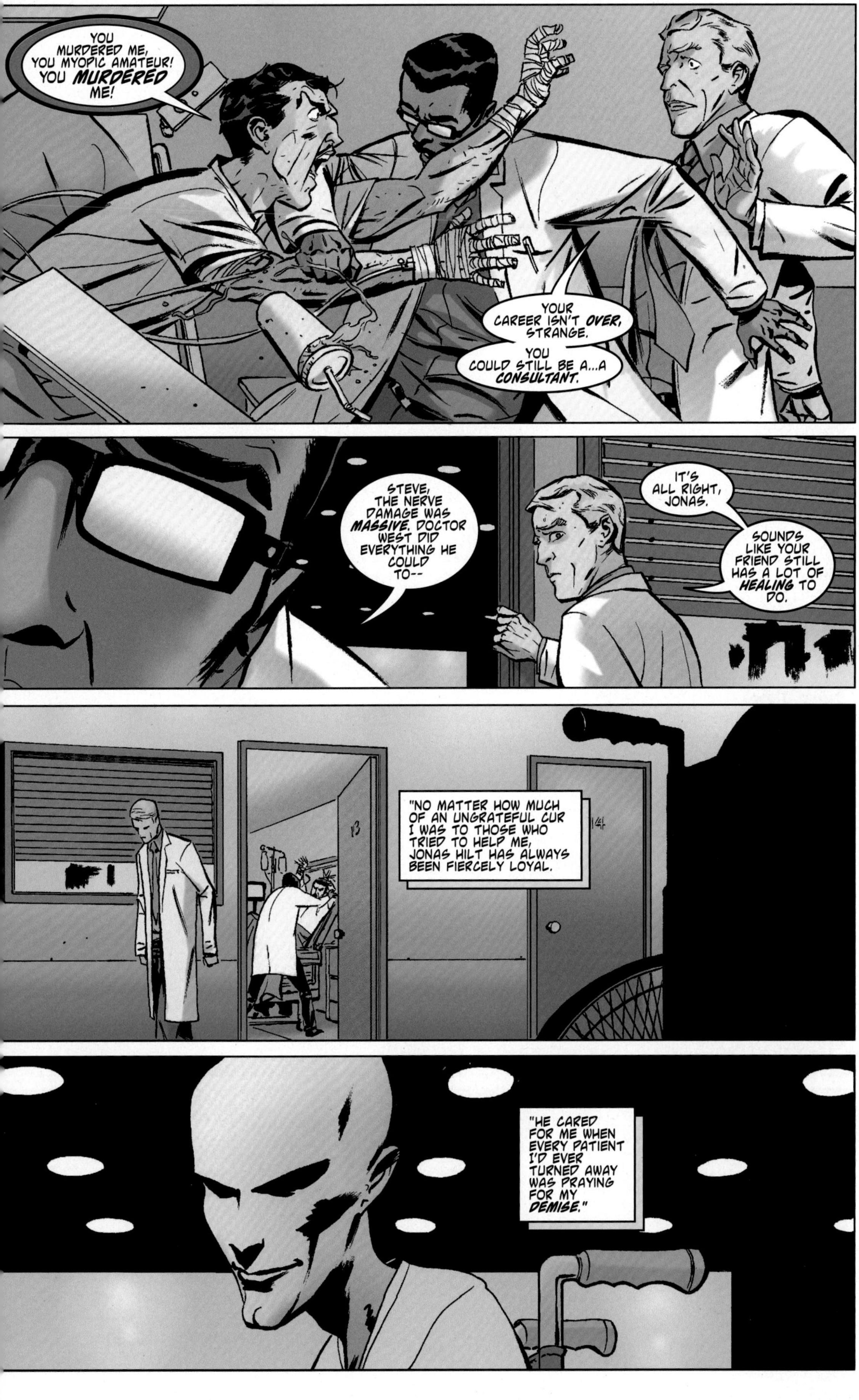
YOU MURDERED ME, YOU MYOPIC AMATEUR! YOU MURDERED ME!
YOUR CAREER ISN'T OVER, STRANGE.
YOU COULD STILL BE A...A CONSULTANT.
STEVE, THE NERVE DAMAGE WAS MASSIVE. DOCTOR WEST DID EVERYTHING HE COULD TO--
IT'S ALL RIGHT, JONAS.
SOUNDS LIKE YOUR FRIEND STILL HAS A LOT OF HEALING TO DO.
13
14
"NO MATTER HOW MUCH OF AN UNGRATEFUL CUR I WAS TO THOSE WHO TRIED TO HELP ME, JONAS HILT HAS ALWAYS BEEN FIERCELY LOYAL.
"HE CARED FOR ME WHEN EVERY PATIENT I'D EVER TURNED AWAY WAS PRAYING FOR MY DEMISE."

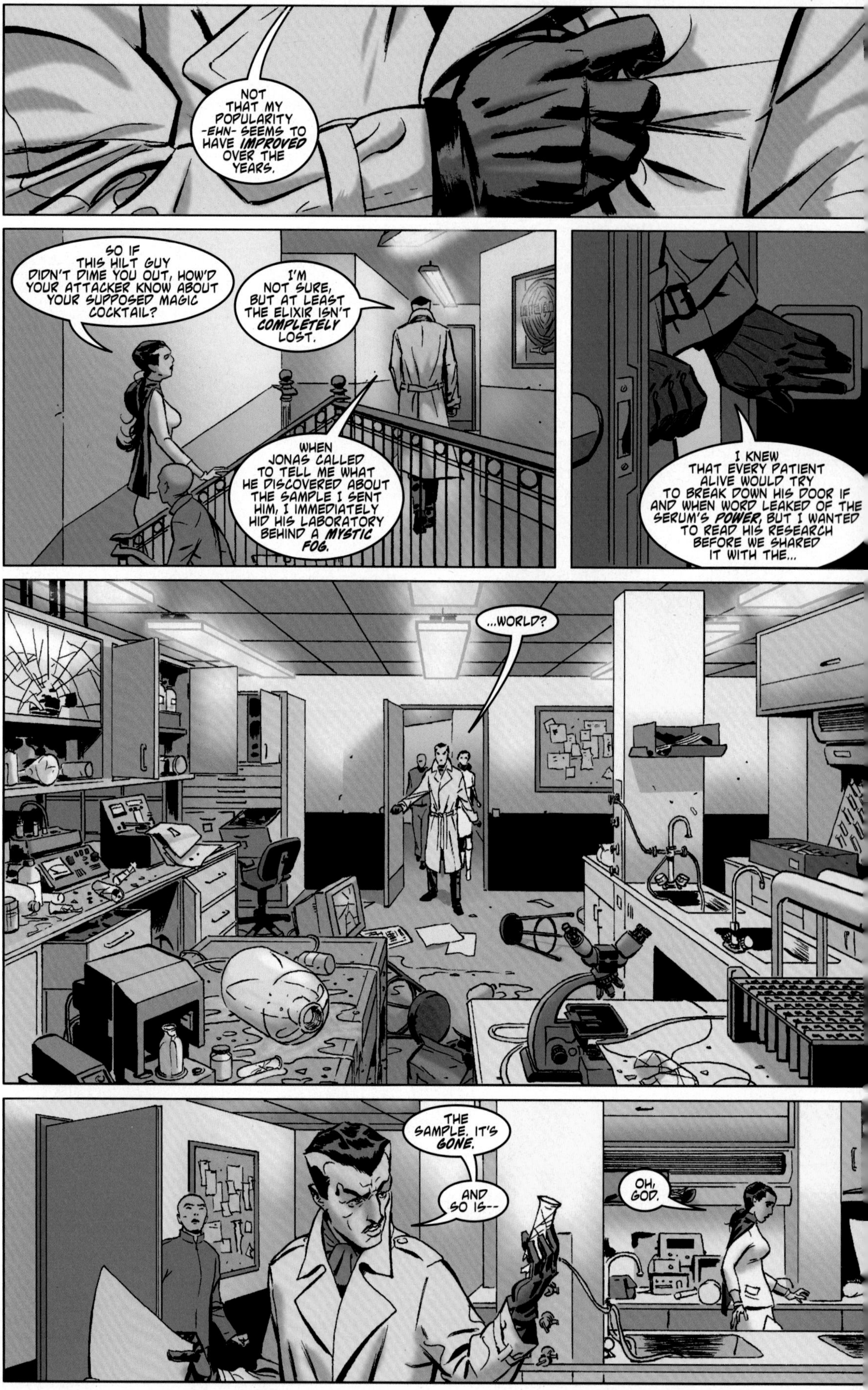
NOT THAT MY POPULARITY -EHN- SEEMS TO HAVE *IMPROVED* OVER THE YEARS.
SO IF THIS HILT GUY DIDN'T DIME YOU OUT, HOW'D YOUR ATTACKER KNOW ABOUT YOUR SUPPOSED MAGIC COCKTAIL?
I'M NOT SURE, BUT AT LEAST THE ELIXIR ISN'T *COMPLETELY* LOST.
WHEN JONAS CALLED TO TELL ME WHAT HE DISCOVERED ABOUT THE SAMPLE I SENT HIM, I IMMEDIATELY HID HIS LABORATORY BEHIND A *MYSTIC FOG.*
I KNEW THAT EVERY PATIENT ALIVE WOULD TRY TO BREAK DOWN HIS DOOR IF AND WHEN WORD LEAKED OF THE SERUM'S *POWER,* BUT I WANTED TO READ HIS RESEARCH BEFORE WE SHARED IT WITH THE...
...WORLD?
THE SAMPLE. IT'S *GONE.*
AND SO IS--
OH, GOD.

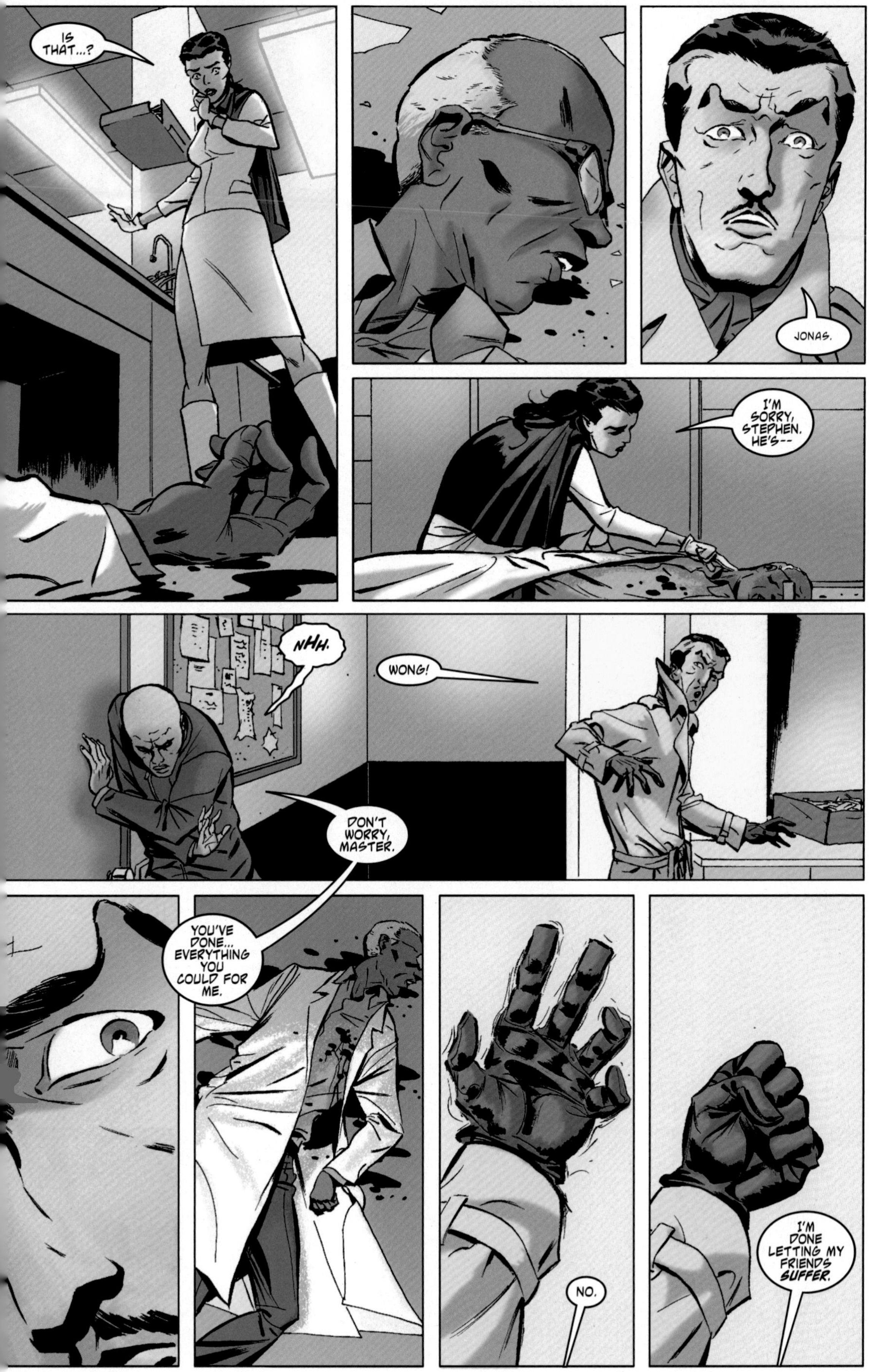

IS THAT...?
JONAS.
I'M SORRY, STEPHEN. HE'S--
NHH.
WONG!
DON'T WORRY, MASTER.
YOU'VE DONE... EVERYTHING YOU COULD FOR ME.
NO.
I'M DONE LETTING MY FRIENDS SUFFER.

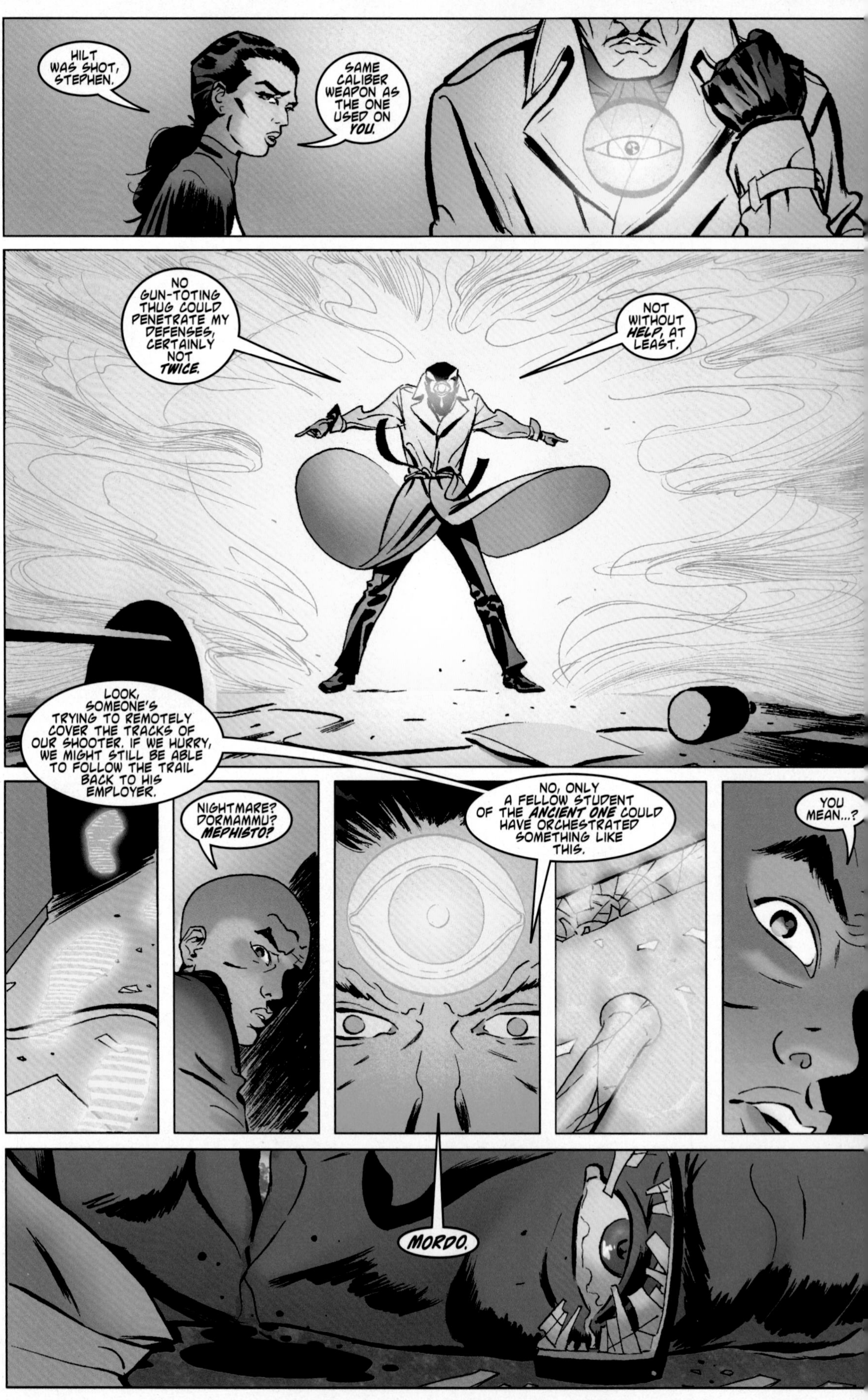
HILT WAS SHOT, STEPHEN.
SAME CALIBER WEAPON AS THE ONE USED ON YOU.
NO GUN-TOTING THUG COULD PENETRATE MY DEFENSES, CERTAINLY NOT TWICE.
NOT WITHOUT HELP, AT LEAST.
LOOK, SOMEONE'S TRYING TO REMOTELY COVER THE TRACKS OF OUR SHOOTER. IF WE HURRY, WE MIGHT STILL BE ABLE TO FOLLOW THE TRAIL BACK TO HIS EMPLOYER.
NIGHTMARE? DORMAMMU? MEPHISTO?
NO, ONLY A FELLOW STUDENT OF THE ANCIENT ONE COULD HAVE ORCHESTRATED SOMETHING LIKE THIS.
YOU MEAN...?
MORDO.

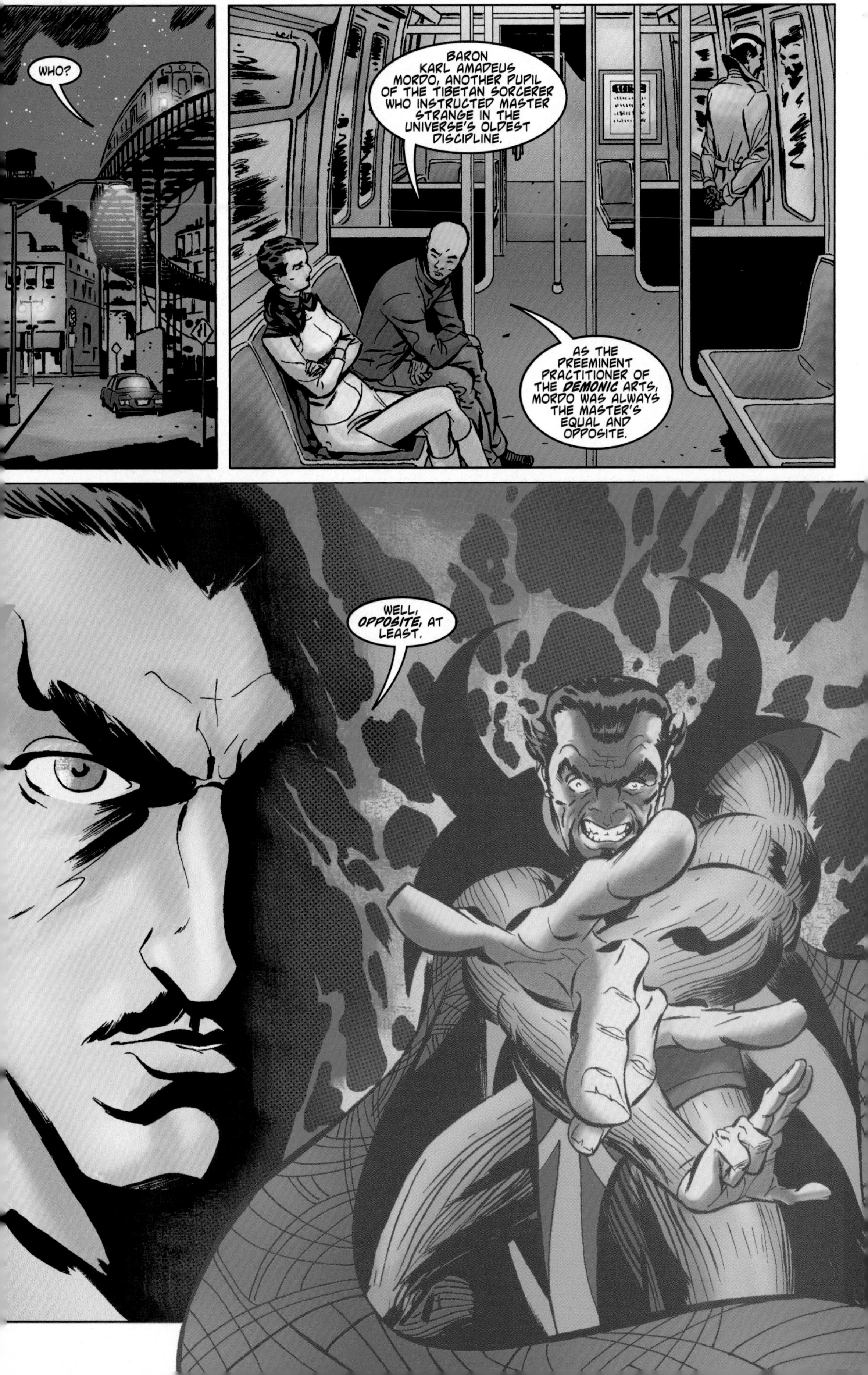
WHO?
BARON KARL AMADEUS MORDO, ANOTHER PUPIL OF THE TIBETAN SORCERER WHO INSTRUCTED MASTER STRANGE IN THE UNIVERSE'S OLDEST DISCIPLINE.
AS THE PREEMINENT PRACTITIONER OF THE *DEMONIC* ARTS, MORDO WAS ALWAYS THE MASTER'S EQUAL AND OPPOSITE.
WELL, *OPPOSITE*, AT LEAST.

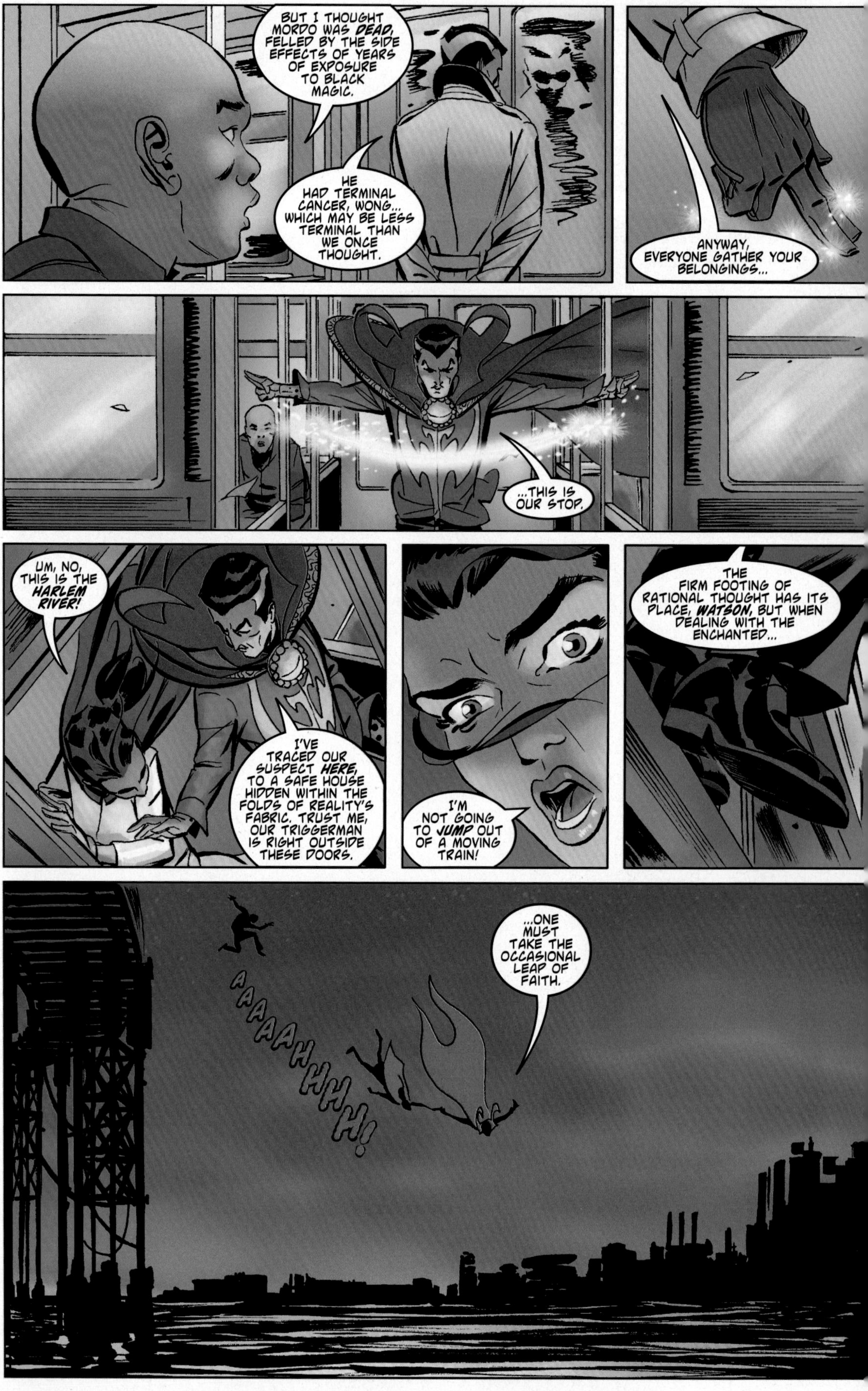
BUT I THOUGHT MORDO WAS DEAD, FELLED BY THE SIDE EFFECTS OF YEARS OF EXPOSURE TO BLACK MAGIC.
HE HAD TERMINAL CANCER, WONG... WHICH MAY BE LESS TERMINAL THAN WE ONCE THOUGHT.
ANYWAY, EVERYONE GATHER YOUR BELONGINGS...
...THIS IS OUR STOP.
UM, NO, THIS IS THE HARLEM RIVER!
I'VE TRACED OUR SUSPECT HERE, TO A SAFE HOUSE HIDDEN WITHIN THE FOLDS OF REALITY'S FABRIC. TRUST ME, OUR TRIGGERMAN IS RIGHT OUTSIDE THESE DOORS.
I'M NOT GOING TO JUMP OUT OF A MOVING TRAIN!
THE FIRM FOOTING OF RATIONAL THOUGHT HAS ITS PLACE, WATSON, BUT WHEN DEALING WITH THE ENCHANTED...
...ONE MUST TAKE THE OCCASIONAL LEAP OF FAITH.
AAAAAAHHHHH!

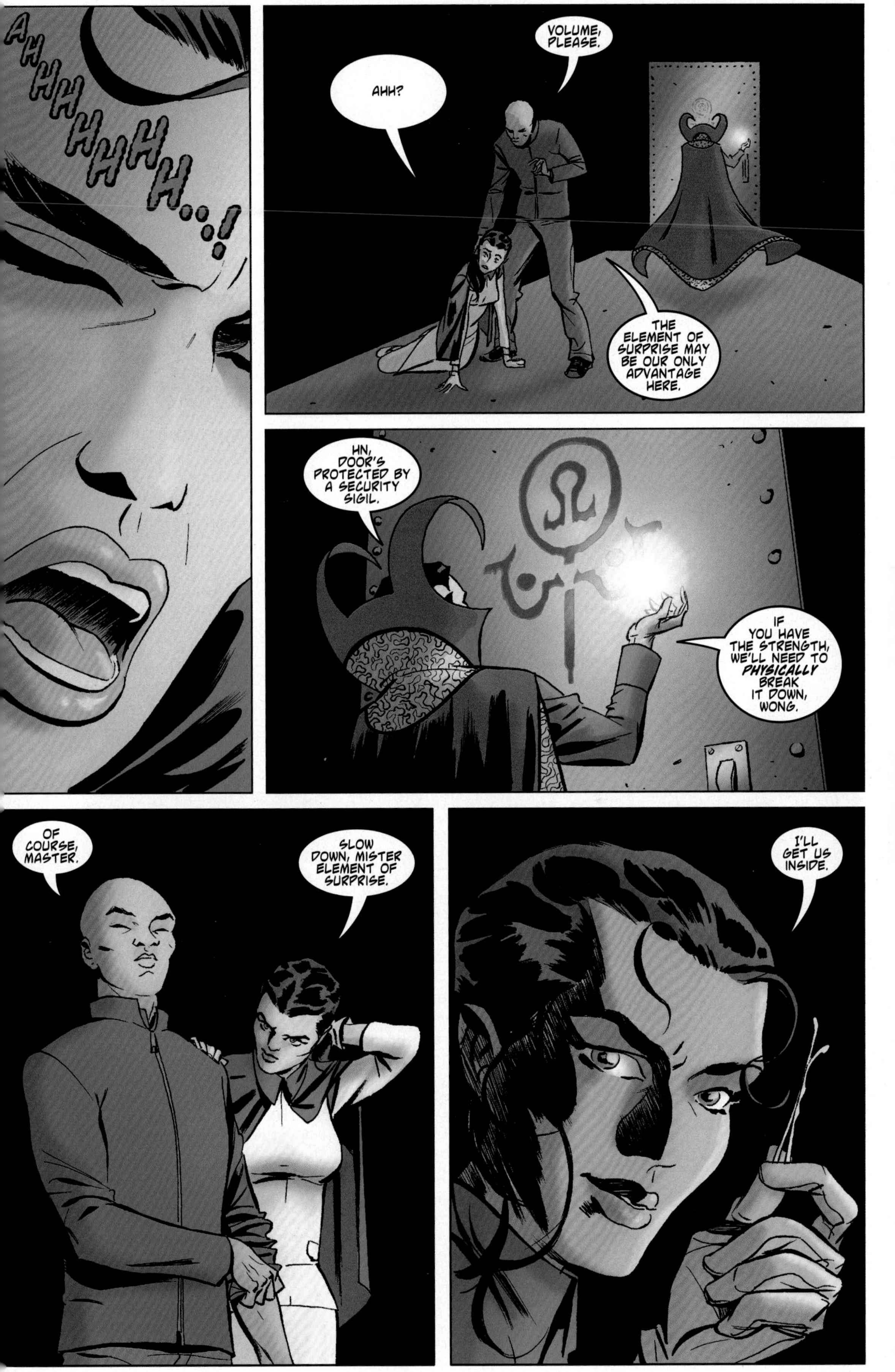
AHHHHHHHH...!
AHH?
VOLUME, PLEASE.
THE ELEMENT OF SURPRISE MAY BE OUR ONLY ADVANTAGE HERE.
HN, DOOR'S PROTECTED BY A SECURITY SIGIL.
IF YOU HAVE THE STRENGTH, WE'LL NEED TO *PHYSICALLY* BREAK IT DOWN, WONG.
OF COURSE, MASTER.
SLOW DOWN, MISTER ELEMENT OF SURPRISE.
I'LL GET US INSIDE.

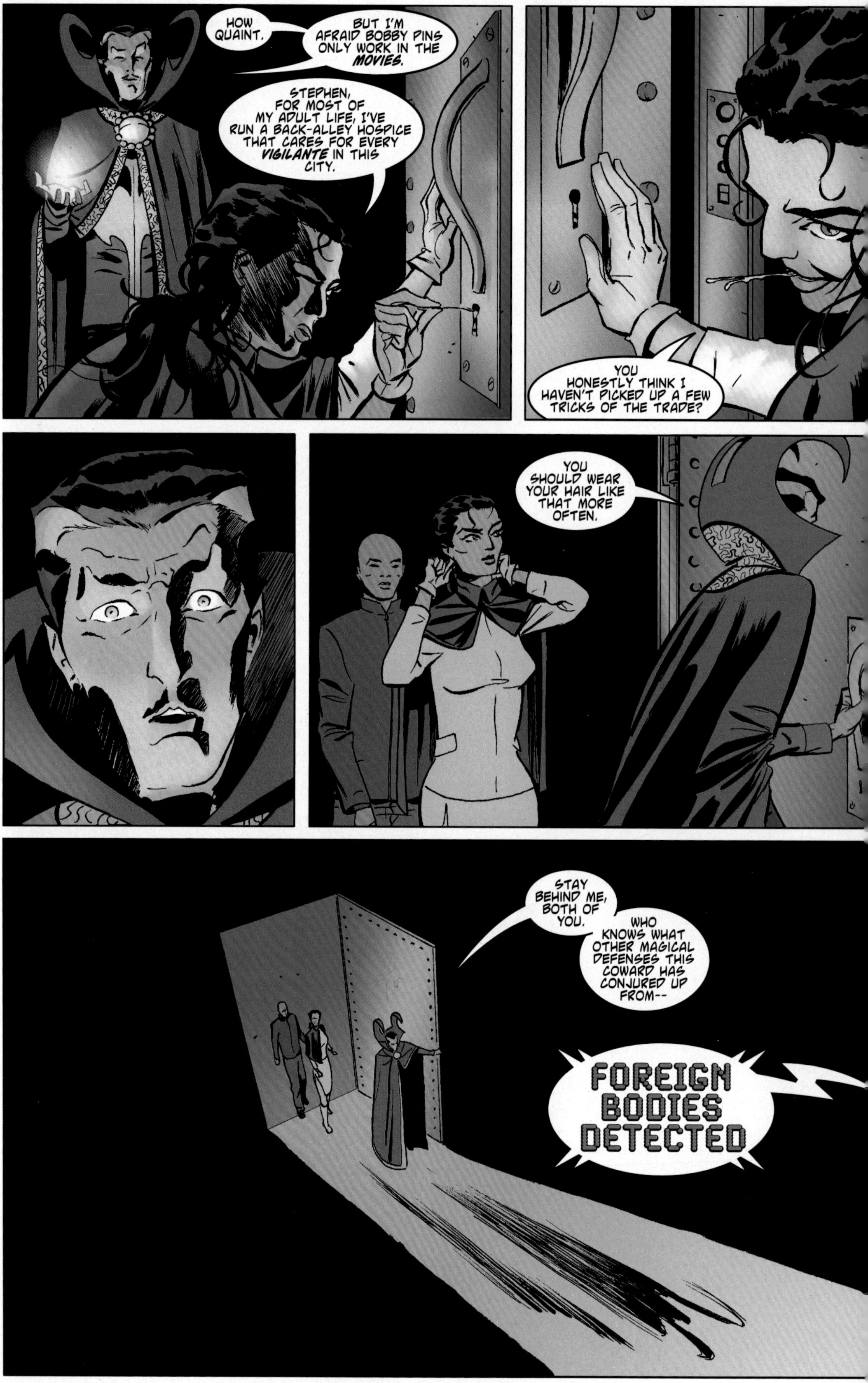
HOW QUAINT.
BUT I'M AFRAID BOBBY PINS ONLY WORK IN THE *MOVIES*.
STEPHEN, FOR MOST OF MY ADULT LIFE, I'VE RUN A BACK-ALLEY HOSPICE THAT CARES FOR EVERY *VIGILANTE* IN THIS CITY.
YOU HONESTLY THINK I HAVEN'T PICKED UP A FEW TRICKS OF THE TRADE?
YOU SHOULD WEAR YOUR HAIR LIKE THAT MORE OFTEN.
STAY BEHIND ME, BOTH OF YOU.
WHO KNOWS WHAT OTHER MAGICAL DEFENSES THIS COWARD HAS CONJURED UP FROM--
FOREIGN BODIES DETECTED

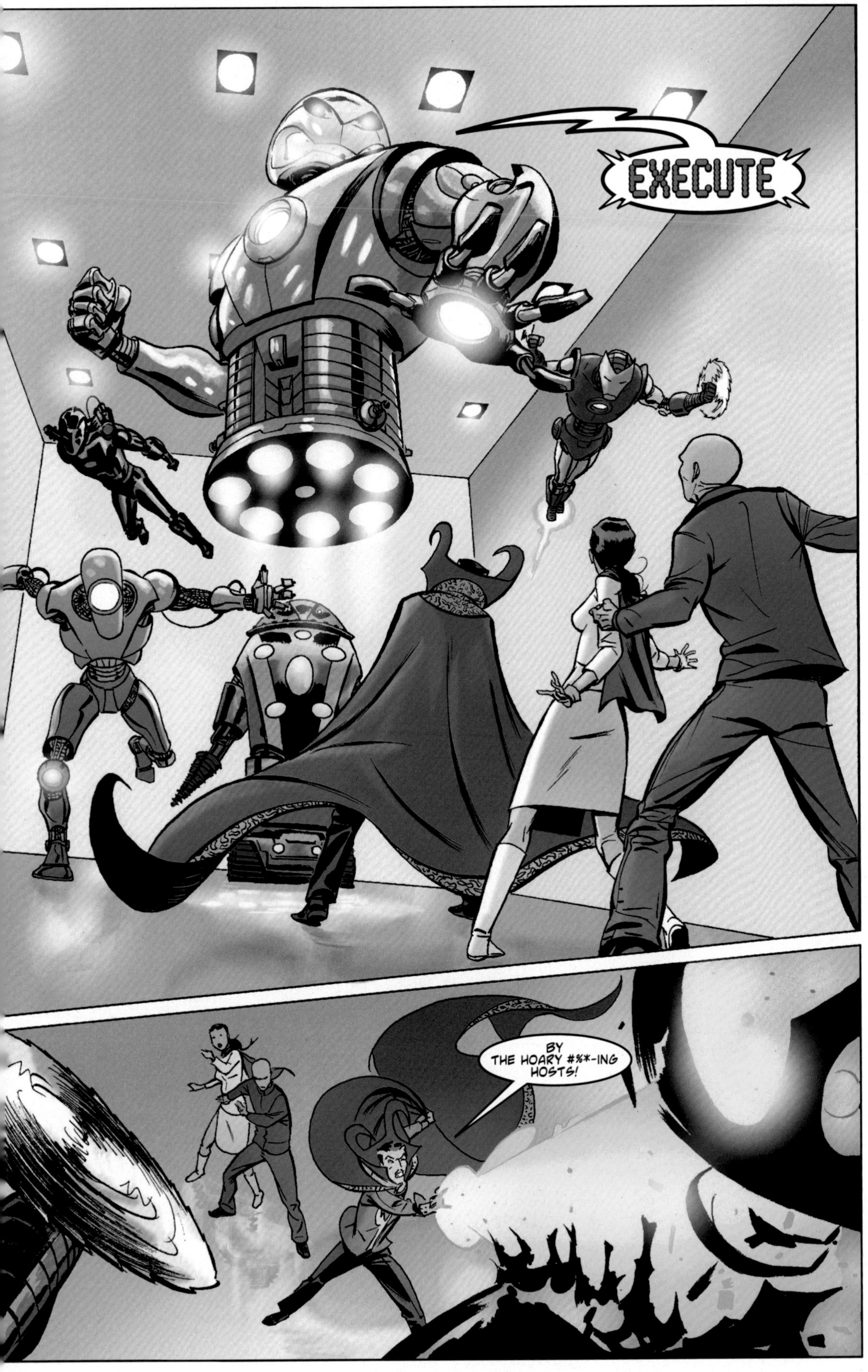
EXECUTE
BY THE HOARY #%*-ING HOSTS!

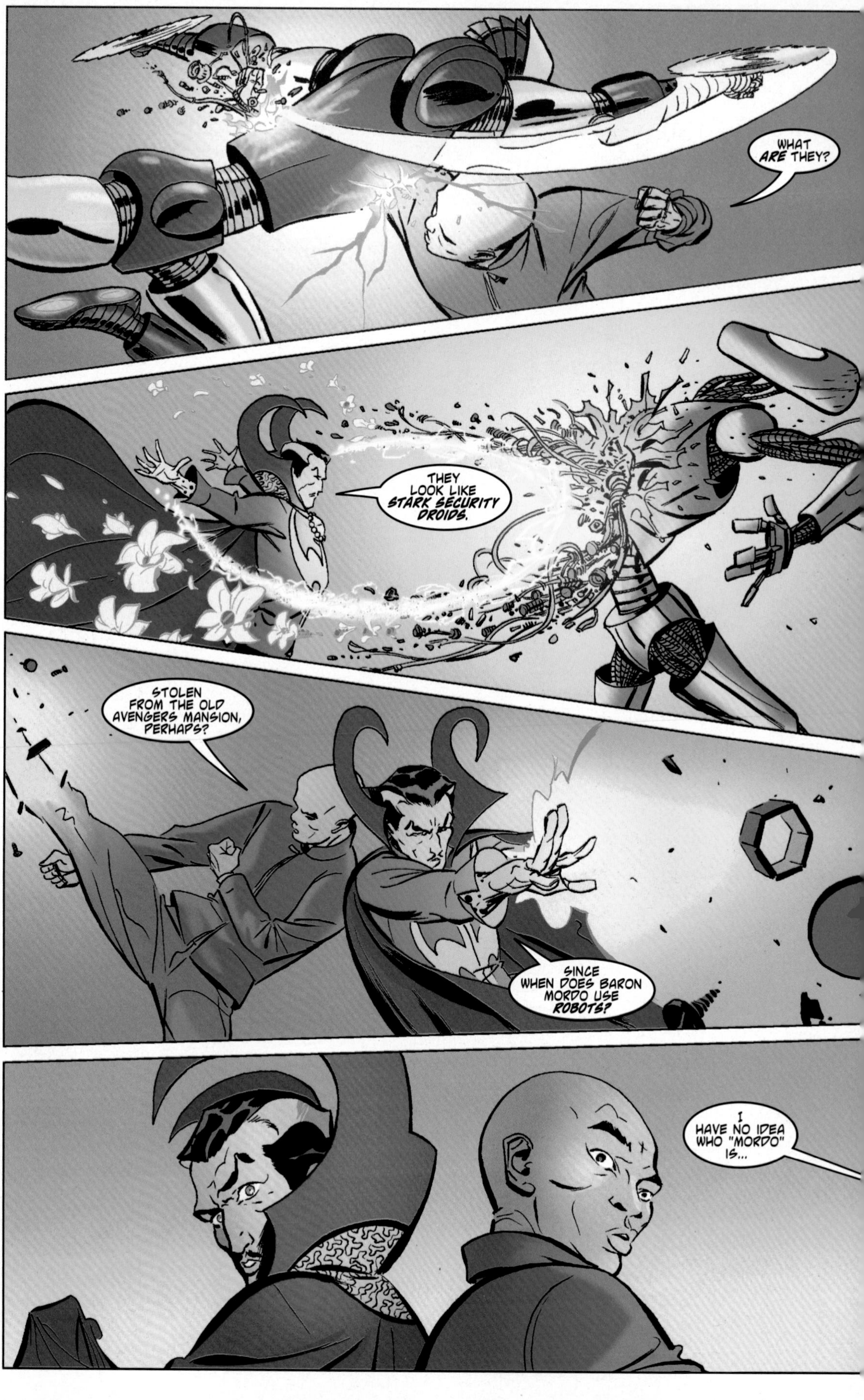
WHAT ARE THEY?
THEY LOOK LIKE STARK SECURITY DROIDS.
STOLEN FROM THE OLD AVENGERS MANSION, PERHAPS?
SINCE WHEN DOES BARON MORDO USE ROBOTS?
I HAVE NO IDEA WHO "MORDO" IS...

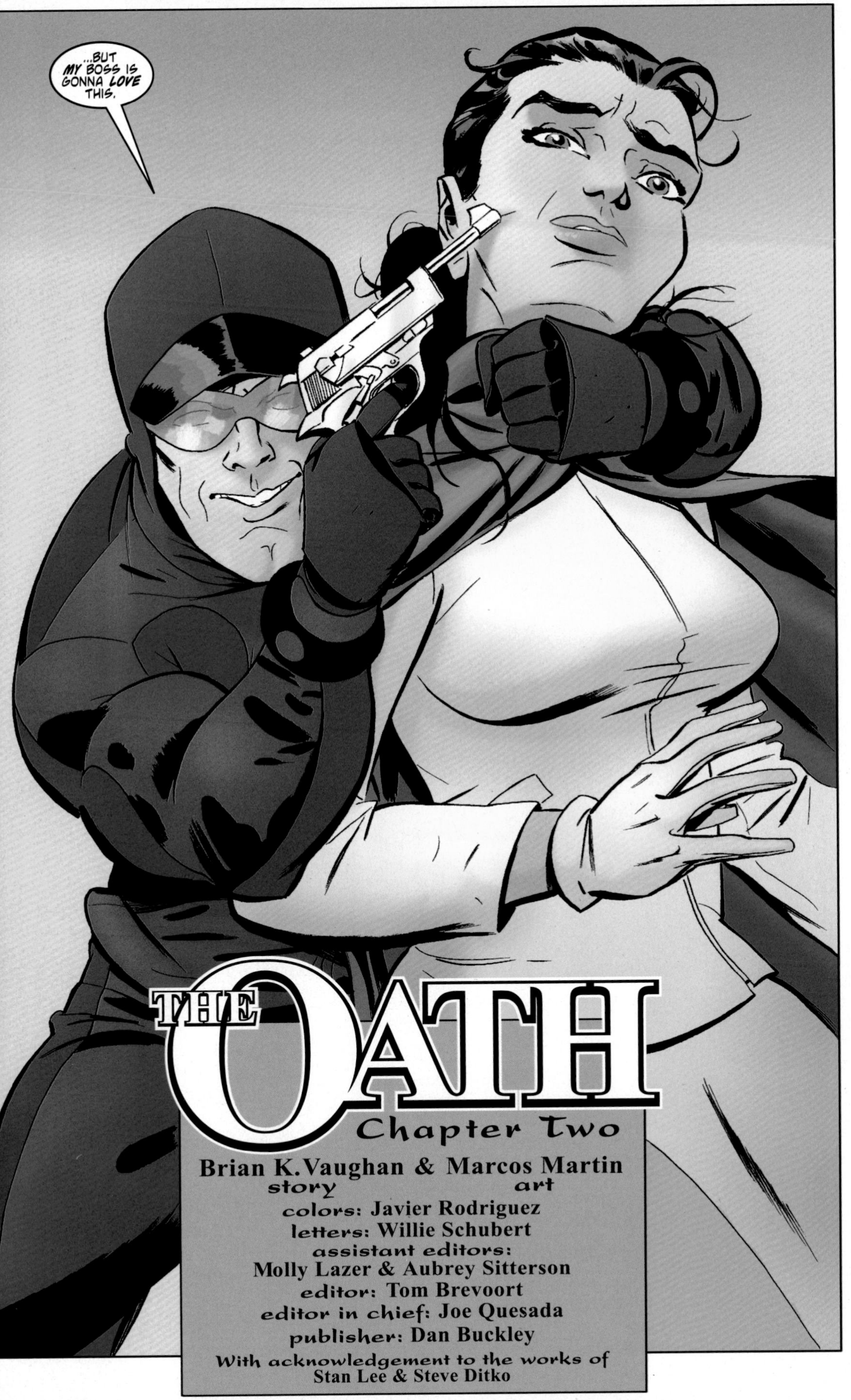
...BUT *MY* BOSS IS GONNA *LOVE* THIS.

THE OATH

Chapter Two

Brian K. Vaughan story & **Marcos Martin** art

colors: **Javier Rodriguez**

letters: **Willie Schubert**

assistant editors:
Molly Lazer & Aubrey Sitterson

editor: **Tom Brevoort**

editor in chief: **Joe Quesada**

publisher: **Dan Buckley**

With acknowledgement to the works of
Stan Lee & Steve Ditko

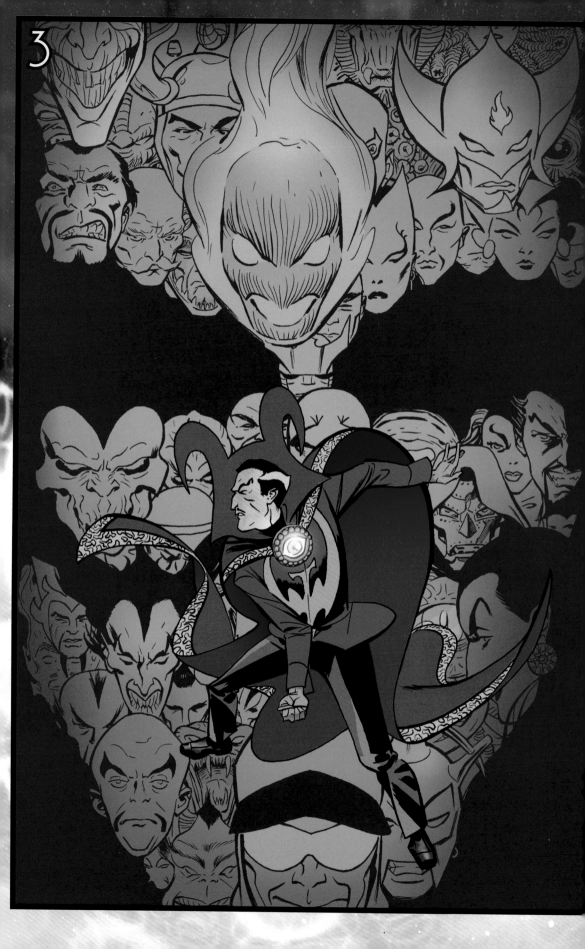

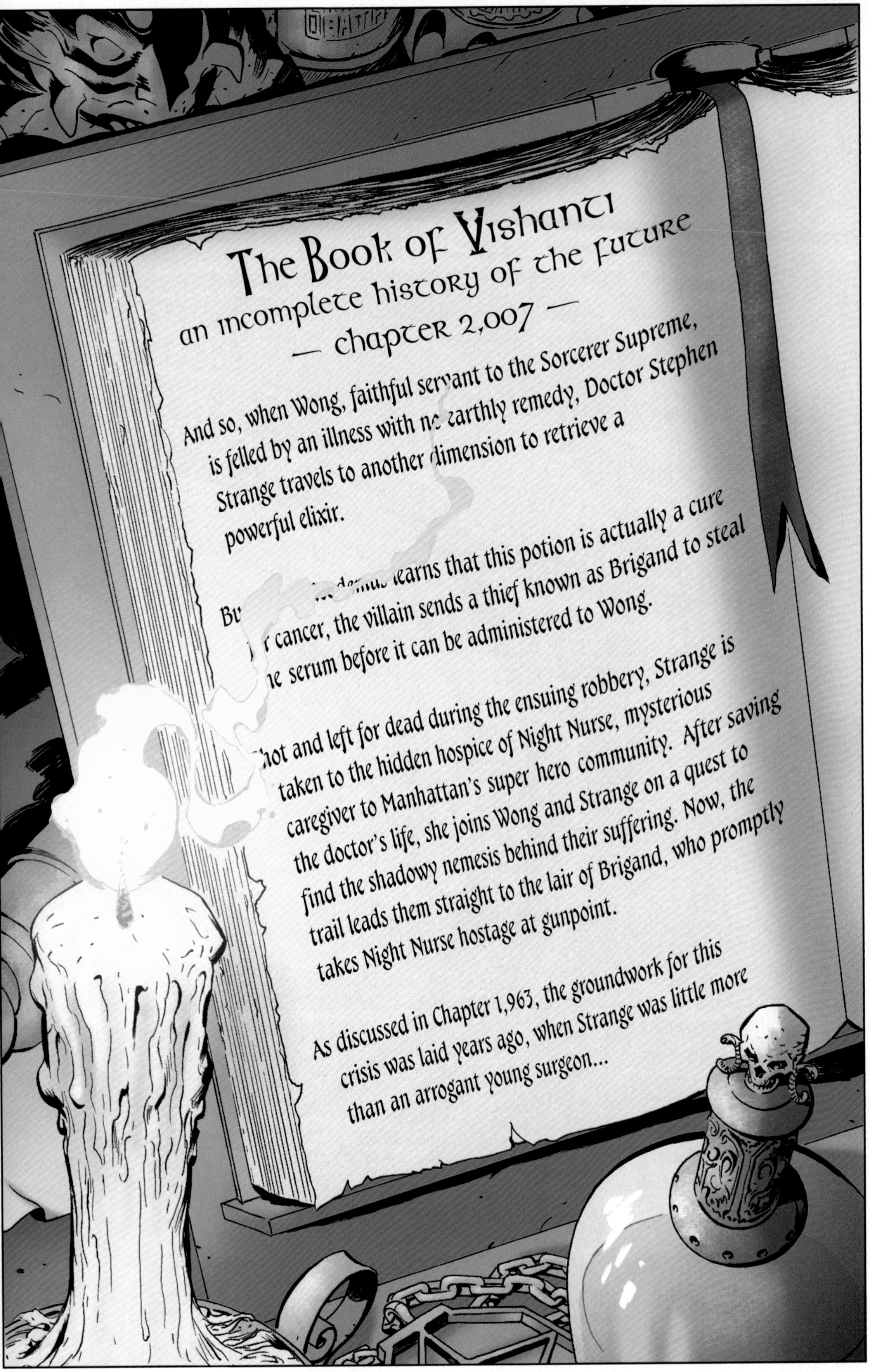
The Book of Vishanti
an incomplete history of the future
— chapter 2,007 —
And so, when Wong, faithful servant to the Sorcerer Supreme, is felled by an illness with no earthly remedy, Doctor Stephen Strange travels to another dimension to retrieve a powerful elixir.
learns that this potion is actually a cure cancer, the villain sends a thief known as Brigand to steal serum before it can be administered to Wong.
hot and left for dead during the ensuing robbery, Strange is taken to the hidden hospice of Night Nurse, mysterious caregiver to Manhattan's super hero community. After saving the doctor's life, she joins Wong and Strange on a quest to find the shadowy nemesis behind their suffering. Now, the trail leads them straight to the lair of Brigand, who promptly takes Night Nurse hostage at gunpoint.
As discussed in Chapter 1,963, the groundwork for this crisis was laid years ago, when Strange was little more than an arrogant young surgeon...

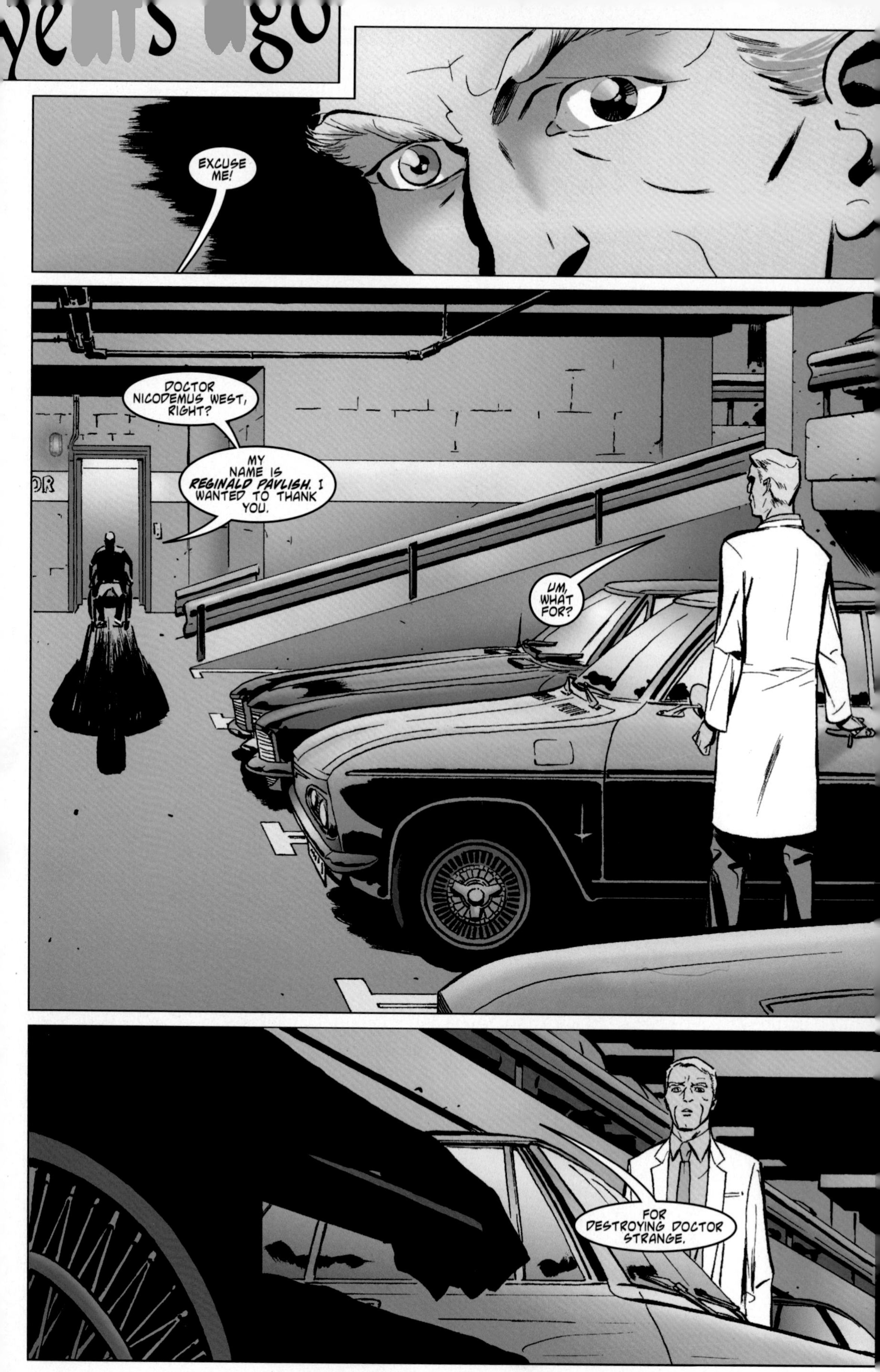
EXCUSE ME!
DOCTOR NICODEMUS WEST, RIGHT?
MY NAME IS REGINALD PAVLISH. I WANTED TO THANK YOU.
UM, WHAT FOR?
FOR DESTROYING DOCTOR STRANGE.

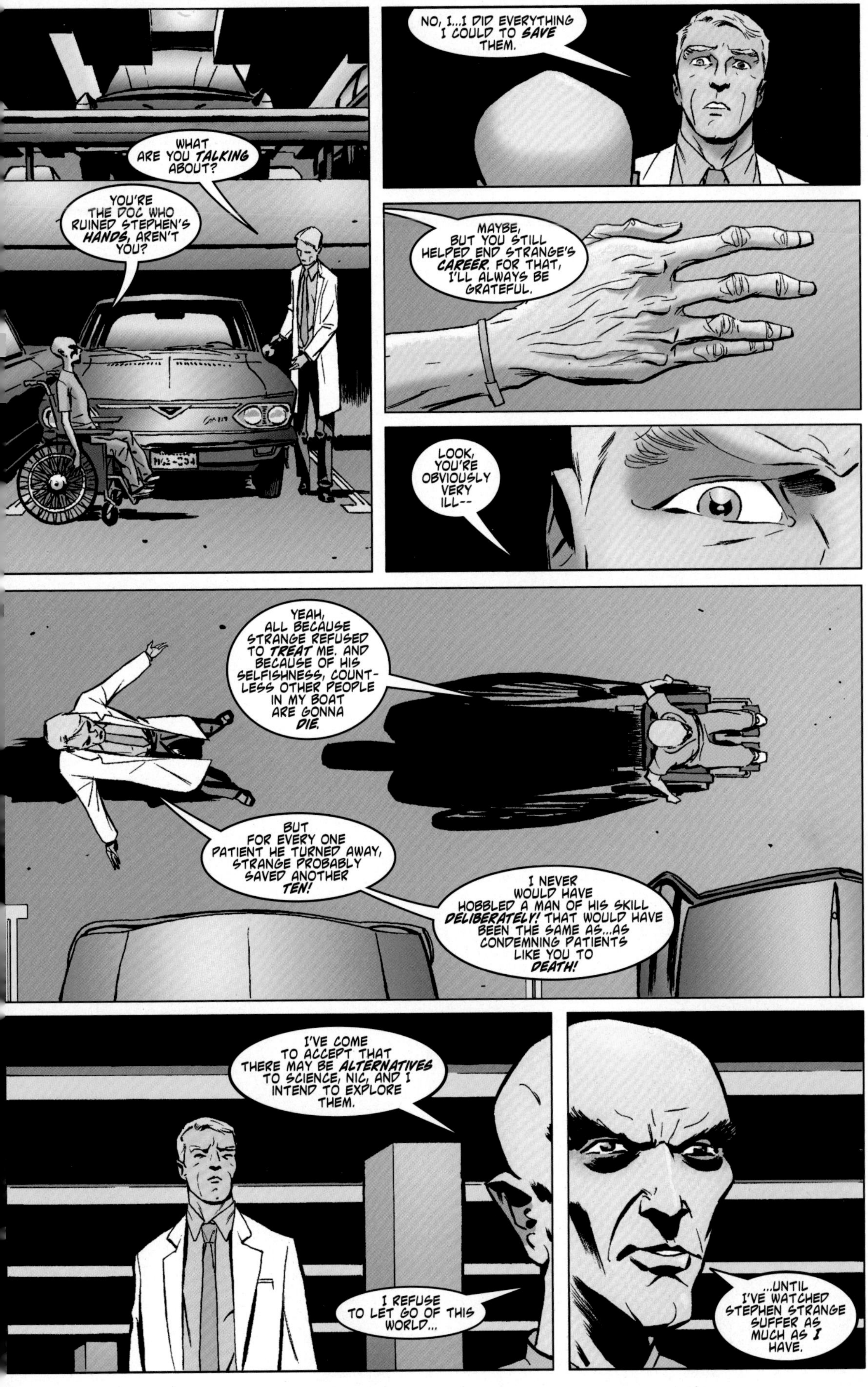
WHAT ARE YOU TALKING ABOUT?
YOU'RE THE DOC WHO RUINED STEPHEN'S HANDS, AREN'T YOU?
NO, I...I DID EVERYTHING I COULD TO SAVE THEM.
MAYBE, BUT YOU STILL HELPED END STRANGE'S CAREER. FOR THAT, I'LL ALWAYS BE GRATEFUL.
LOOK, YOU'RE OBVIOUSLY VERY ILL--
YEAH, ALL BECAUSE STRANGE REFUSED TO TREAT ME. AND BECAUSE OF HIS SELFISHNESS, COUNTLESS OTHER PEOPLE IN MY BOAT ARE GONNA DIE.
BUT FOR EVERY ONE PATIENT HE TURNED AWAY, STRANGE PROBABLY SAVED ANOTHER TEN!
I NEVER WOULD HAVE HOBBLED A MAN OF HIS SKILL DELIBERATELY! THAT WOULD HAVE BEEN THE SAME AS...AS CONDEMNING PATIENTS LIKE YOU TO DEATH!
I'VE COME TO ACCEPT THAT THERE MAY BE ALTERNATIVES TO SCIENCE, NIC, AND I INTEND TO EXPLORE THEM.
I REFUSE TO LET GO OF THIS WORLD...
...UNTIL I'VE WATCHED STEPHEN STRANGE SUFFER AS MUCH AS I HAVE.

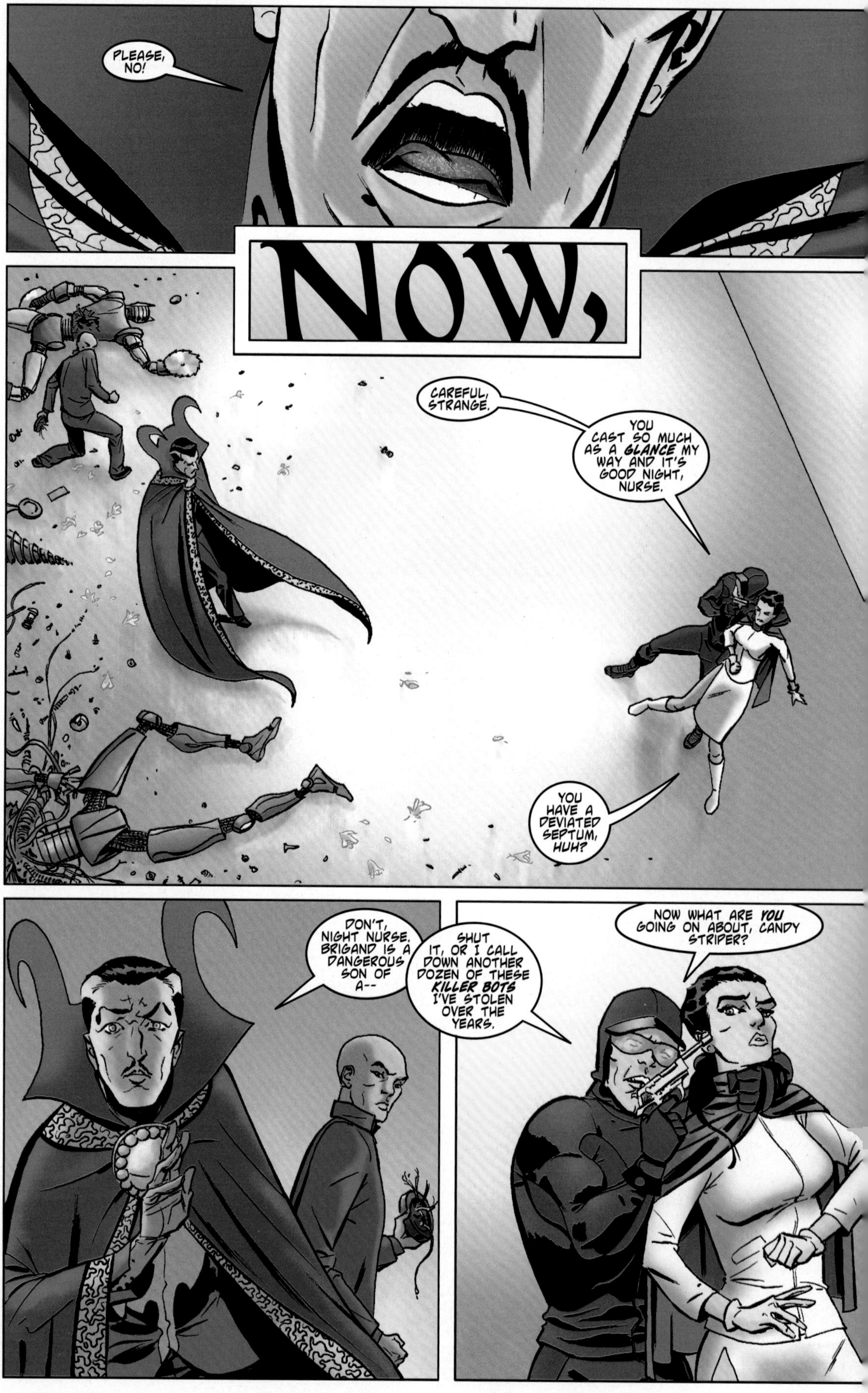

PLEASE, NO!
NOW,
CAREFUL, STRANGE.
YOU CAST SO MUCH AS A GLANCE MY WAY AND IT'S GOOD NIGHT, NURSE.
YOU HAVE A DEVIATED SEPTUM, HUH?
DON'T, NIGHT NURSE. BRIGAND IS A DANGEROUS SON OF A--
SHUT IT, OR I CALL DOWN ANOTHER DOZEN OF THESE KILLER BOTS I'VE STOLEN OVER THE YEARS.
NOW WHAT ARE YOU GOING ON ABOUT, CANDY STRIPER?

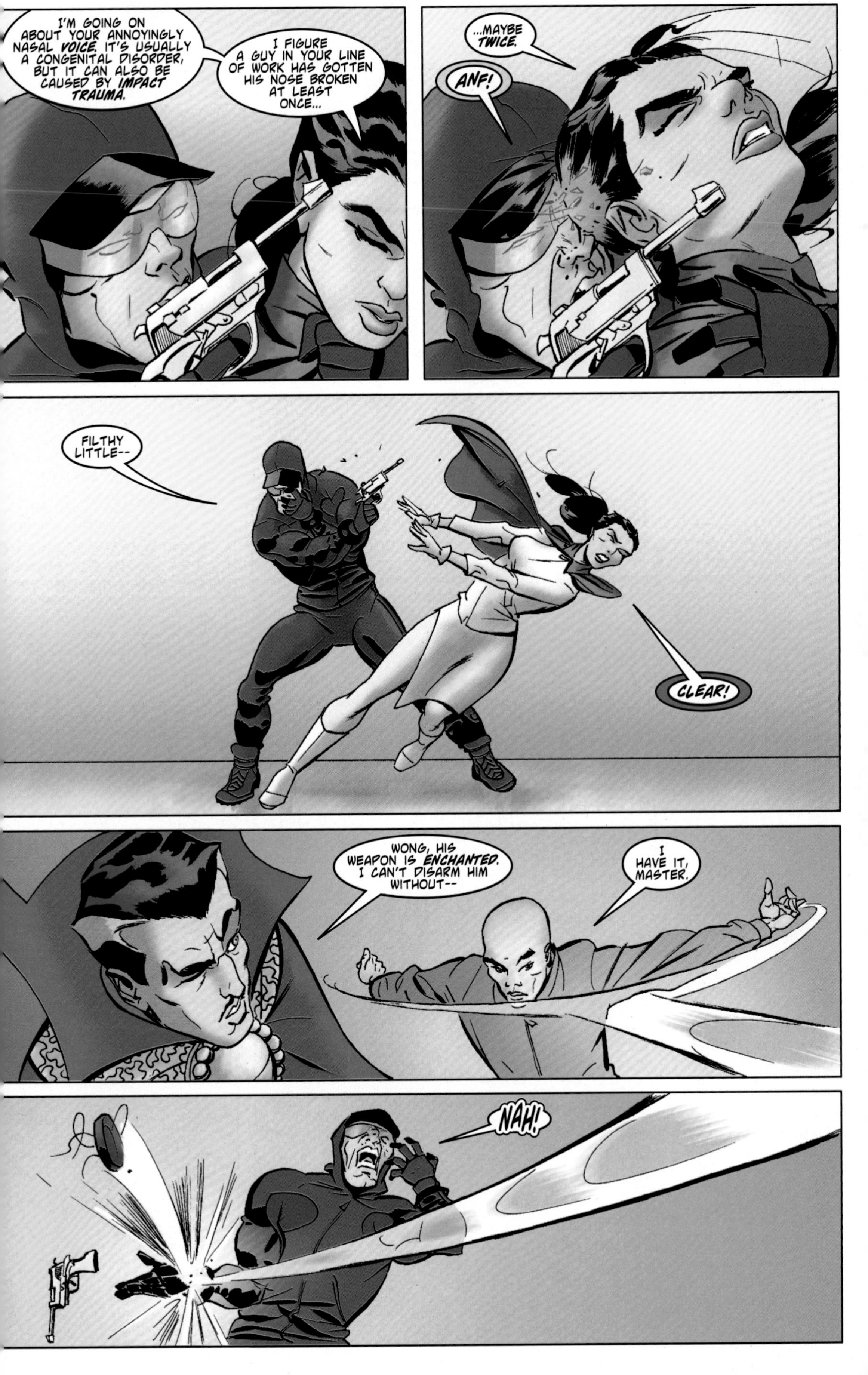
I'M GOING ON ABOUT YOUR ANNOYINGLY NASAL VOICE. IT'S USUALLY A CONGENITAL DISORDER, BUT IT CAN ALSO BE CAUSED BY IMPACT TRAUMA.
I FIGURE A GUY IN YOUR LINE OF WORK HAS GOTTEN HIS NOSE BROKEN AT LEAST ONCE...
...MAYBE TWICE.
ANF!
FILTHY LITTLE--
CLEAR!
WONG, HIS WEAPON IS ENCHANTED. I CAN'T DISARM HIM WITHOUT--
I HAVE IT, MASTER.
NAH!

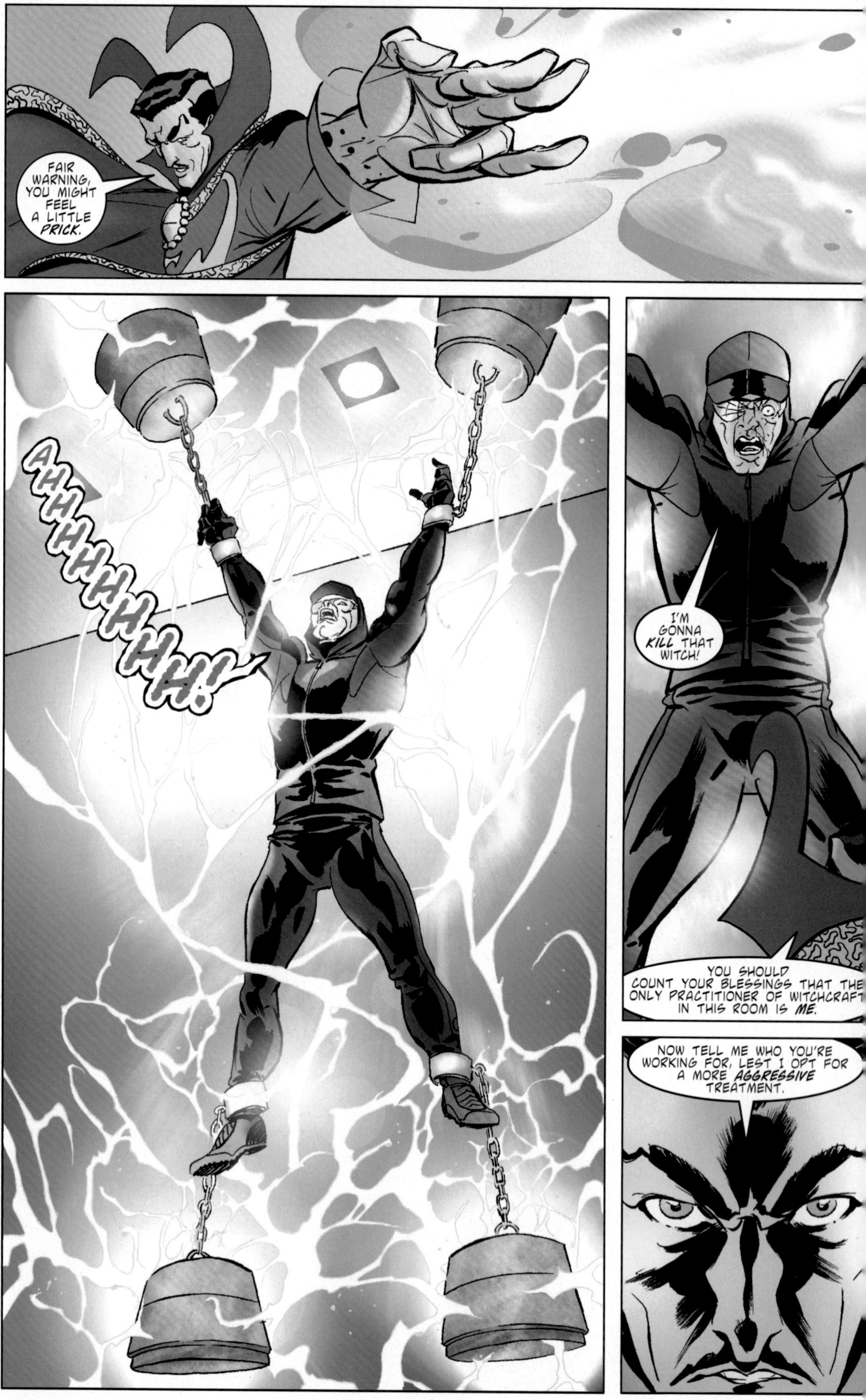
FAIR WARNING, YOU MIGHT FEEL A LITTLE PRICK.
AHHHHHHHHH!
I'M GONNA KILL THAT WITCH!
YOU SHOULD COUNT YOUR BLESSINGS THAT THE ONLY PRACTITIONER OF WITCHCRAFT IN THIS ROOM IS ME.
NOW TELL ME WHO YOU'RE WORKING FOR, LEST I OPT FOR A MORE AGGRESSIVE TREATMENT.

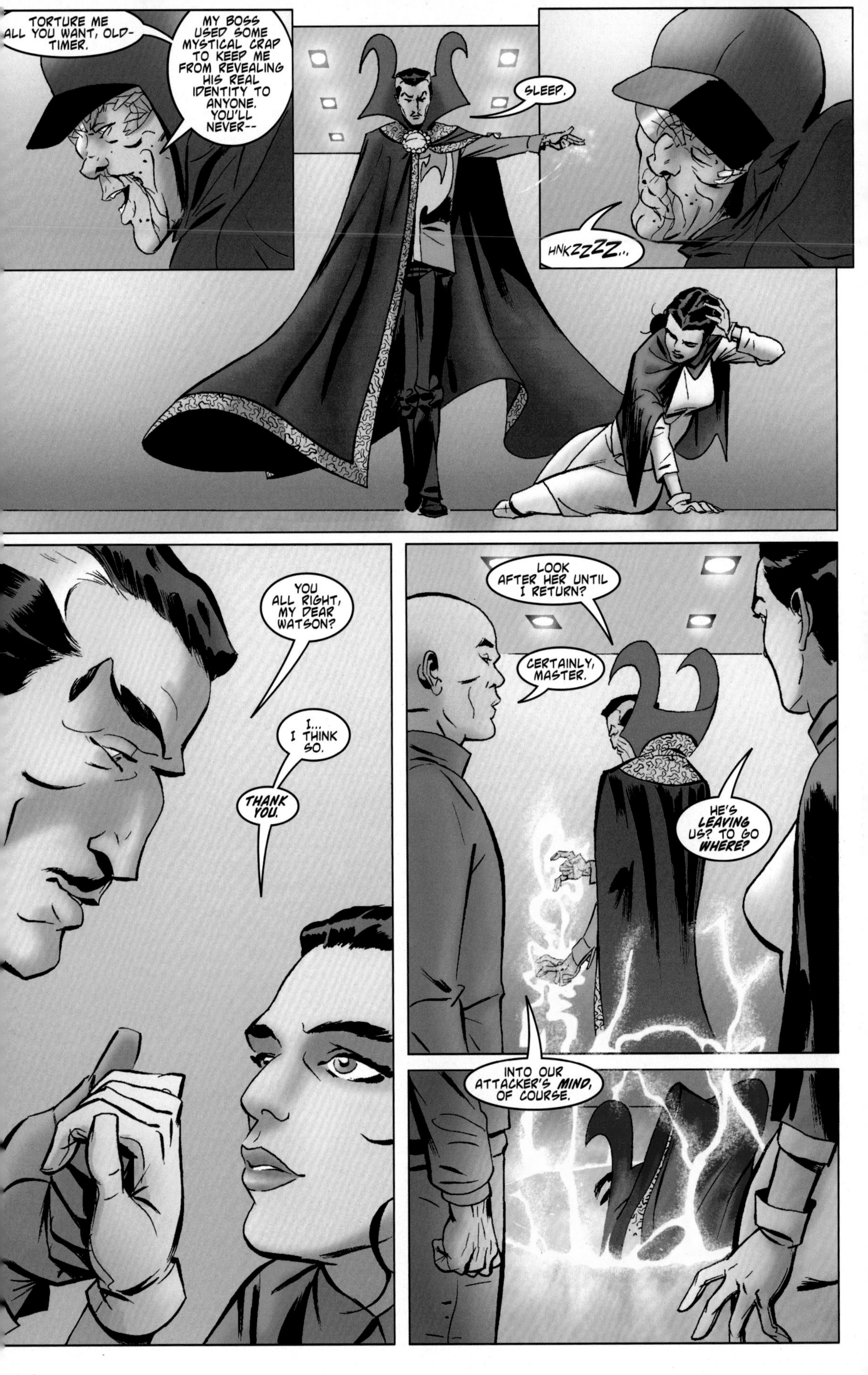
TORTURE ME ALL YOU WANT, OLD-TIMER.
MY BOSS USED SOME MYSTICAL CRAP TO KEEP ME FROM REVEALING HIS REAL IDENTITY TO ANYONE. YOU'LL NEVER--
SLEEP.
HNKZZZZ...
YOU ALL RIGHT, MY DEAR WATSON?
I... I THINK SO.
THANK YOU.
LOOK AFTER HER UNTIL I RETURN?
CERTAINLY, MASTER.
HE'S LEAVING US? TO GO WHERE?
INTO OUR ATTACKER'S MIND, OF COURSE.

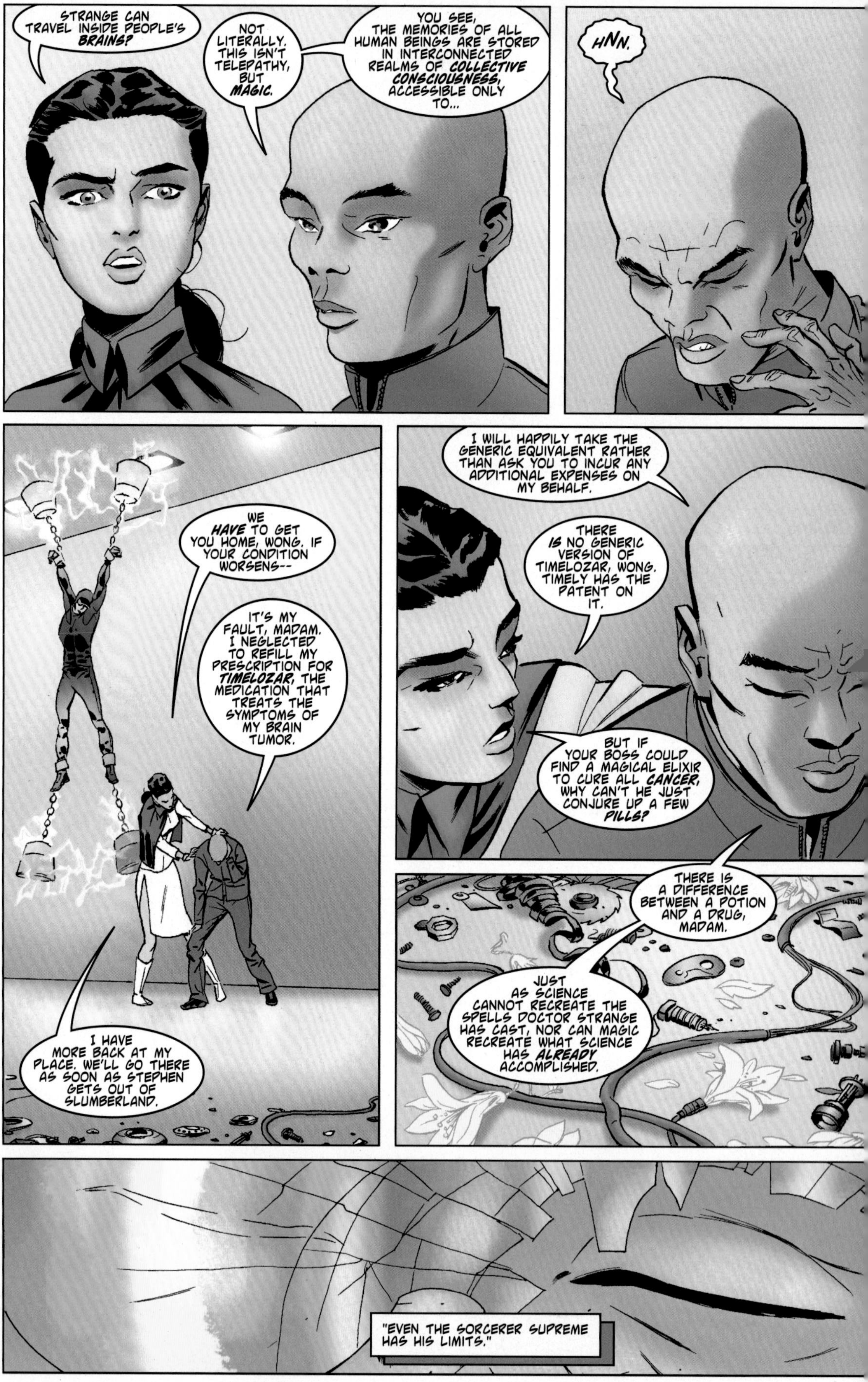
STRANGE CAN TRAVEL INSIDE PEOPLE'S BRAINS?
NOT LITERALLY. THIS ISN'T TELEPATHY, BUT MAGIC.
YOU SEE, THE MEMORIES OF ALL HUMAN BEINGS ARE STORED IN INTERCONNECTED REALMS OF COLLECTIVE CONSCIOUSNESS, ACCESSIBLE ONLY TO...
HNN.
WE HAVE TO GET YOU HOME, WONG. IF YOUR CONDITION WORSENS--
IT'S MY FAULT, MADAM. I NEGLECTED TO REFILL MY PRESCRIPTION FOR TIMELOZAR, THE MEDICATION THAT TREATS THE SYMPTOMS OF MY BRAIN TUMOR.
I HAVE MORE BACK AT MY PLACE. WE'LL GO THERE AS SOON AS STEPHEN GETS OUT OF SLUMBERLAND.
I WILL HAPPILY TAKE THE GENERIC EQUIVALENT RATHER THAN ASK YOU TO INCUR ANY ADDITIONAL EXPENSES ON MY BEHALF.
THERE IS NO GENERIC VERSION OF TIMELOZAR, WONG. TIMELY HAS THE PATENT ON IT.
BUT IF YOUR BOSS COULD FIND A MAGICAL ELIXIR TO CURE ALL CANCER, WHY CAN'T HE JUST CONJURE UP A FEW PILLS?
THERE IS A DIFFERENCE BETWEEN A POTION AND A DRUG, MADAM.
JUST AS SCIENCE CANNOT RECREATE THE SPELLS DOCTOR STRANGE HAS CAST, NOR CAN MAGIC RECREATE WHAT SCIENCE HAS ALREADY ACCOMPLISHED.
"EVEN THE SORCERER SUPREME HAS HIS LIMITS."

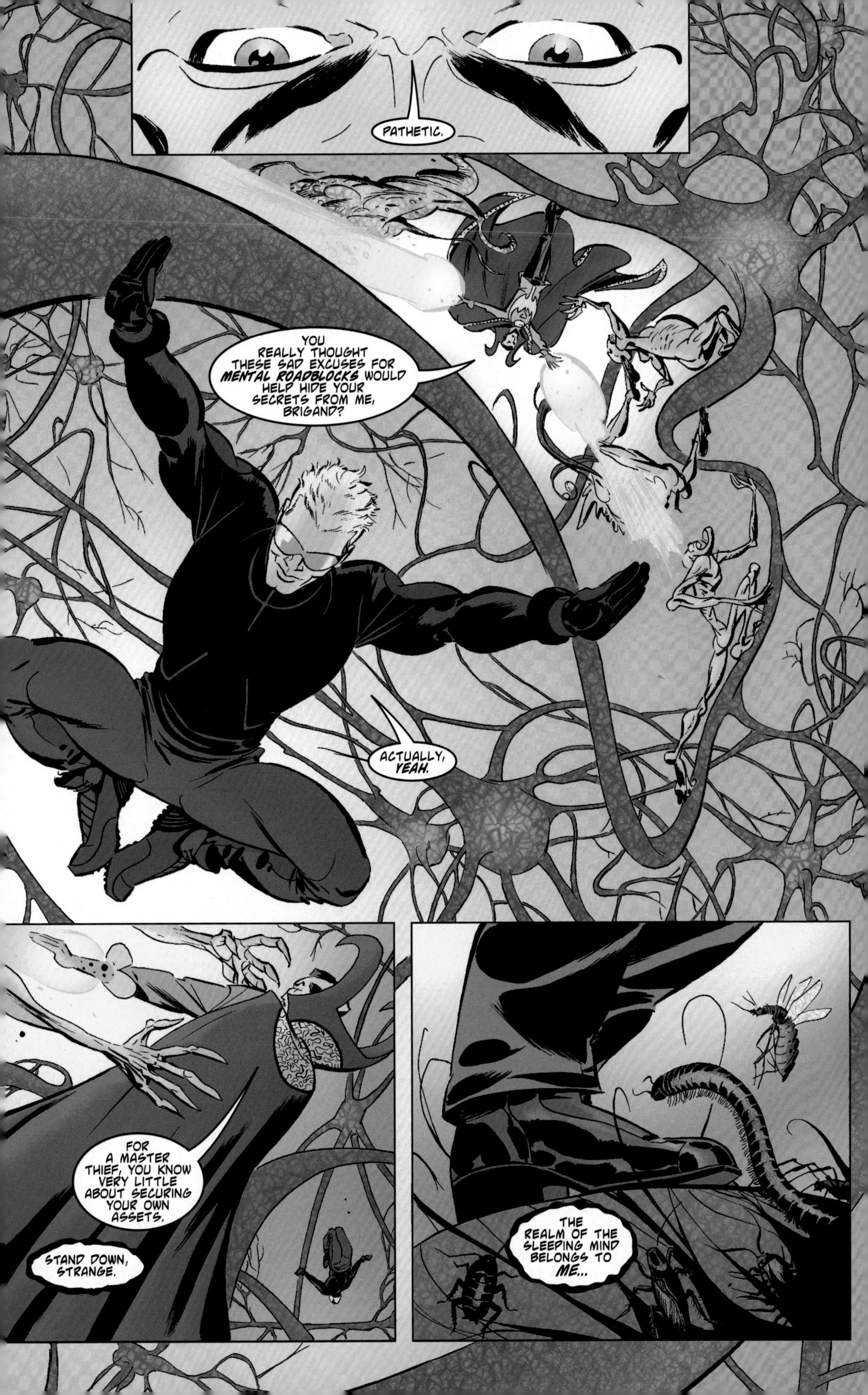
PATHETIC.
YOU REALLY THOUGHT THESE SAD EXCUSES FOR MENTAL ROADBLOCKS WOULD HELP HIDE YOUR SECRETS FROM ME, BRIGAND?
ACTUALLY, YEAH.
FOR A MASTER THIEF, YOU KNOW VERY LITTLE ABOUT SECURING YOUR OWN ASSETS.
STAND DOWN, STRANGE.
THE REALM OF THE SLEEPING MIND BELONGS TO ME...

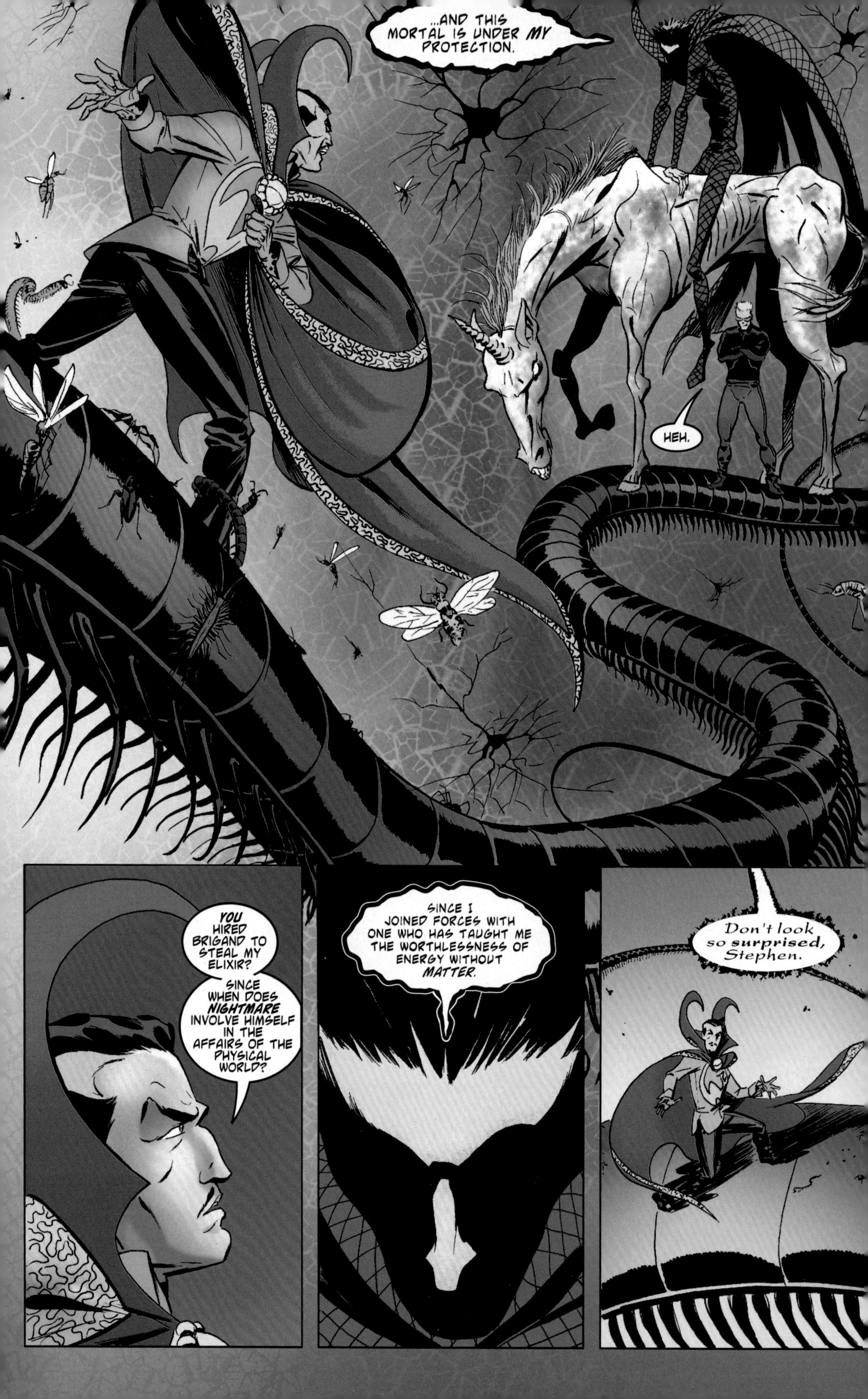
...AND THIS MORTAL IS UNDER MY PROTECTION.
HEH.
YOU HIRED BRIGAND TO STEAL MY ELIXIR?
SINCE WHEN DOES NIGHTMARE INVOLVE HIMSELF IN THE AFFAIRS OF THE PHYSICAL WORLD?
SINCE I JOINED FORCES WITH ONE WHO HAS TAUGHT ME THE WORTHLESSNESS OF ENERGY WITHOUT MATTER.
Don't look so surprised, Stephen.

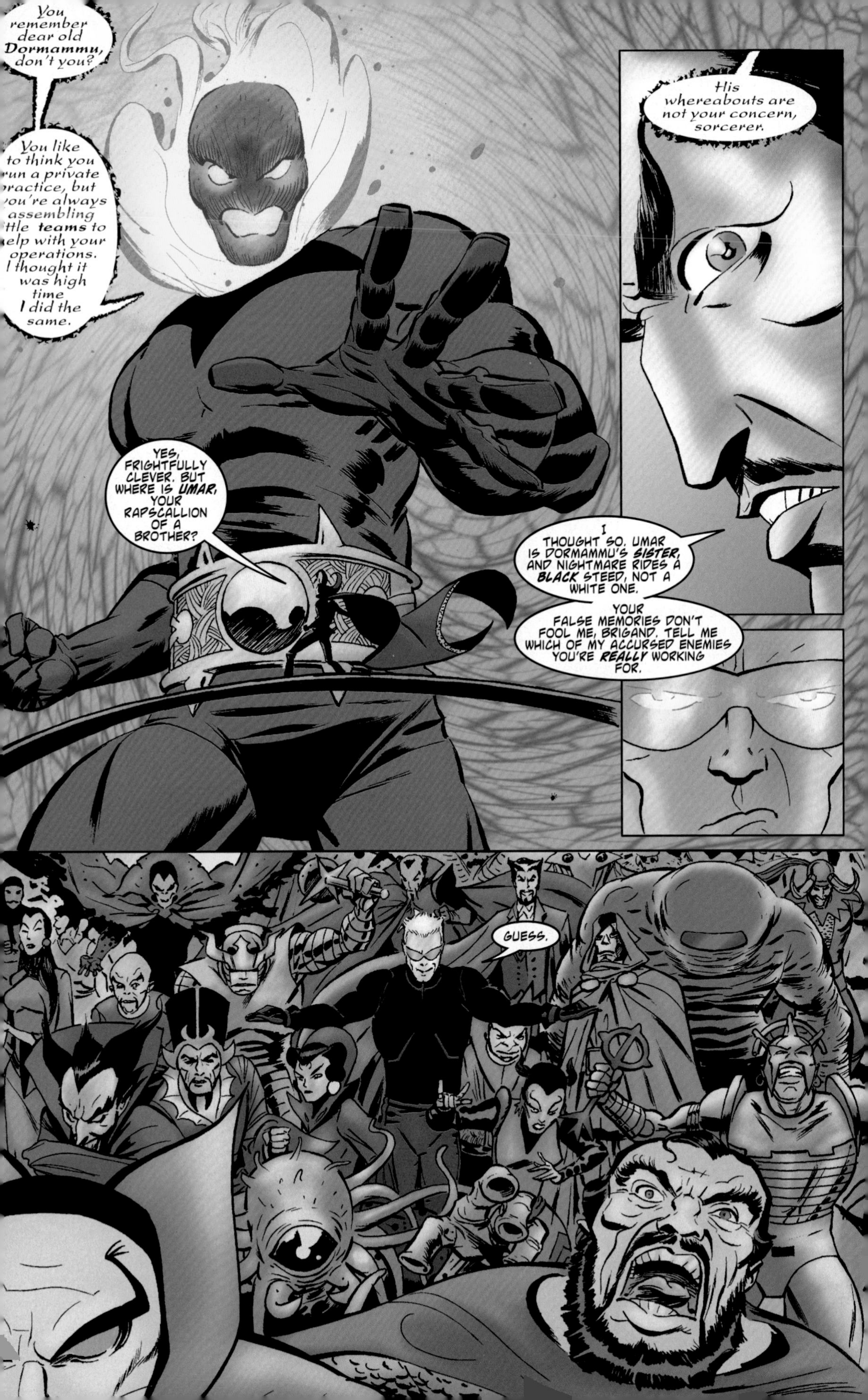
You remember dear old **Dormammu**, don't you?
You like to think you run a private ractice, but ou're always assembling ttle **teams** to elp with your operations. I thought it was high time **I** did the same.
YES, FRIGHTFULLY CLEVER. BUT WHERE IS ***UMAR***, YOUR RAPSCALLION OF A BROTHER?
His whereabouts are not your concern, sorcerer.
I THOUGHT SO. UMAR IS DORMAMMU'S ***SISTER***, AND NIGHTMARE RIDES A ***BLACK*** STEED, NOT A WHITE ONE.
YOUR FALSE MEMORIES DON'T FOOL ME, BRIGAND. TELL ME WHICH OF MY ACCURSED ENEMIES YOU'RE ***REALLY*** WORKING FOR.
GUESS.

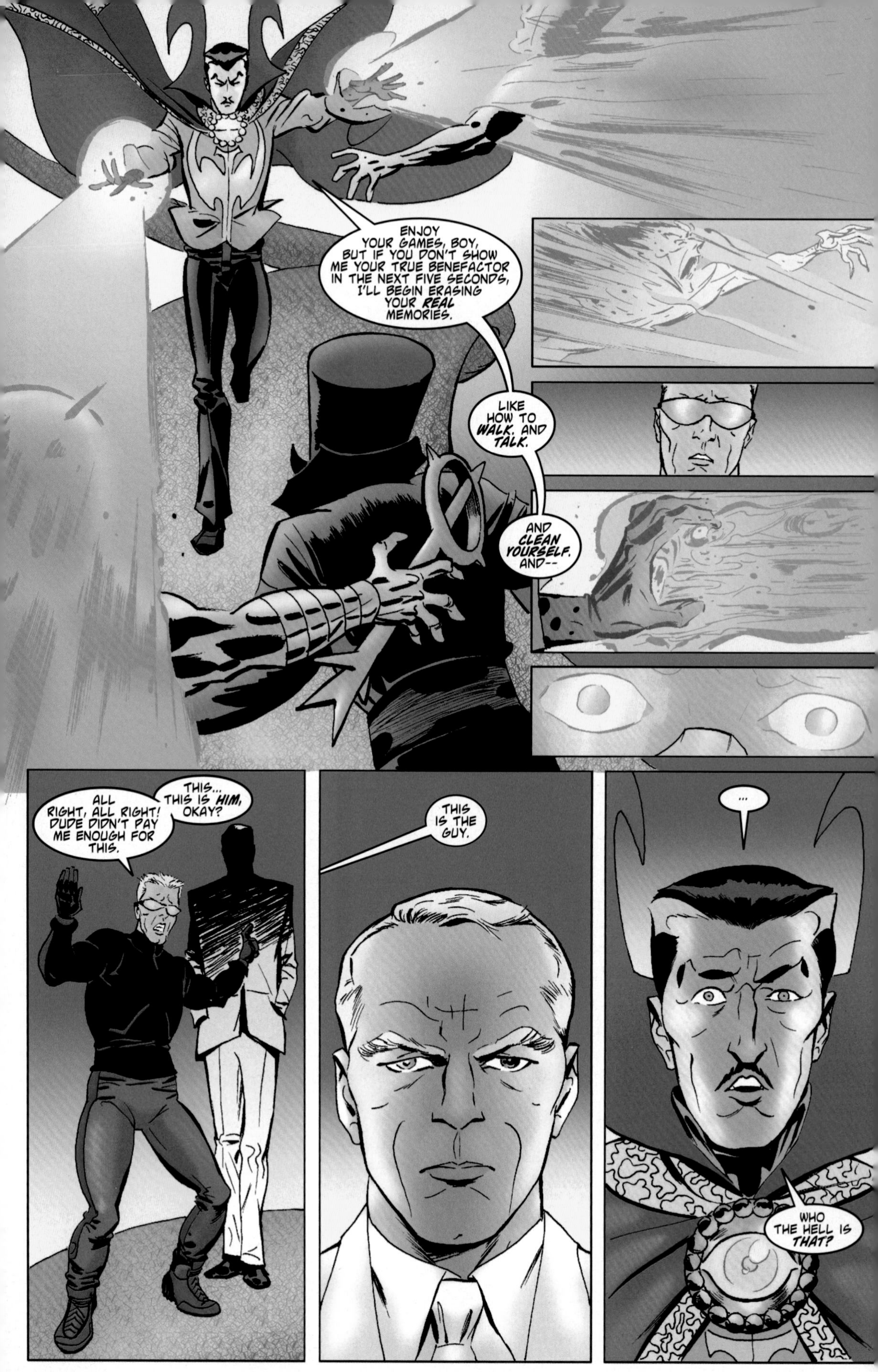
ENJOY YOUR GAMES, BOY, BUT IF YOU DON'T SHOW ME YOUR TRUE BENEFACTOR IN THE NEXT FIVE SECONDS, I'LL BEGIN ERASING YOUR REAL MEMORIES.
LIKE HOW TO WALK. AND TALK.
AND CLEAN YOURSELF. AND--
ALL RIGHT, ALL RIGHT! DUDE DIDN'T PAY ME ENOUGH FOR THIS.
THIS... THIS IS HIM, OKAY?
THIS IS THE GUY.
...
WHO THE HELL IS THAT?

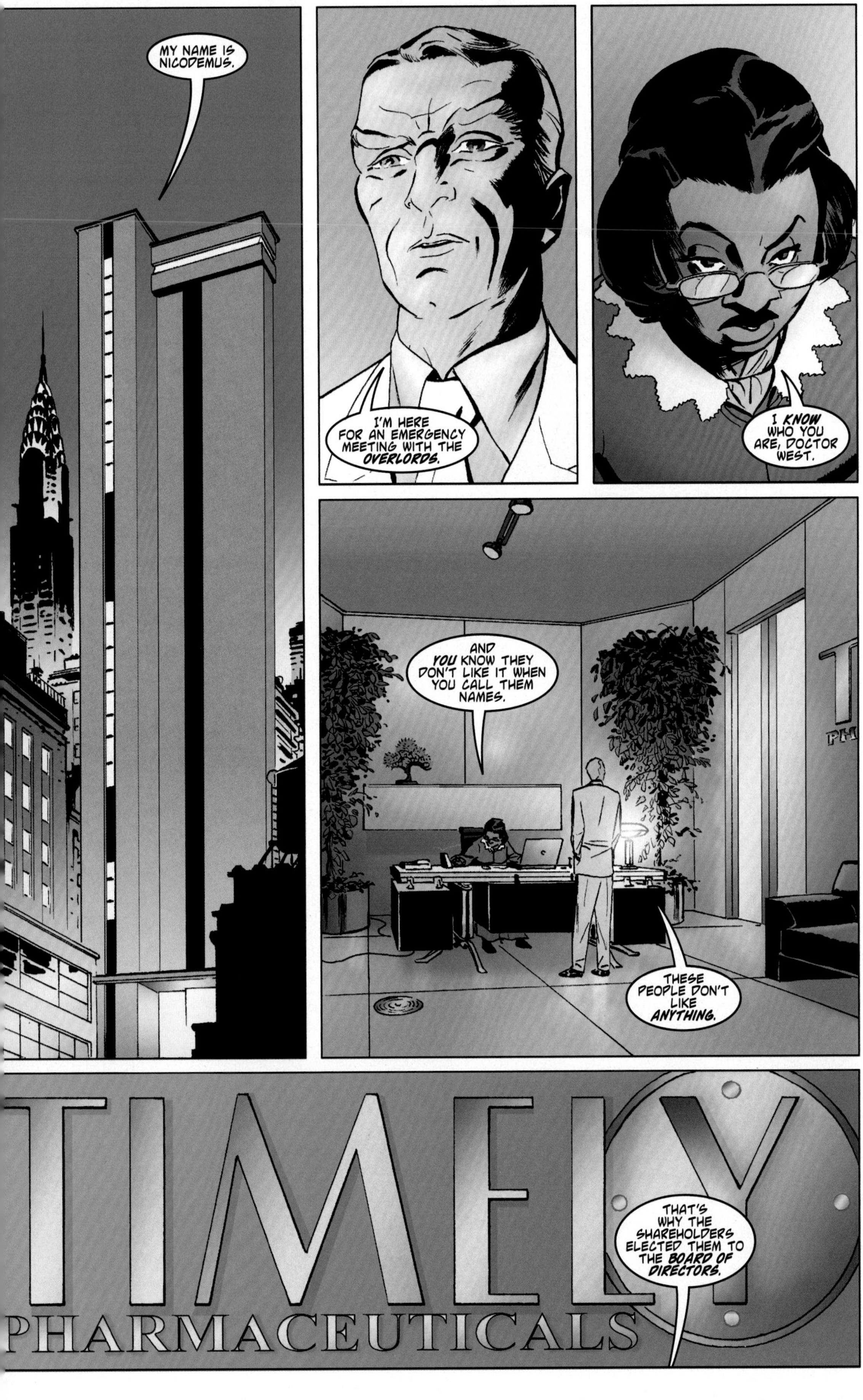
MY NAME IS NICODEMUS.
I'M HERE FOR AN EMERGENCY MEETING WITH THE OVERLORDS.
I KNOW WHO YOU ARE, DOCTOR WEST.
AND YOU KNOW THEY DON'T LIKE IT WHEN YOU CALL THEM NAMES.
THESE PEOPLE DON'T LIKE ANYTHING.
TIMELY PHARMACEUTICALS
THAT'S WHY THE SHAREHOLDERS ELECTED THEM TO THE BOARD OF DIRECTORS.

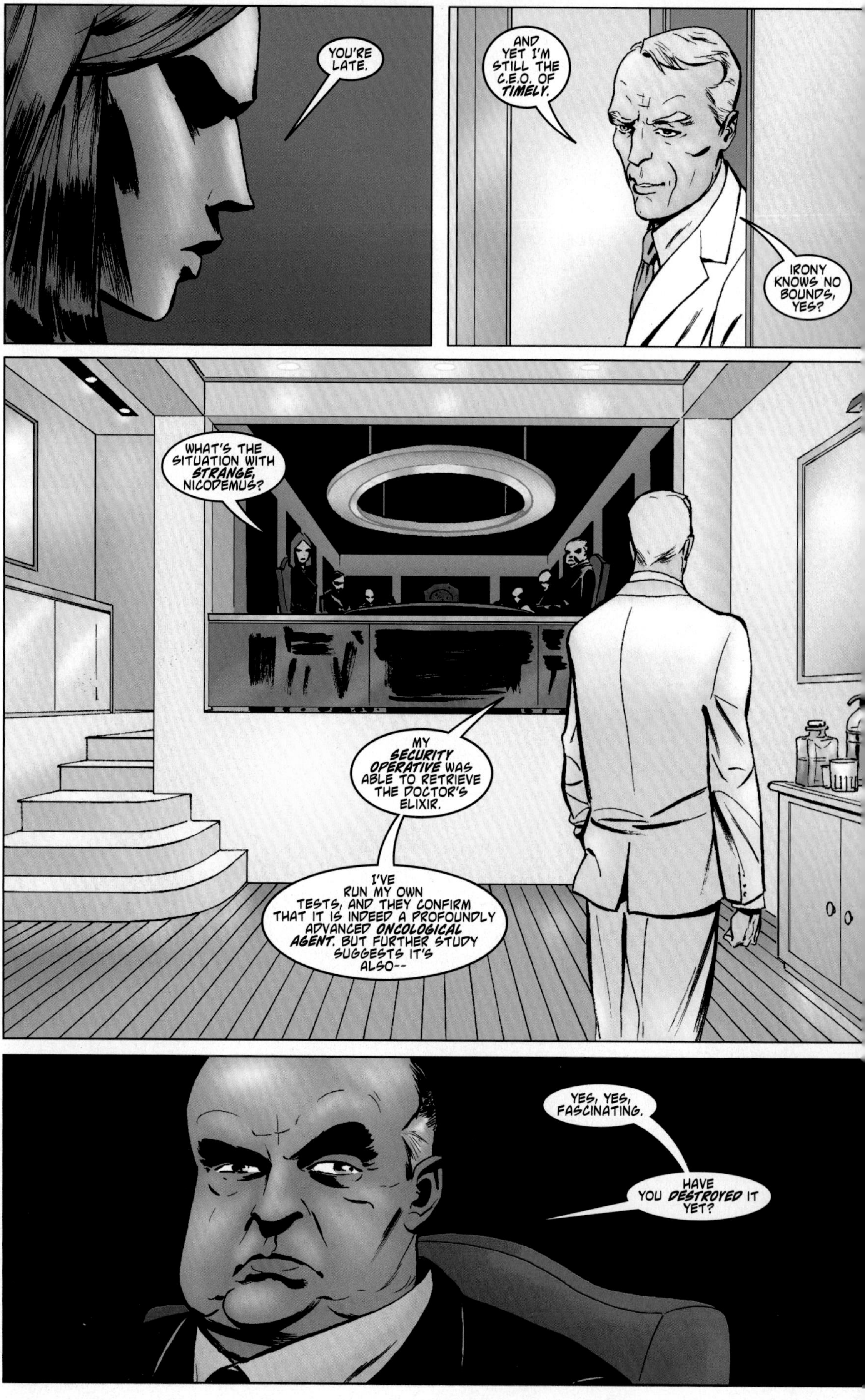
YOU'RE LATE.
AND YET I'M STILL THE C.E.O. OF TIMELY.
IRONY KNOWS NO BOUNDS, YES?
WHAT'S THE SITUATION WITH STRANGE, NICODEMUS?
MY SECURITY OPERATIVE WAS ABLE TO RETRIEVE THE DOCTOR'S ELIXIR.
I'VE RUN MY OWN TESTS, AND THEY CONFIRM THAT IT IS INDEED A PROFOUNDLY ADVANCED ONCOLOGICAL AGENT. BUT FURTHER STUDY SUGGESTS IT'S ALSO--
YES, YES, FASCINATING.
HAVE YOU DESTROYED IT YET?

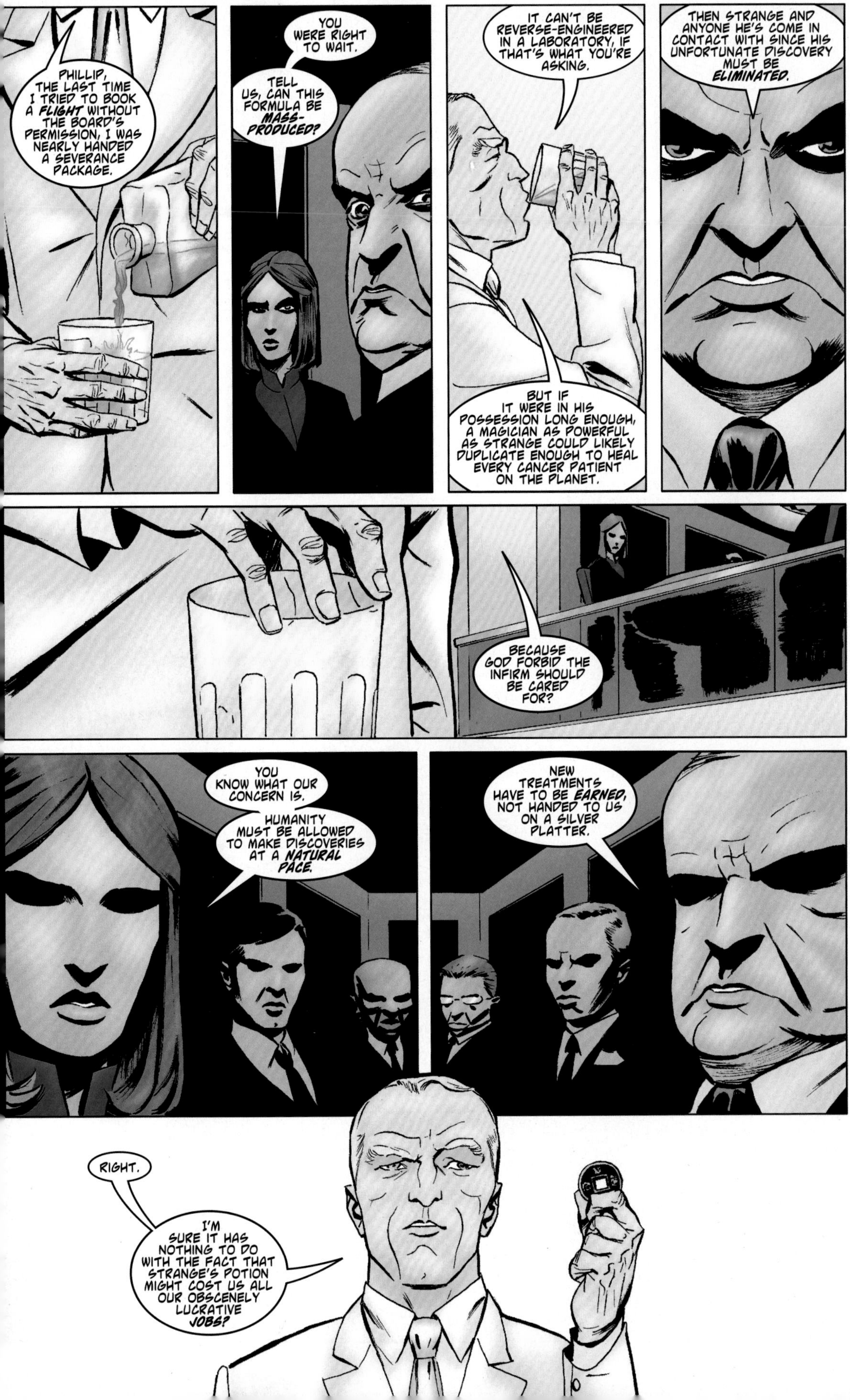
PHILLIP, THE LAST TIME I TRIED TO BOOK A FLIGHT WITHOUT THE BOARD'S PERMISSION, I WAS NEARLY HANDED A SEVERANCE PACKAGE.
YOU WERE RIGHT TO WAIT.
TELL US, CAN THIS FORMULA BE MASS-PRODUCED?
IT CAN'T BE REVERSE-ENGINEERED IN A LABORATORY, IF THAT'S WHAT YOU'RE ASKING.
BUT IF IT WERE IN HIS POSSESSION LONG ENOUGH, A MAGICIAN AS POWERFUL AS STRANGE COULD LIKELY DUPLICATE ENOUGH TO HEAL EVERY CANCER PATIENT ON THE PLANET.
THEN STRANGE AND ANYONE HE'S COME IN CONTACT WITH SINCE HIS UNFORTUNATE DISCOVERY MUST BE ELIMINATED.
BECAUSE GOD FORBID THE INFIRM SHOULD BE CARED FOR?
YOU KNOW WHAT OUR CONCERN IS.
HUMANITY MUST BE ALLOWED TO MAKE DISCOVERIES AT A NATURAL PACE.
NEW TREATMENTS HAVE TO BE EARNED, NOT HANDED TO US ON A SILVER PLATTER.
RIGHT.
I'M SURE IT HAS NOTHING TO DO WITH THE FACT THAT STRANGE'S POTION MIGHT COST US ALL OUR OBSCENELY LUCRATIVE JOBS?

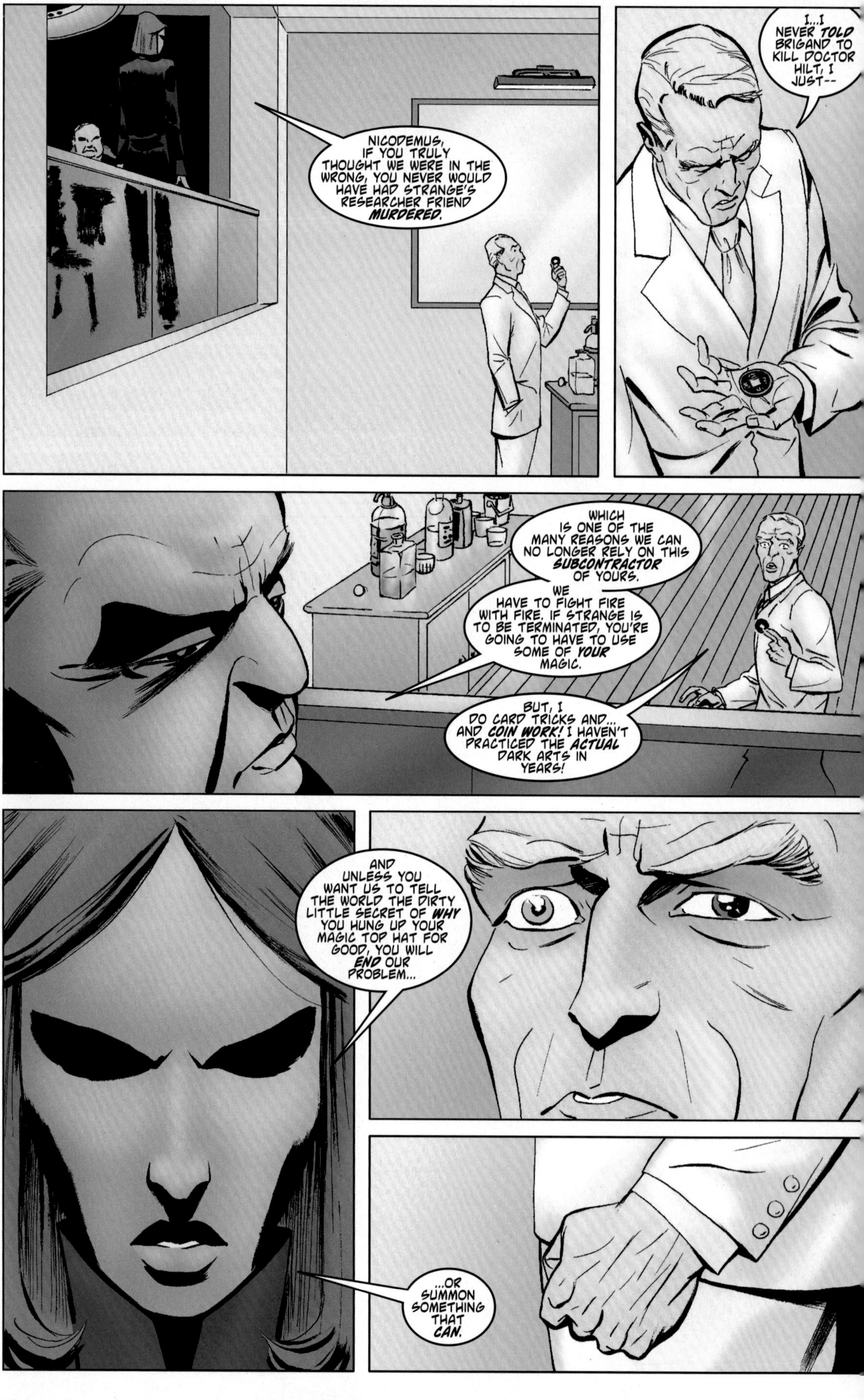
NICODEMUS, IF YOU TRULY THOUGHT WE WERE IN THE WRONG, YOU NEVER WOULD HAVE HAD STRANGE'S RESEARCHER FRIEND MURDERED.
I...I NEVER TOLD BRIGAND TO KILL DOCTOR HILT, I JUST--
WHICH IS ONE OF THE MANY REASONS WE CAN NO LONGER RELY ON THIS SUBCONTRACTOR OF YOURS.
WE HAVE TO FIGHT FIRE WITH FIRE. IF STRANGE IS TO BE TERMINATED, YOU'RE GOING TO HAVE TO USE SOME OF YOUR MAGIC.
BUT, I DO CARD TRICKS AND... AND COIN WORK! I HAVEN'T PRACTICED THE ACTUAL DARK ARTS IN YEARS!
AND UNLESS YOU WANT US TO TELL THE WORLD THE DIRTY LITTLE SECRET OF WHY YOU HUNG UP YOUR MAGIC TOP HAT FOR GOOD, YOU WILL END OUR PROBLEM...
...OR SUMMON SOMETHING THAT CAN.

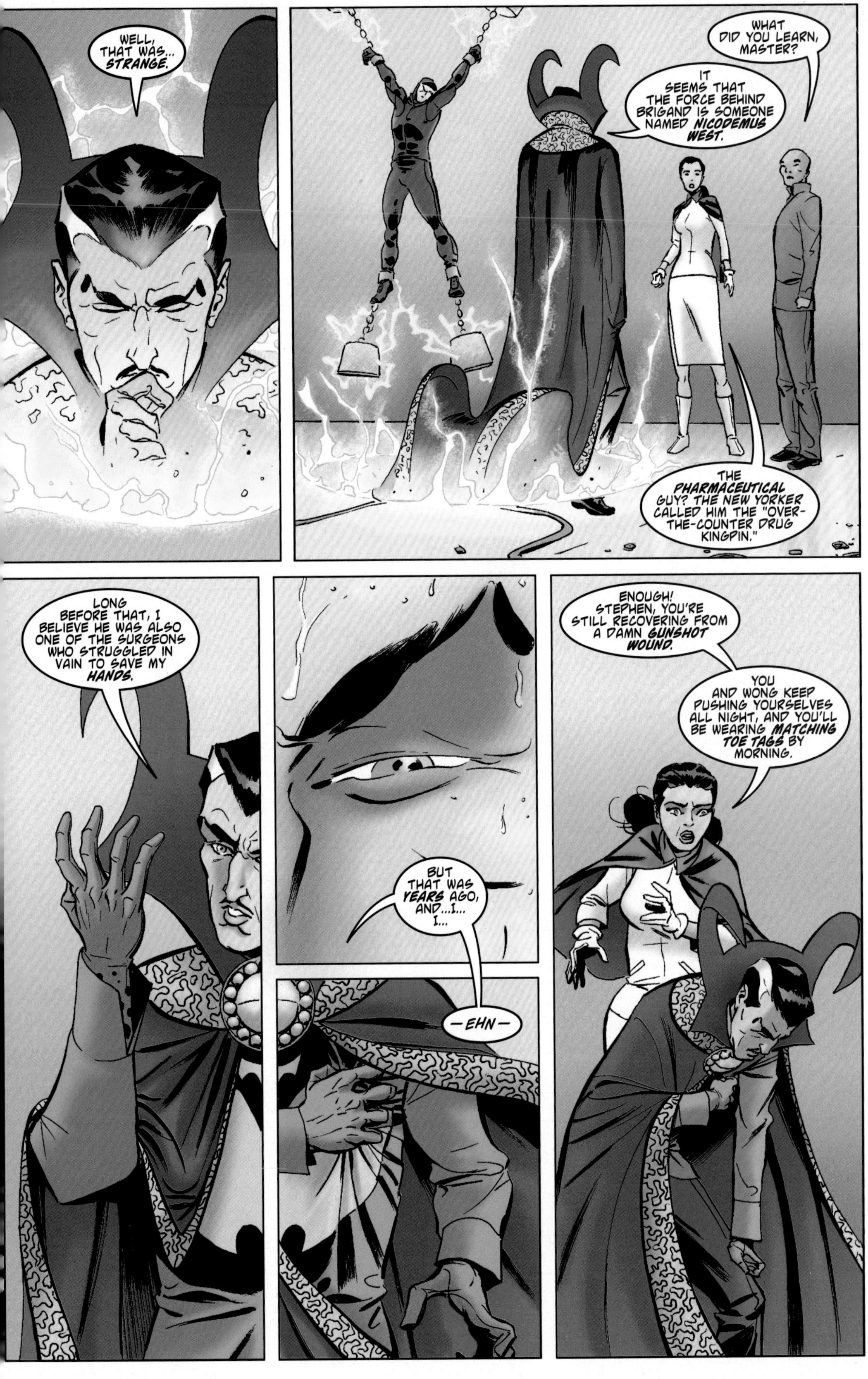
WELL, THAT WAS... STRANGE.
WHAT DID YOU LEARN, MASTER?
IT SEEMS THAT THE FORCE BEHIND BRIGAND IS SOMEONE NAMED NICODEMUS WEST.
THE PHARMACEUTICAL GUY? THE NEW YORKER CALLED HIM THE "OVER-THE-COUNTER DRUG KINGPIN."
LONG BEFORE THAT, I BELIEVE HE WAS ALSO ONE OF THE SURGEONS WHO STRUGGLED IN VAIN TO SAVE MY HANDS.
BUT THAT WAS YEARS AGO, AND...I... I...
—EHN—
ENOUGH! STEPHEN, YOU'RE STILL RECOVERING FROM A DAMN GUNSHOT WOUND.
YOU AND WONG KEEP PUSHING YOURSELVES ALL NIGHT, AND YOU'LL BE WEARING MATCHING TOE TAGS BY MORNING.

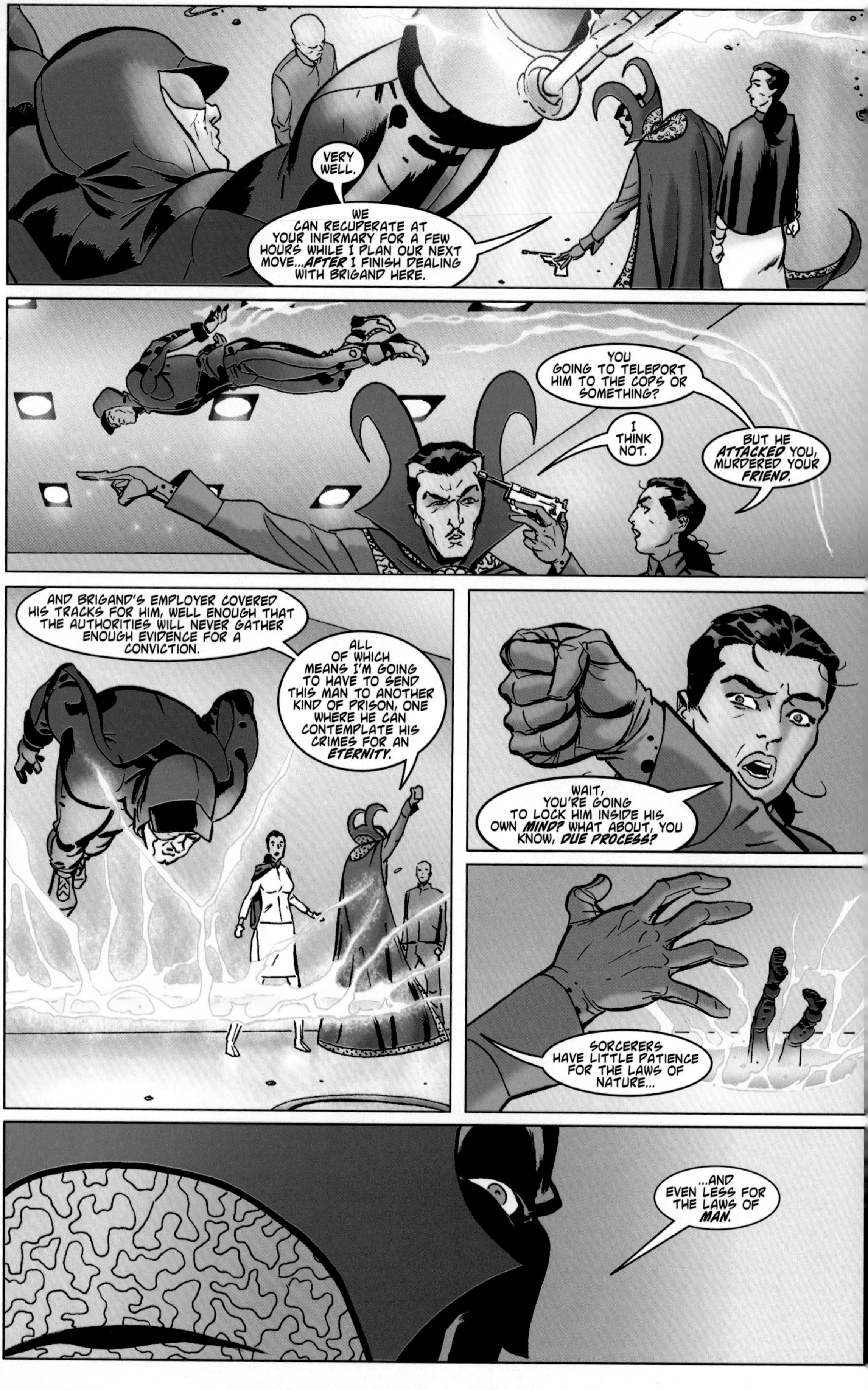

VERY WELL.
WE CAN RECUPERATE AT YOUR INFIRMARY FOR A FEW HOURS WHILE I PLAN OUR NEXT MOVE...**AFTER** I FINISH DEALING WITH BRIGAND HERE.
YOU GOING TO TELEPORT HIM TO THE COPS OR SOMETHING?
I THINK NOT.
BUT HE **ATTACKED** YOU, MURDERED YOUR **FRIEND**.
AND BRIGAND'S EMPLOYER COVERED HIS TRACKS FOR HIM, WELL ENOUGH THAT THE AUTHORITIES WILL NEVER GATHER ENOUGH EVIDENCE FOR A CONVICTION.
ALL OF WHICH MEANS I'M GOING TO HAVE TO SEND THIS MAN TO ANOTHER KIND OF PRISON, ONE WHERE HE CAN CONTEMPLATE HIS CRIMES FOR AN **ETERNITY**.
WAIT, YOU'RE GOING TO LOCK HIM INSIDE HIS OWN **MIND**? WHAT ABOUT, YOU KNOW, **DUE PROCESS**?
SORCERERS HAVE LITTLE PATIENCE FOR THE LAWS OF NATURE...
...AND EVEN LESS FOR THE LAWS OF **MAN**.

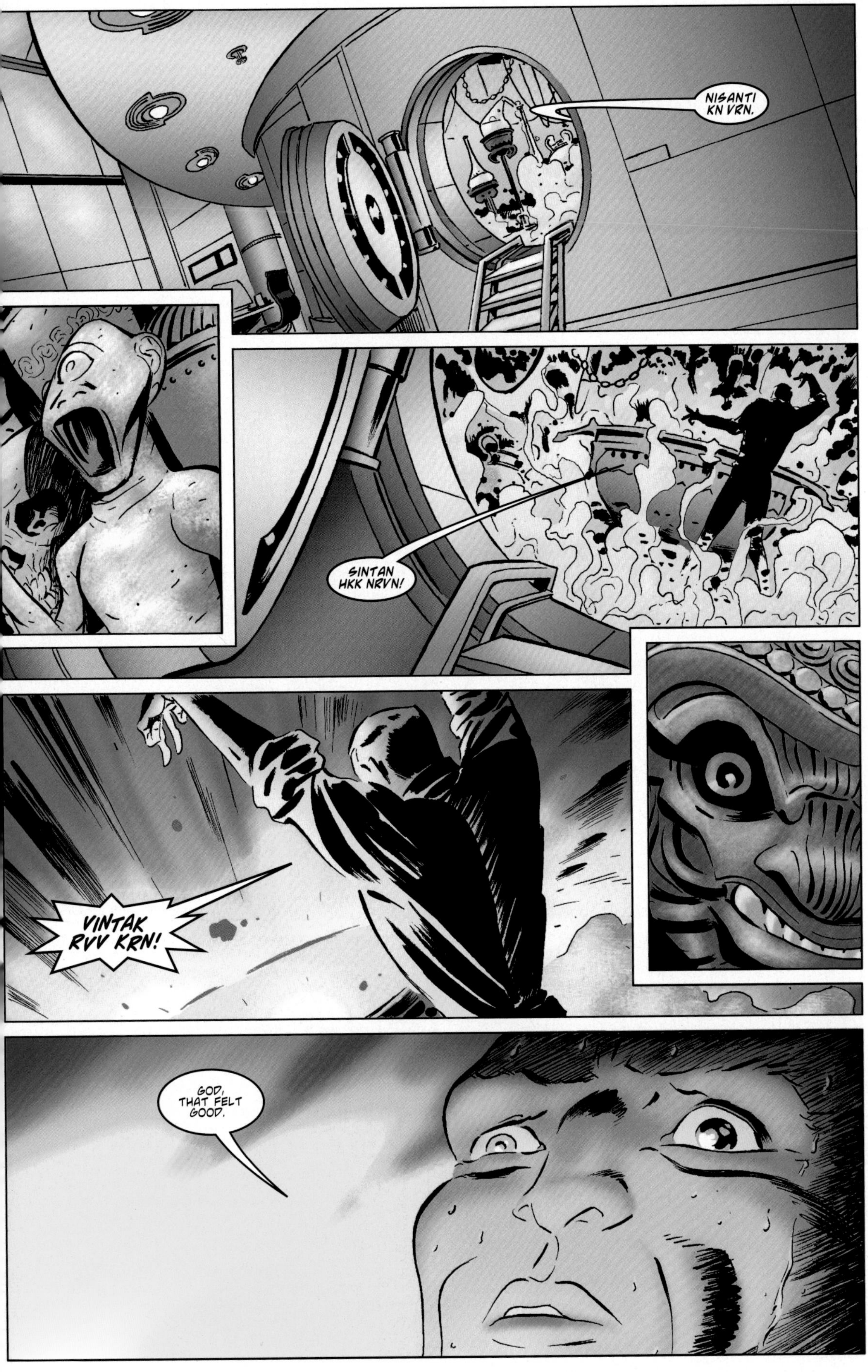
NISANTI KN VRN.
SINTAN HKK NRVN!
VINTAK RVV KRN!
GOD, THAT FELT GOOD.

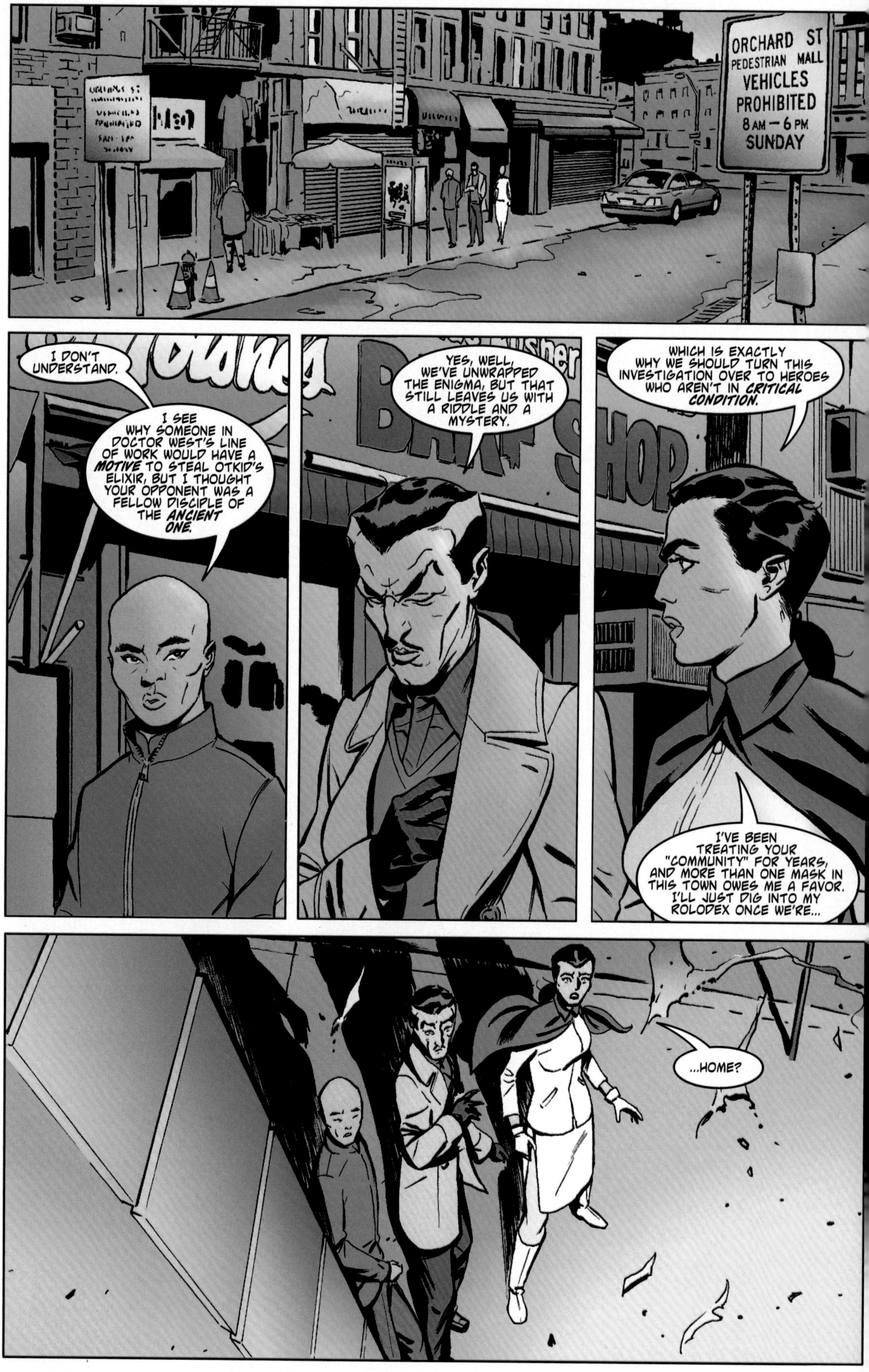
ORCHARD ST
PEDESTRIAN MALL
VEHICLES
PROHIBITED
8 AM — 6 PM
SUNDAY
I DON'T UNDERSTAND.
I SEE WHY SOMEONE IN DOCTOR WEST'S LINE OF WORK WOULD HAVE A MOTIVE TO STEAL OTKID'S ELIXIR, BUT I THOUGHT YOUR OPPONENT WAS A FELLOW DISCIPLE OF THE ANCIENT ONE.
YES, WELL, WE'VE UNWRAPPED THE ENIGMA, BUT THAT STILL LEAVES US WITH A RIDDLE AND A MYSTERY.
WHICH IS EXACTLY WHY WE SHOULD TURN THIS INVESTIGATION OVER TO HEROES WHO AREN'T IN CRITICAL CONDITION.
I'VE BEEN TREATING YOUR "COMMUNITY" FOR YEARS, AND MORE THAN ONE MASK IN THIS TOWN OWES ME A FAVOR. I'LL JUST DIG INTO MY ROLODEX ONCE WE'RE...
...HOME?

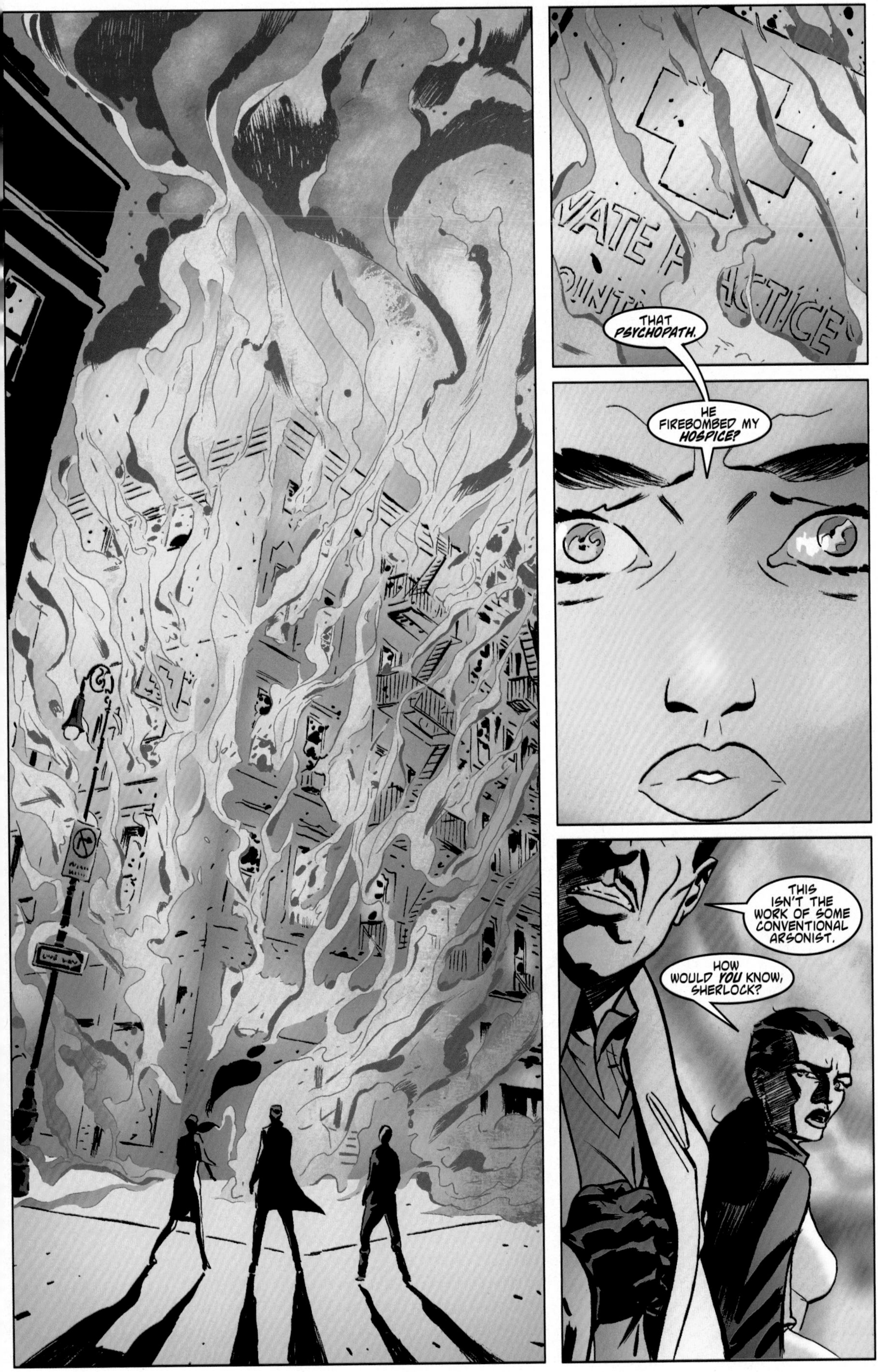
THAT *PSYCHOPATH.*
HE FIREBOMBED MY *HOSPICE?*
THIS ISN'T THE WORK OF SOME CONVENTIONAL ARSONIST.
HOW WOULD *YOU* KNOW, SHERLOCK?

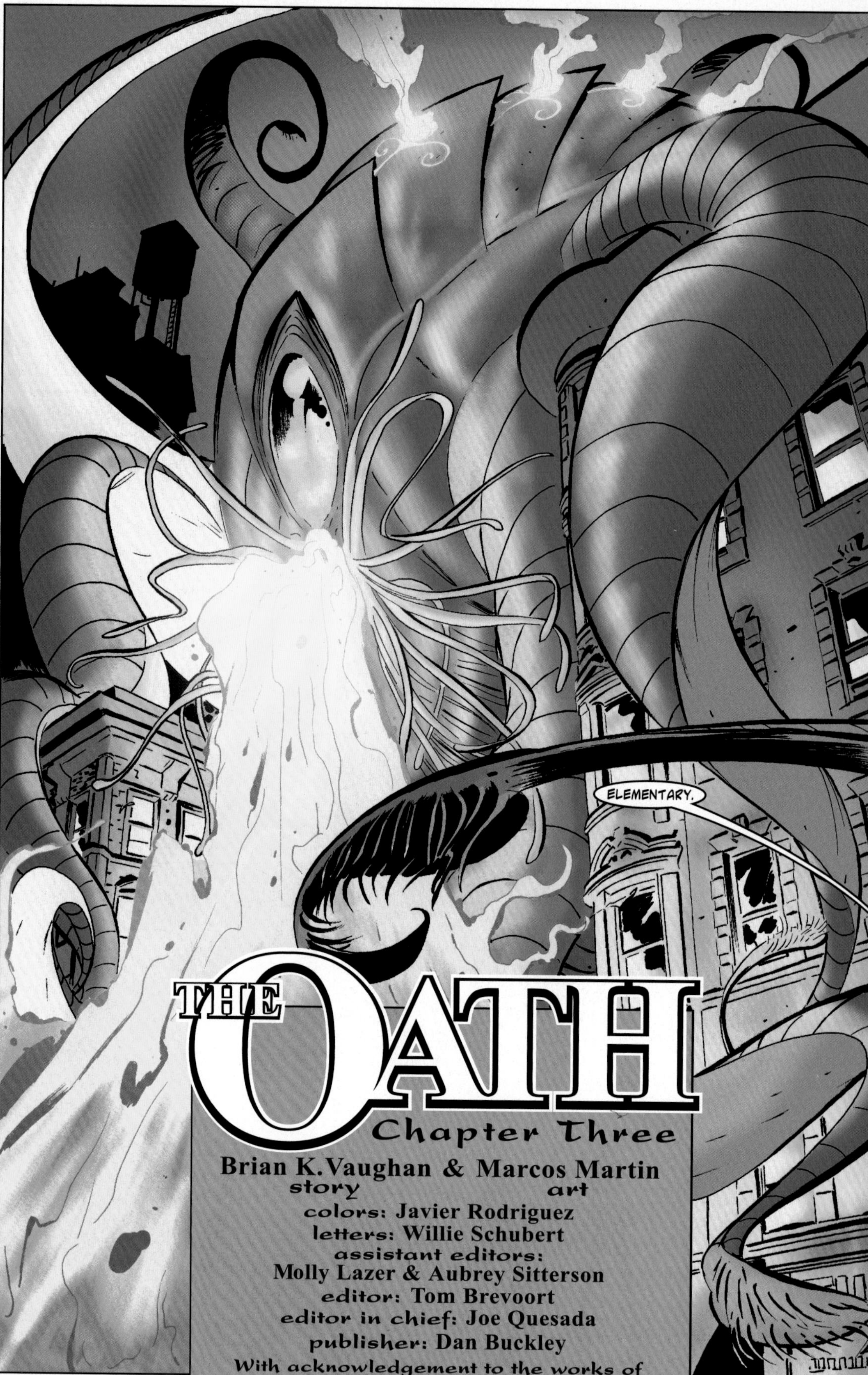
ELEMENTARY.
THE OATH
Chapter Three
Brian K. Vaughan & Marcos Martin
story art
colors: Javier Rodriguez
letters: Willie Schubert
assistant editors:
Molly Lazer & Aubrey Sitterson
editor: Tom Brevoort
editor in chief: Joe Quesada
publisher: Dan Buckley
With acknowledgement to the works of
Stan Lee & Steve Ditko

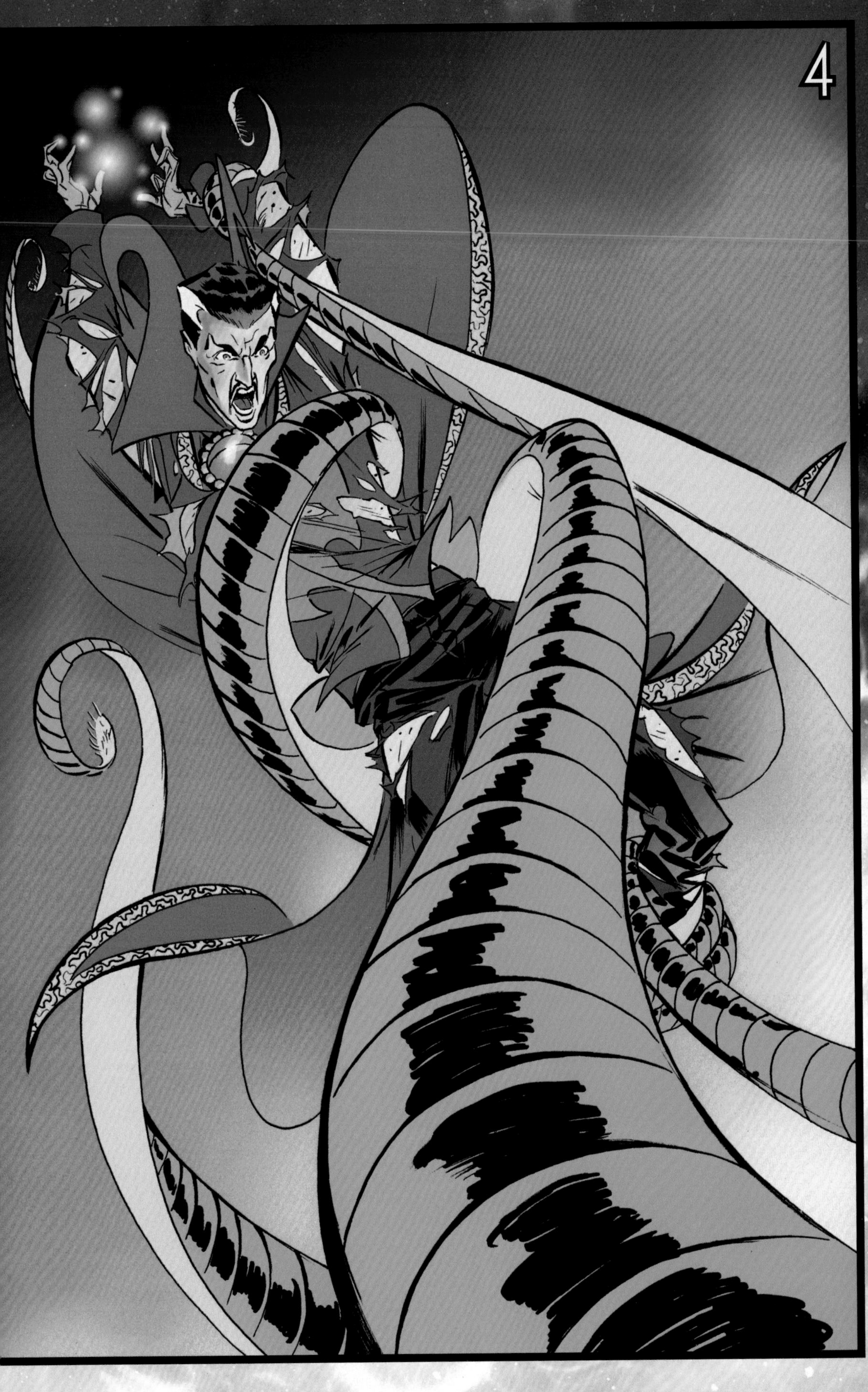
4

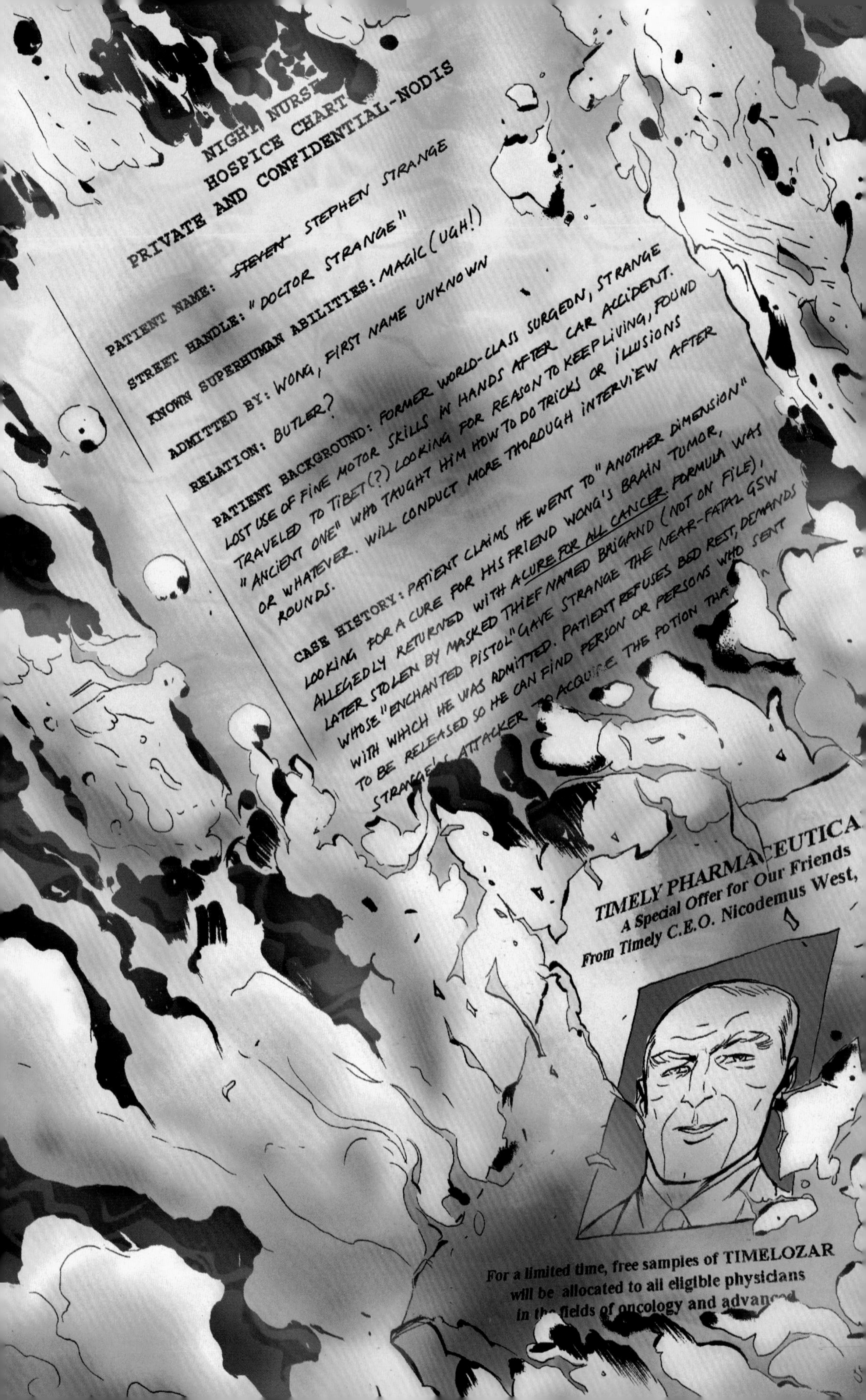
NIGHT NURSE
HOSPICE CHART
PRIVATE AND CONFIDENTIAL-NODIS
PATIENT NAME: ~~STEVEN~~ STEPHEN STRANGE
STREET HANDLE: "DOCTOR STRANGE"
KNOWN SUPERHUMAN ABILITIES: MAGIC (UGH!)
ADMITTED BY: WONG, FIRST NAME UNKNOWN
RELATION: BUTLER?
PATIENT BACKGROUND: FORMER WORLD-CLASS SURGEON, STRANGE LOST USE OF FINE MOTOR SKILLS IN HANDS AFTER CAR ACCIDENT. TRAVELED TO TIBET(?) LOOKING FOR REASON TO KEEP LIVING, FOUND "ANCIENT ONE" WHO TAUGHT HIM HOW TO DO TRICKS OR ILLUSIONS OR WHATEVER. WILL CONDUCT MORE THOROUGH INTERVIEW AFTER ROUNDS.
CASE HISTORY: PATIENT CLAIMS HE WENT TO "ANOTHER DIMENSION" LOOKING FOR A CURE FOR HIS FRIEND WONG'S BRAIN TUMOR, ALLEGEDLY RETURNED WITH A CURE FOR ALL CANCER. FORMULA WAS LATER STOLEN BY MASKED THIEF NAMED BRIGAND (NOT ON FILE), WHOSE "ENCHANTED PISTOL" GAVE STRANGE THE NEAR-FATAL GSW WITH WHICH HE WAS ADMITTED. PATIENT REFUSES BED REST, DEMANDS TO BE RELEASED SO HE CAN FIND PERSON OR PERSONS WHO SENT STRANGE'S ATTACKER TO ACQUIRE THE POTION THA
TIMELY PHARMACEUTICA
A Special Offer for Our Friends
From Timely C.E.O. Nicodemus West,
For a limited time, free samples of TIMELOZAR
will be allocated to all eligible physicians
in the fields of oncology and advan

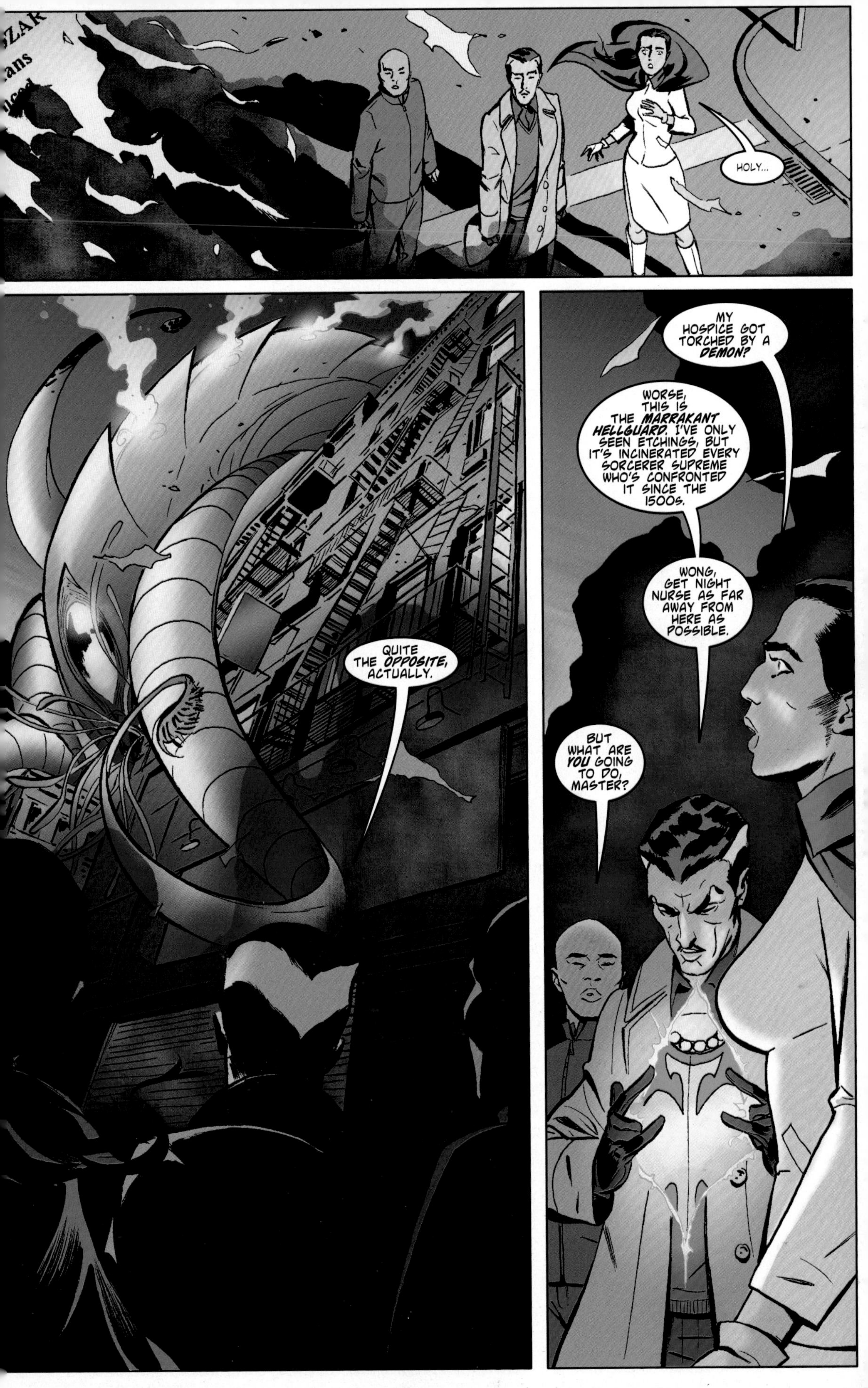
HOLY...
QUITE THE OPPOSITE, ACTUALLY.
MY HOSPICE GOT TORCHED BY A DEMON?
WORSE, THIS IS THE MARRAKANT HELLGUARD. I'VE ONLY SEEN ETCHINGS, BUT IT'S INCINERATED EVERY SORCERER SUPREME WHO'S CONFRONTED IT SINCE THE 1500S.
WONG, GET NIGHT NURSE AS FAR AWAY FROM HERE AS POSSIBLE.
BUT WHAT ARE YOU GOING TO DO, MASTER?

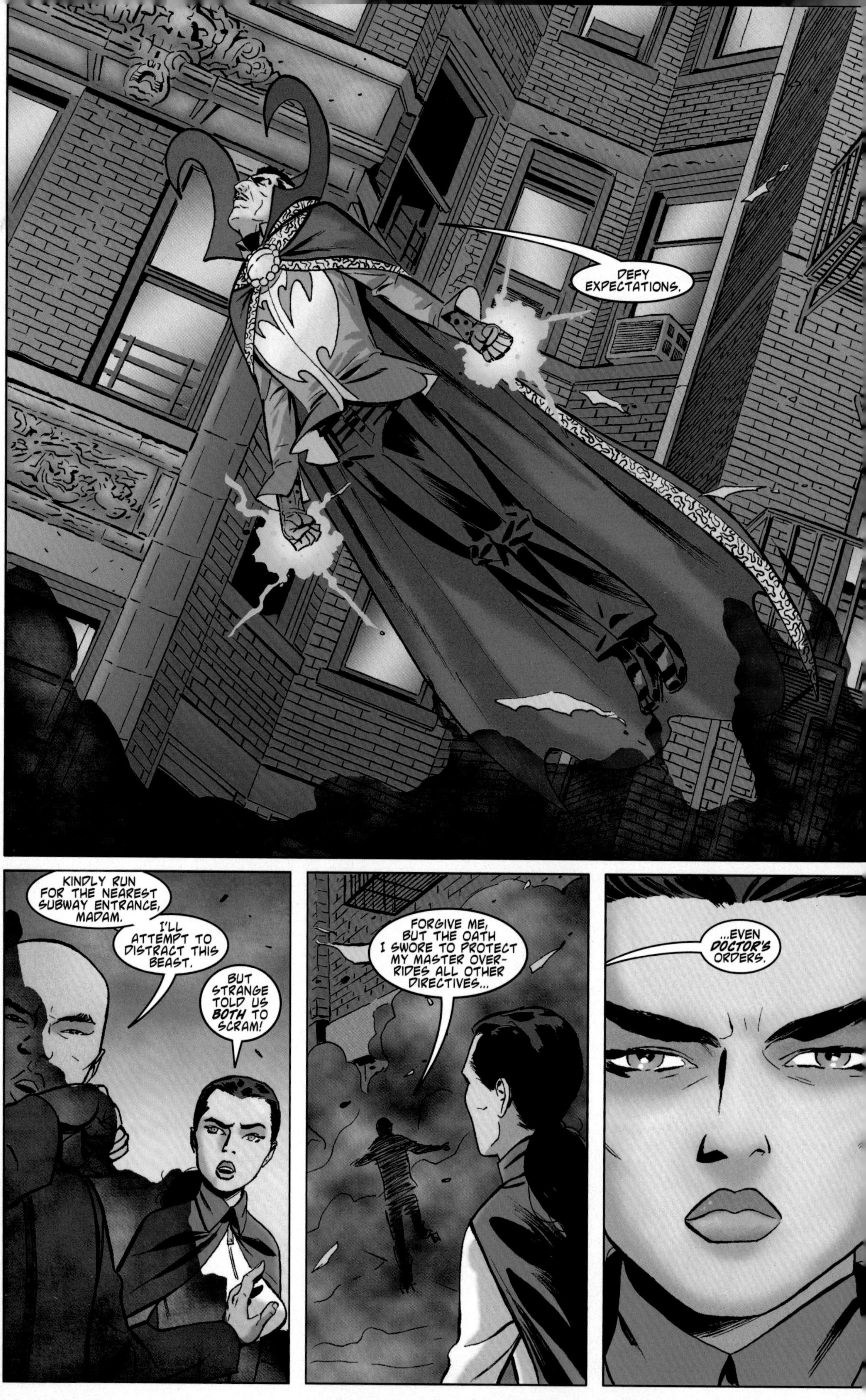
DEFY EXPECTATIONS.
KINDLY RUN FOR THE NEAREST SUBWAY ENTRANCE, MADAM.
I'LL ATTEMPT TO DISTRACT THIS BEAST.
BUT STRANGE TOLD US BOTH TO SCRAM!
FORGIVE ME, BUT THE OATH I SWORE TO PROTECT MY MASTER OVER-RIDES ALL OTHER DIRECTIVES...
...EVEN DOCTOR'S ORDERS.

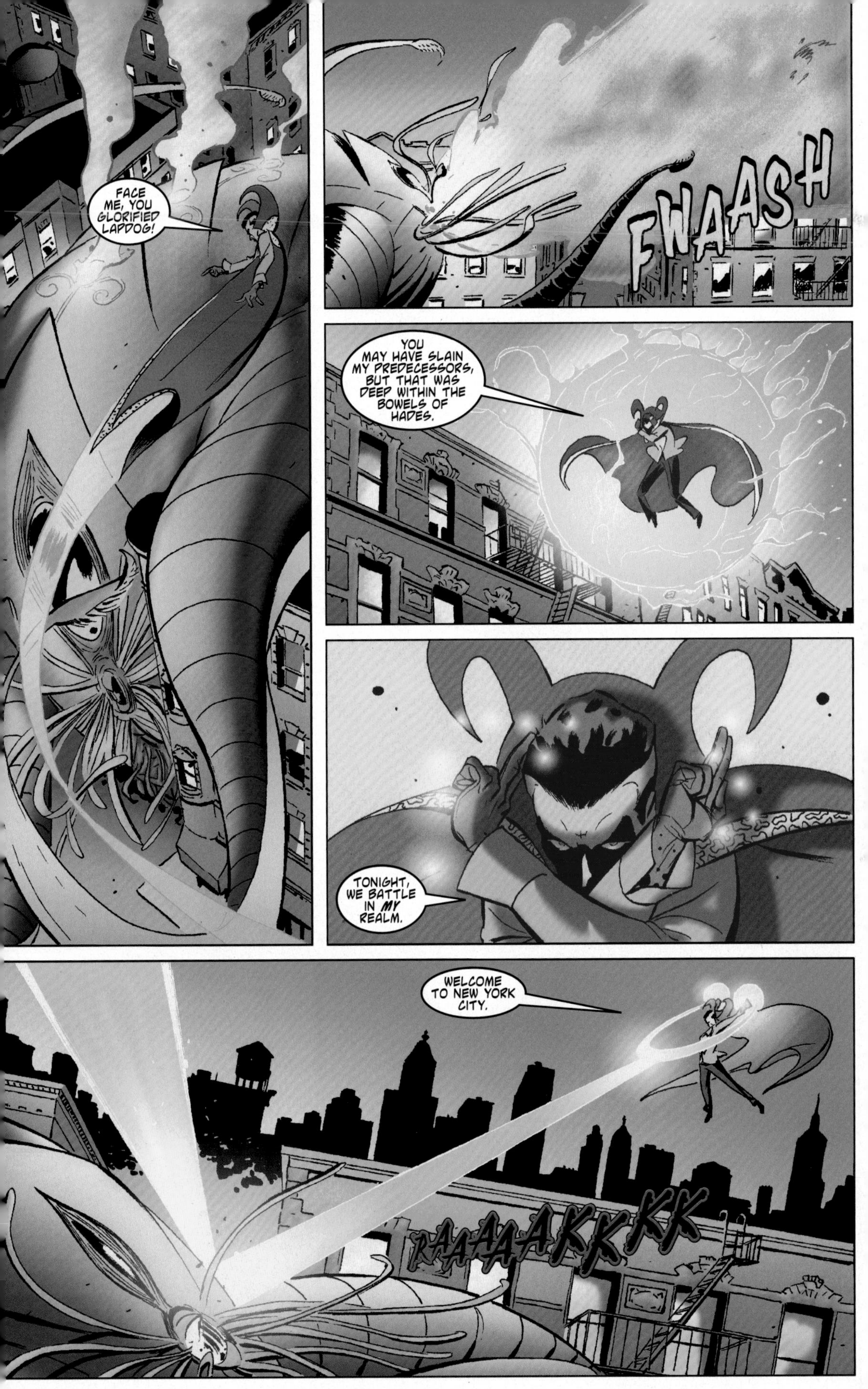
FACE ME, YOU GLORIFIED LAPDOG!
FWAASH
YOU MAY HAVE SLAIN MY PREDECESSORS, BUT THAT WAS DEEP WITHIN THE BOWELS OF HADES.
TONIGHT, WE BATTLE IN *MY* REALM.
WELCOME TO NEW YORK CITY.
RAAAAAKKKKK

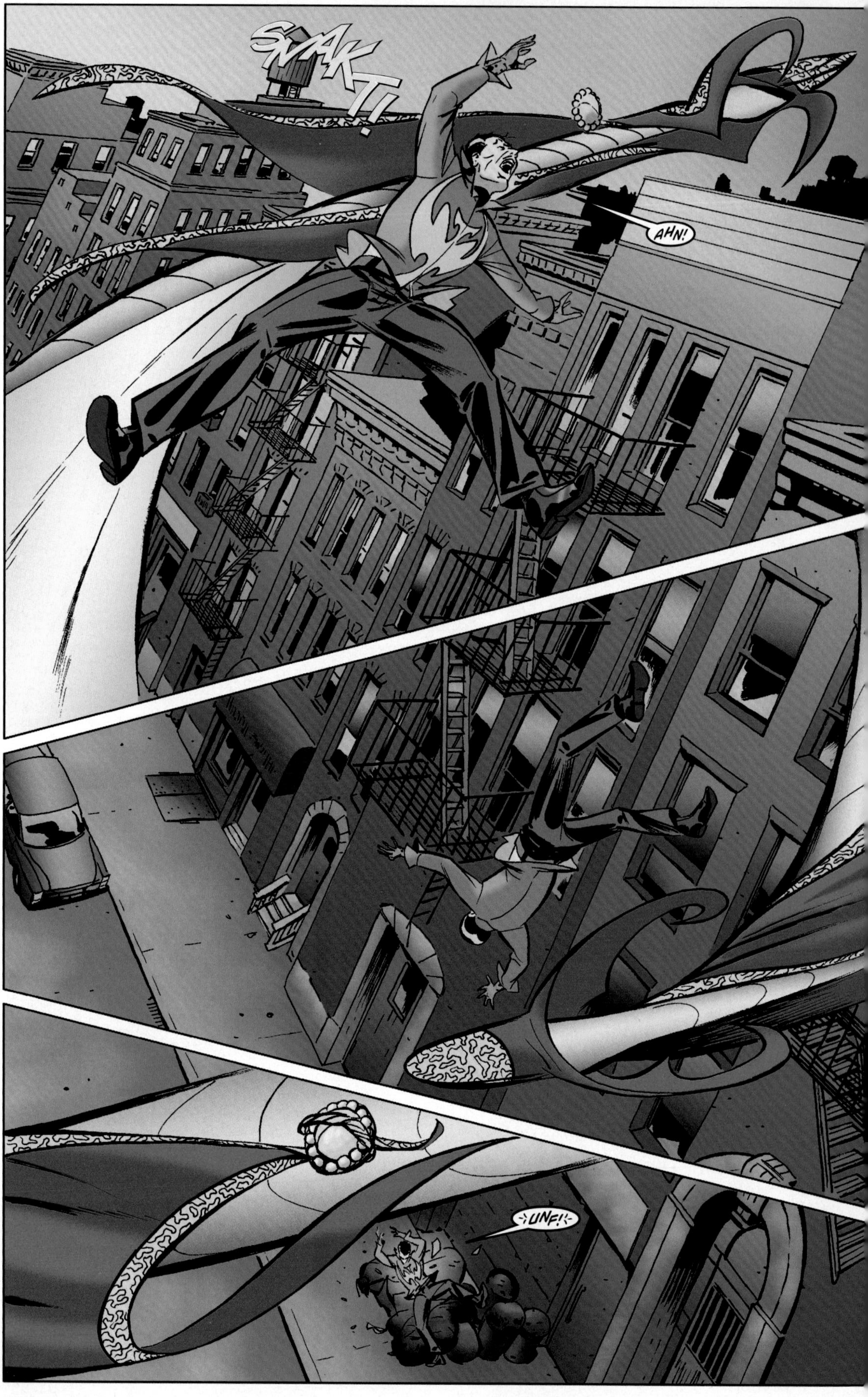
SNAKT!!
AHN!
UNF!

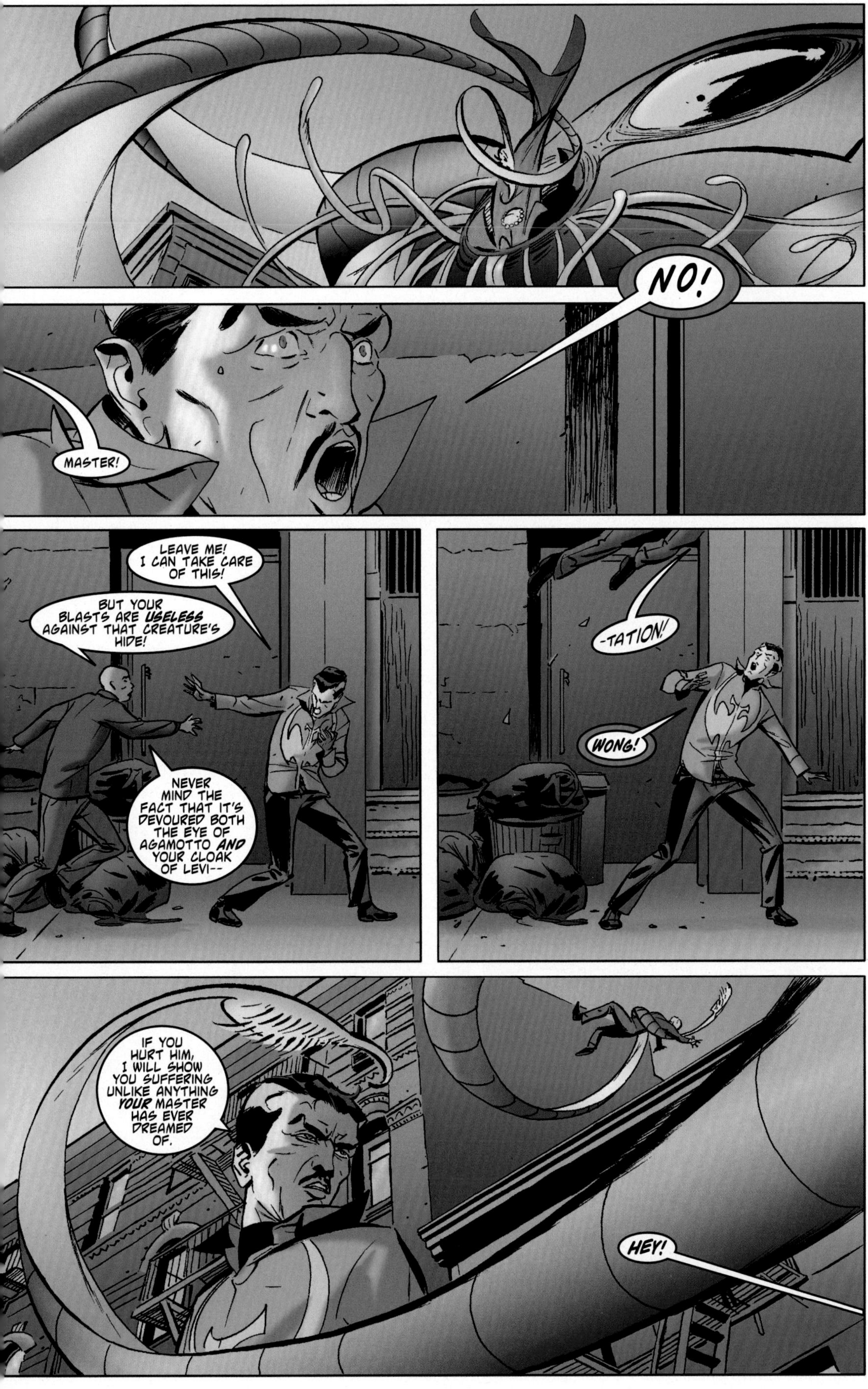
NO!
MASTER!
LEAVE ME! I CAN TAKE CARE OF THIS!
BUT YOUR BLASTS ARE USELESS AGAINST THAT CREATURE'S HIDE!
NEVER MIND THE FACT THAT IT'S DEVOURED BOTH THE EYE OF AGAMOTTO AND YOUR CLOAK OF LEVI--
-TATION!
WONG!
IF YOU HURT HIM, I WILL SHOW YOU SUFFERING UNLIKE ANYTHING YOUR MASTER HAS EVER DREAMED OF.
HEY!

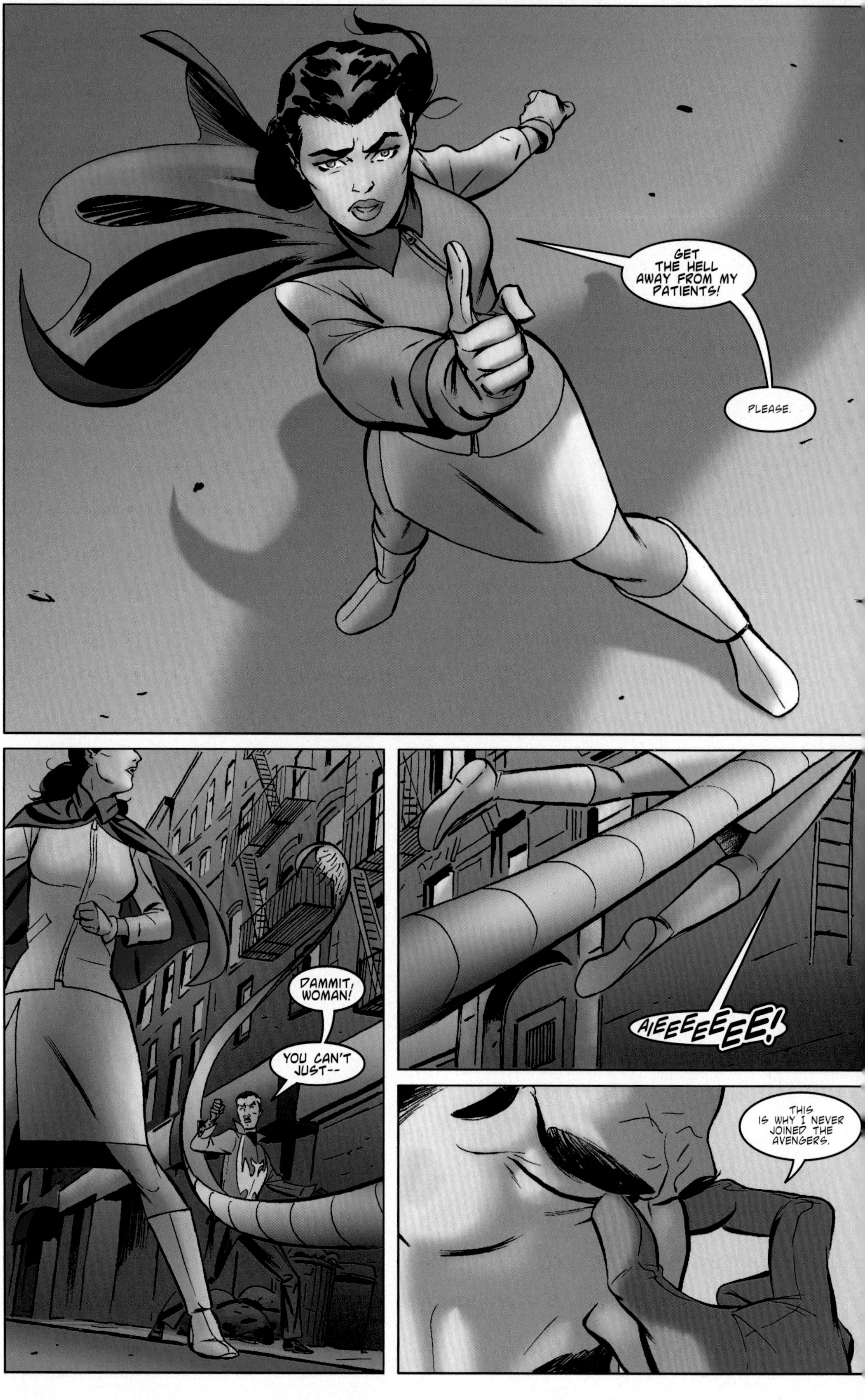
GET THE HELL AWAY FROM MY PATIENTS!
PLEASE.
DAMMIT, WOMAN!
YOU CAN'T JUST--
AIEEEEEEEE!
THIS IS WHY I NEVER JOINED THE AVENGERS.

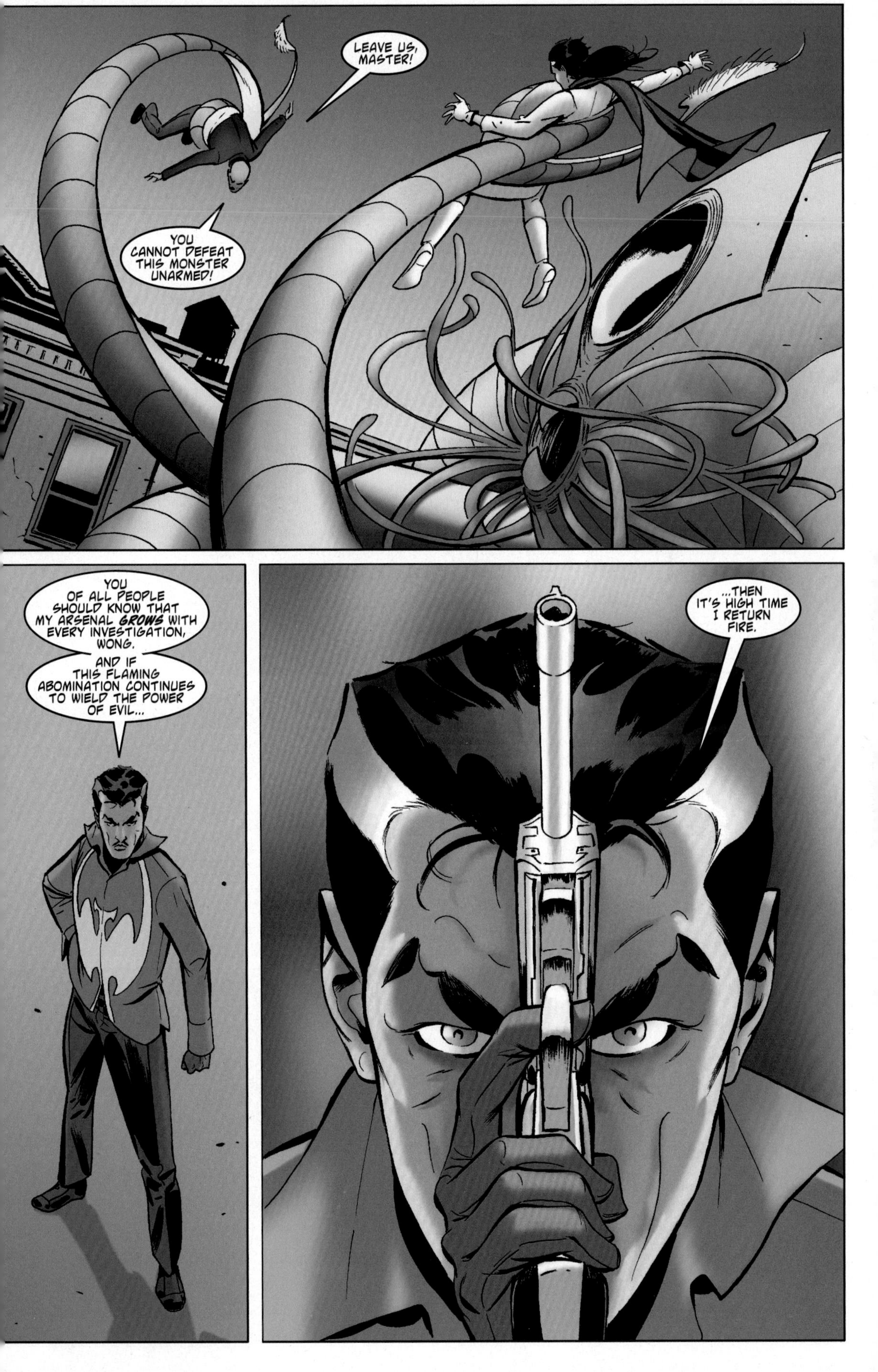
LEAVE US, MASTER!
YOU CANNOT DEFEAT THIS MONSTER UNARMED!
YOU OF ALL PEOPLE SHOULD KNOW THAT MY ARSENAL GROWS WITH EVERY INVESTIGATION, WONG.
AND IF THIS FLAMING ABOMINATION CONTINUES TO WIELD THE POWER OF EVIL...
...THEN IT'S HIGH TIME I RETURN FIRE.

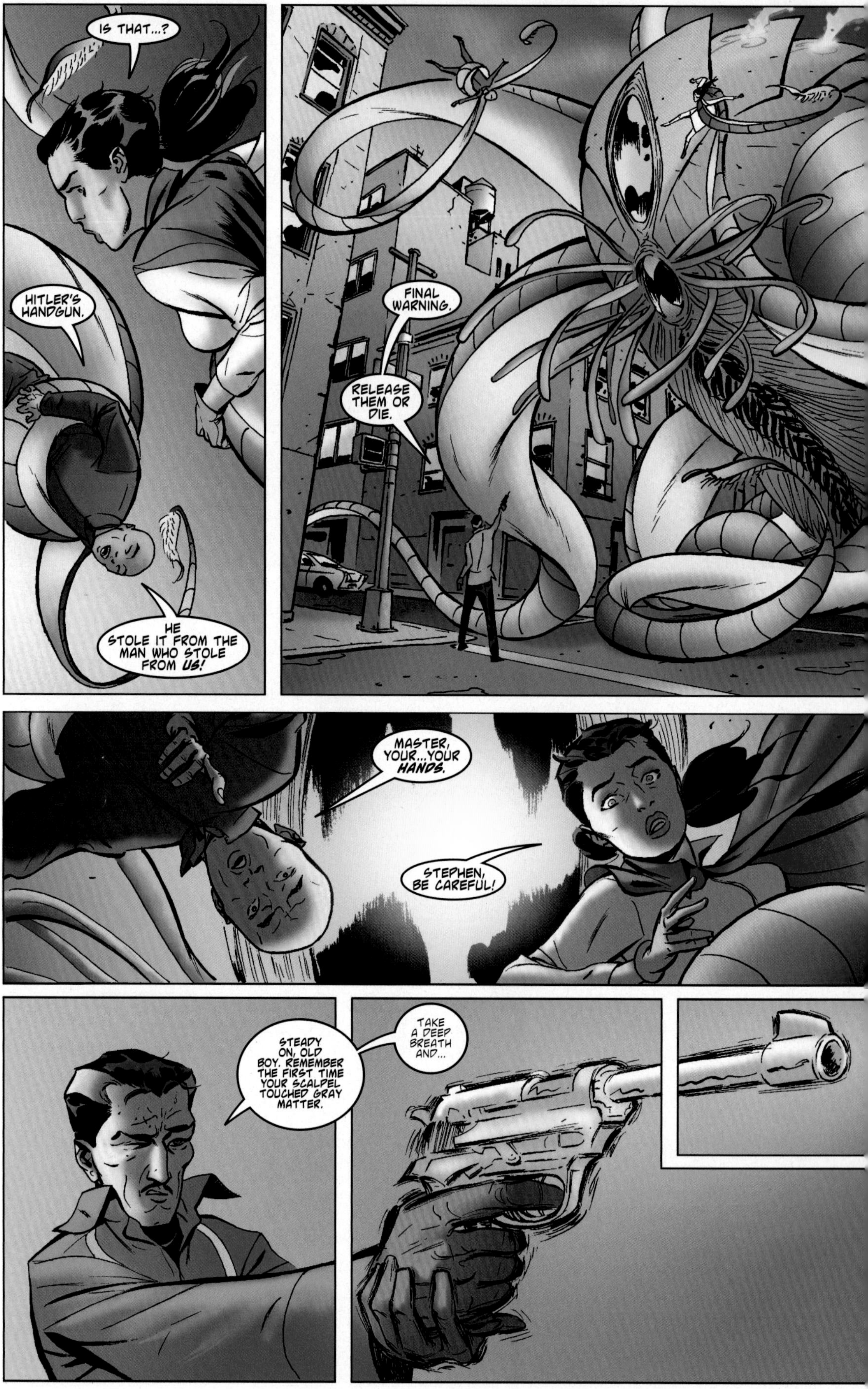
IS THAT...?
HITLER'S HANDGUN.
HE STOLE IT FROM THE MAN WHO STOLE FROM US!
FINAL WARNING.
RELEASE THEM OR DIE.
MASTER, YOUR...YOUR HANDS.
STEPHEN, BE CAREFUL!
STEADY ON, OLD BOY. REMEMBER THE FIRST TIME YOUR SCALPEL TOUCHED GRAY MATTER.
TAKE A DEEP BREATH AND...

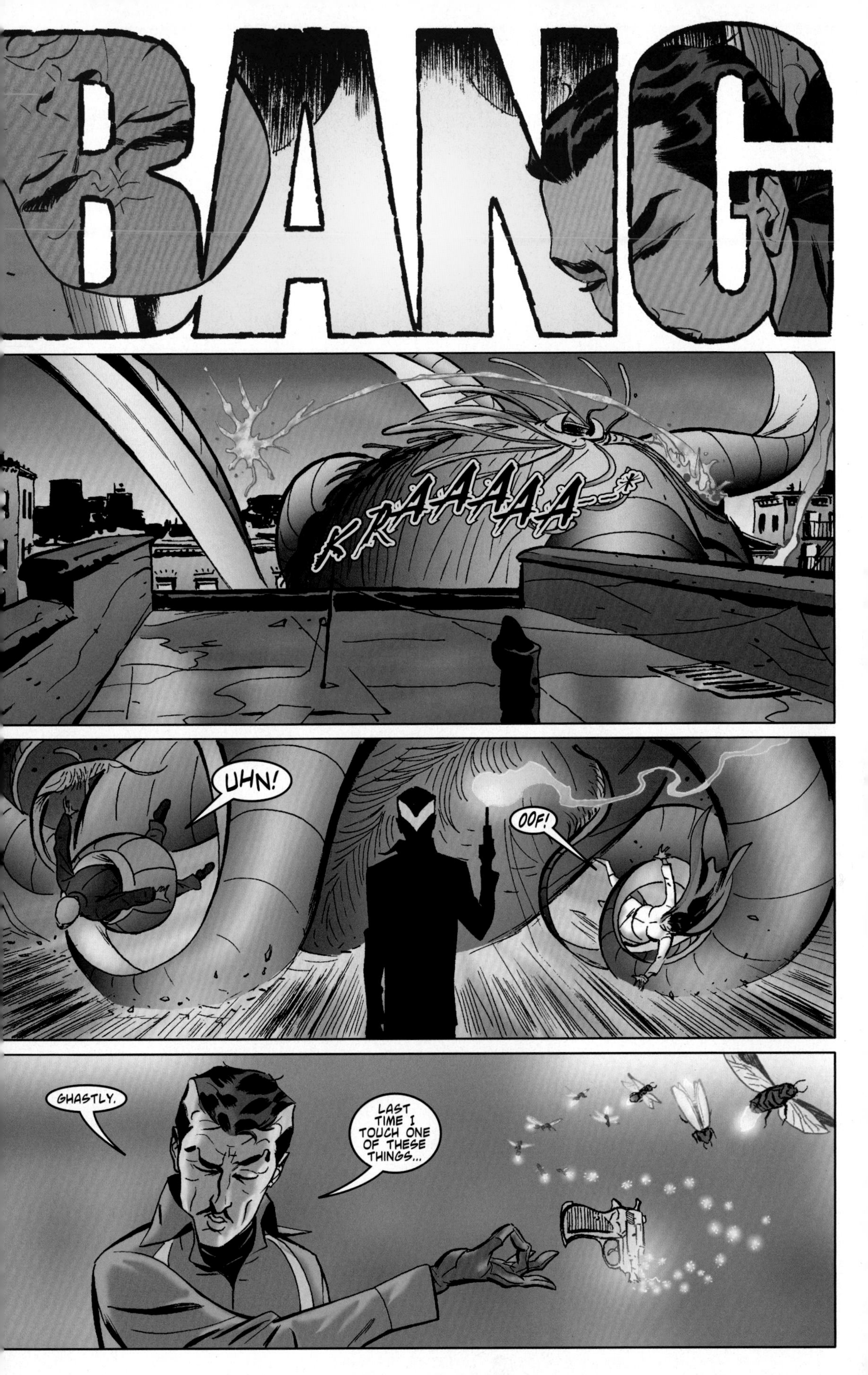
BANG
KRAAAAAA--*
UHN!
OOF!
GHASTLY.
LAST TIME I TOUCH ONE OF THESE THINGS...

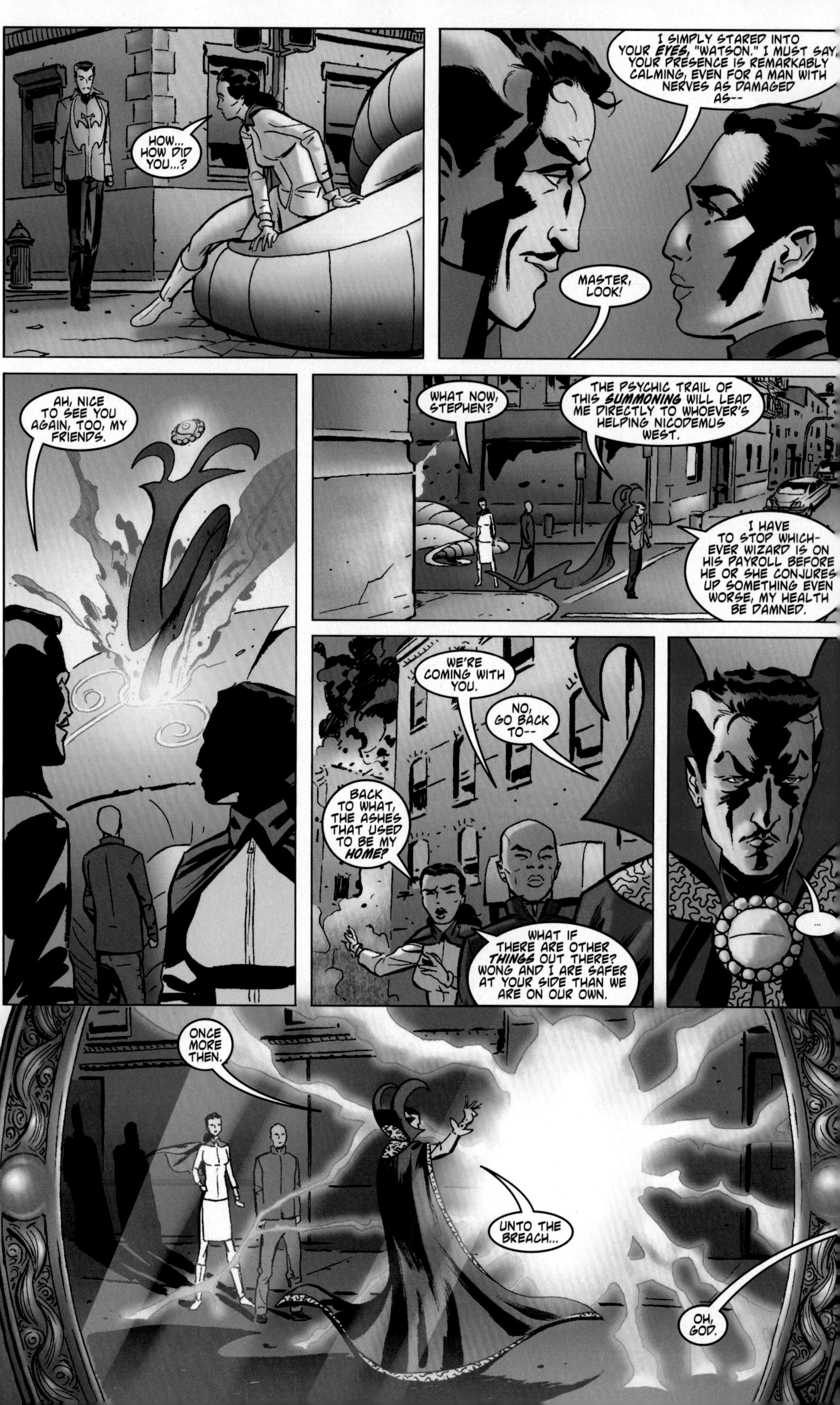
HOW... HOW DID YOU...?
I SIMPLY STARED INTO YOUR EYES, "WATSON." I MUST SAY, YOUR PRESENCE IS REMARKABLY CALMING, EVEN FOR A MAN WITH NERVES AS DAMAGED AS--
MASTER, LOOK!
AH, NICE TO SEE YOU AGAIN, TOO, MY FRIENDS.
WHAT NOW, STEPHEN?
THE PSYCHIC TRAIL OF THIS SUMMONING WILL LEAD ME DIRECTLY TO WHOEVER'S HELPING NICODEMUS WEST.
I HAVE TO STOP WHICH-EVER WIZARD IS ON HIS PAYROLL BEFORE HE OR SHE CONJURES UP SOMETHING EVEN WORSE, MY HEALTH BE DAMNED.
WE'RE COMING WITH YOU.
NO, GO BACK TO--
BACK TO WHAT, THE ASHES THAT USED TO BE MY HOME?
WHAT IF THERE ARE OTHER THINGS OUT THERE? WONG AND I ARE SAFER AT YOUR SIDE THAN WE ARE ON OUR OWN.
...
ONCE MORE THEN.
UNTO THE BREACH...
OH, GOD.

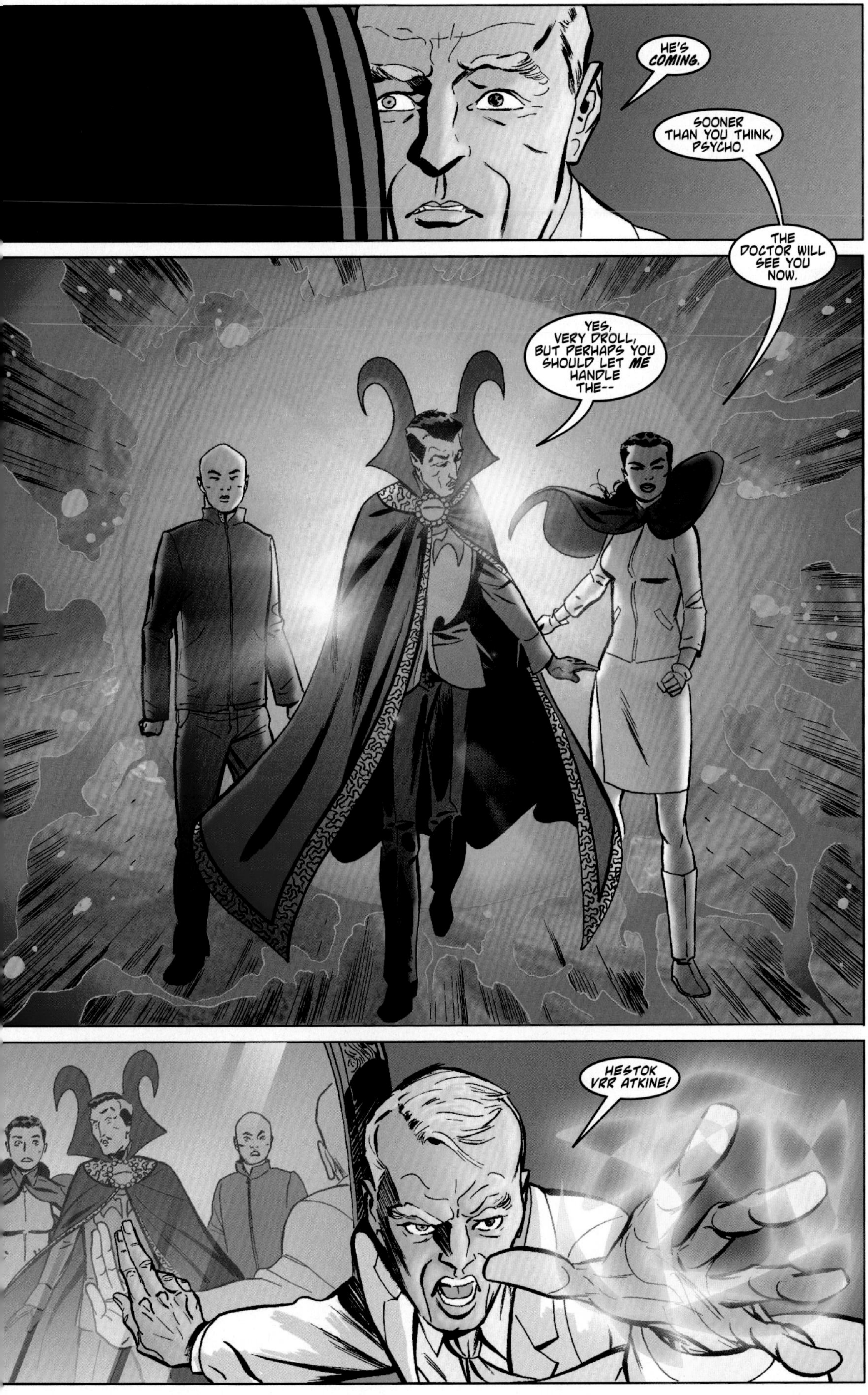
HE'S COMING.
SOONER THAN YOU THINK, PSYCHO.
THE DOCTOR WILL SEE YOU NOW.
YES, VERY DROLL, BUT PERHAPS YOU SHOULD LET ME HANDLE THE--
HESTOK VRR ATKINE!

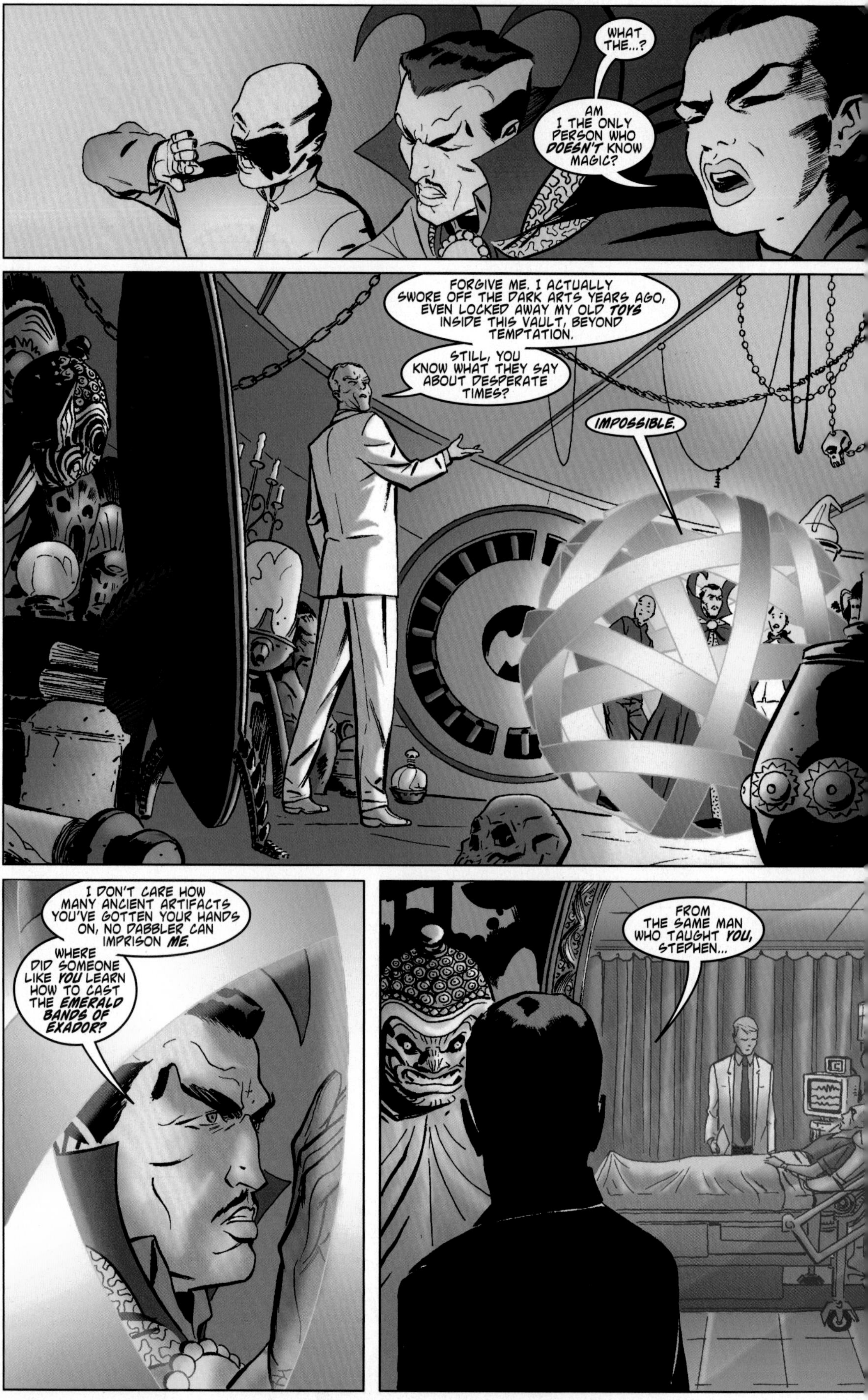
WHAT THE...?
AM I THE ONLY PERSON WHO DOESN'T KNOW MAGIC?
FORGIVE ME. I ACTUALLY SWORE OFF THE DARK ARTS YEARS AGO, EVEN LOCKED AWAY MY OLD TOYS INSIDE THIS VAULT, BEYOND TEMPTATION.
STILL, YOU KNOW WHAT THEY SAY ABOUT DESPERATE TIMES?
IMPOSSIBLE.
I DON'T CARE HOW MANY ANCIENT ARTIFACTS YOU'VE GOTTEN YOUR HANDS ON, NO DABBLER CAN IMPRISON ME.
WHERE DID SOMEONE LIKE YOU LEARN HOW TO CAST THE EMERALD BANDS OF EXADOR?
FROM THE SAME MAN WHO TAUGHT YOU, STEPHEN...

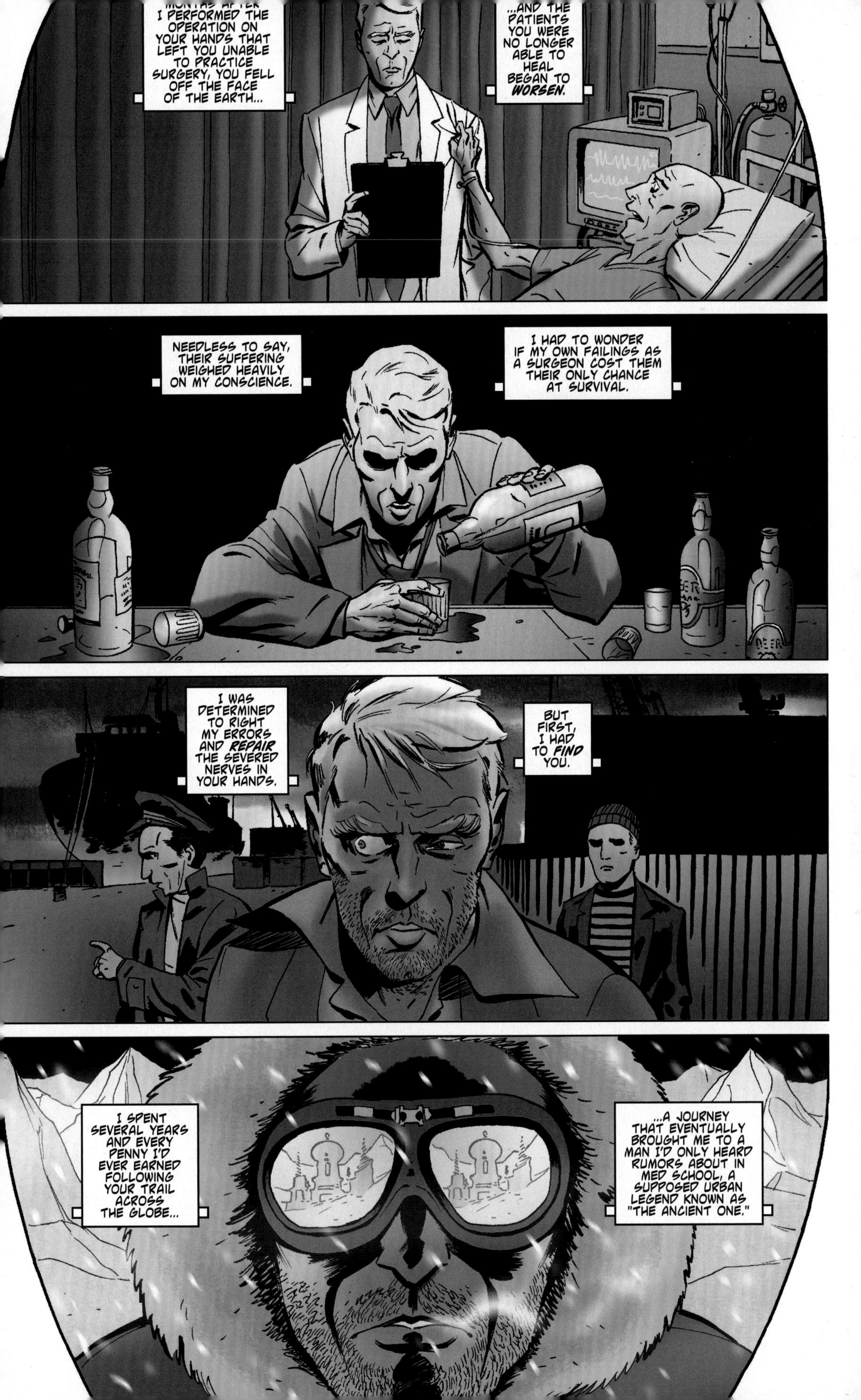
I PERFORMED THE OPERATION ON YOUR HANDS THAT LEFT YOU UNABLE TO PRACTICE SURGERY, YOU FELL OFF THE FACE OF THE EARTH...
...AND THE PATIENTS YOU WERE NO LONGER ABLE TO HEAL BEGAN TO *WORSEN*.
NEEDLESS TO SAY, THEIR SUFFERING WEIGHED HEAVILY ON MY CONSCIENCE.
I HAD TO WONDER IF MY OWN FAILINGS AS A SURGEON COST THEM THEIR ONLY CHANCE AT SURVIVAL.
I WAS DETERMINED TO RIGHT MY ERRORS AND *REPAIR* THE SEVERED NERVES IN YOUR HANDS.
BUT FIRST, I HAD TO *FIND* YOU.
I SPENT SEVERAL YEARS AND EVERY PENNY I'D EVER EARNED FOLLOWING YOUR TRAIL ACROSS THE GLOBE...
...A JOURNEY THAT EVENTUALLY BROUGHT ME TO A MAN I'D ONLY HEARD RUMORS ABOUT IN MED SCHOOL, A SUPPOSED URBAN LEGEND KNOWN AS "THE ANCIENT ONE."

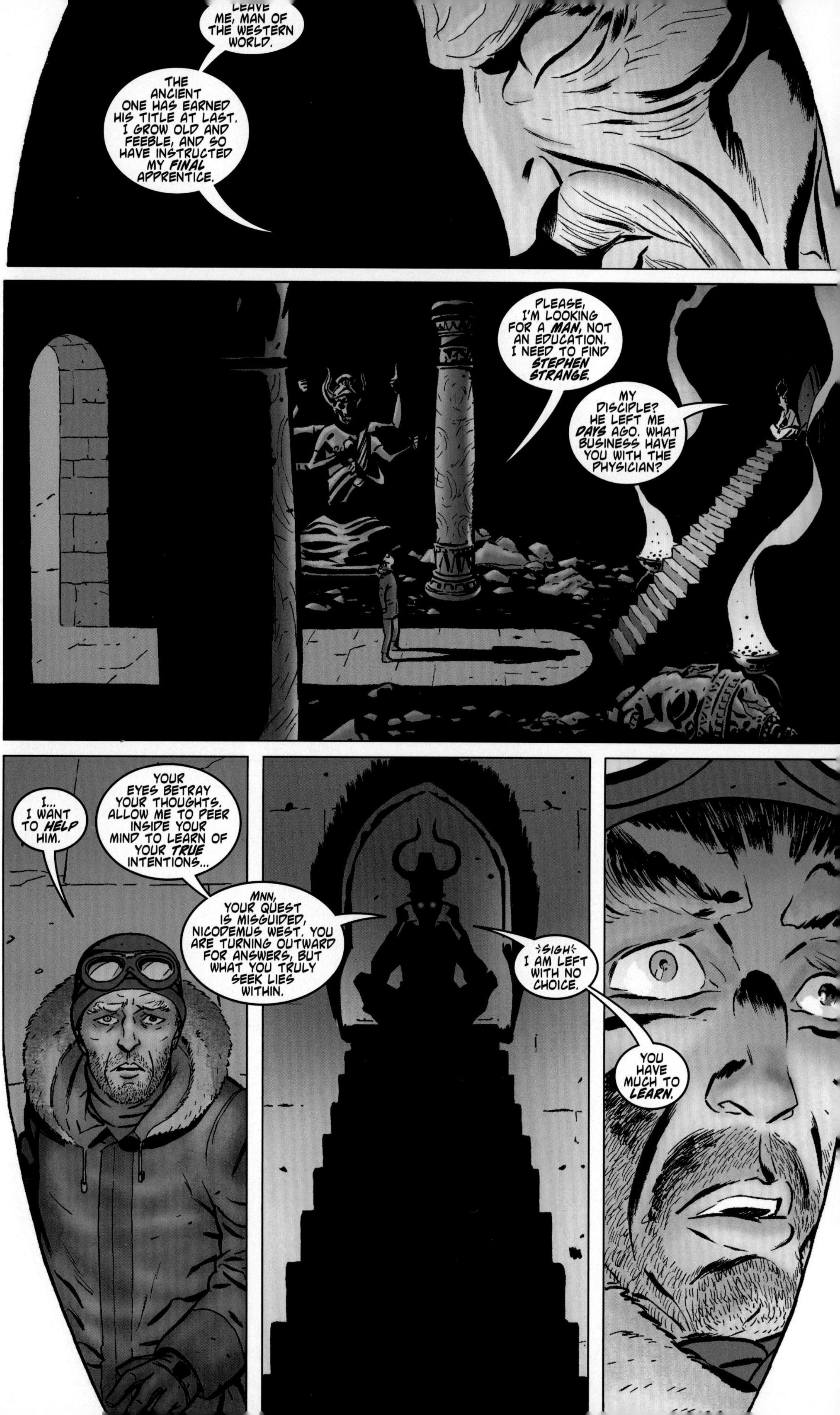
LEAVE ME, MAN OF THE WESTERN WORLD.
THE ANCIENT ONE HAS EARNED HIS TITLE AT LAST. I GROW OLD AND FEEBLE, AND SO HAVE INSTRUCTED MY FINAL APPRENTICE.
PLEASE, I'M LOOKING FOR A MAN, NOT AN EDUCATION. I NEED TO FIND STEPHEN STRANGE.
MY DISCIPLE? HE LEFT ME DAYS AGO. WHAT BUSINESS HAVE YOU WITH THE PHYSICIAN?
I... I WANT TO HELP HIM.
YOUR EYES BETRAY YOUR THOUGHTS. ALLOW ME TO PEER INSIDE YOUR MIND TO LEARN OF YOUR TRUE INTENTIONS...
MNN, YOUR QUEST IS MISGUIDED, NICODEMUS WEST. YOU ARE TURNING OUTWARD FOR ANSWERS, BUT WHAT YOU TRULY SEEK LIES WITHIN.
SIGH I AM LEFT WITH NO CHOICE.
YOU HAVE MUCH TO LEARN.

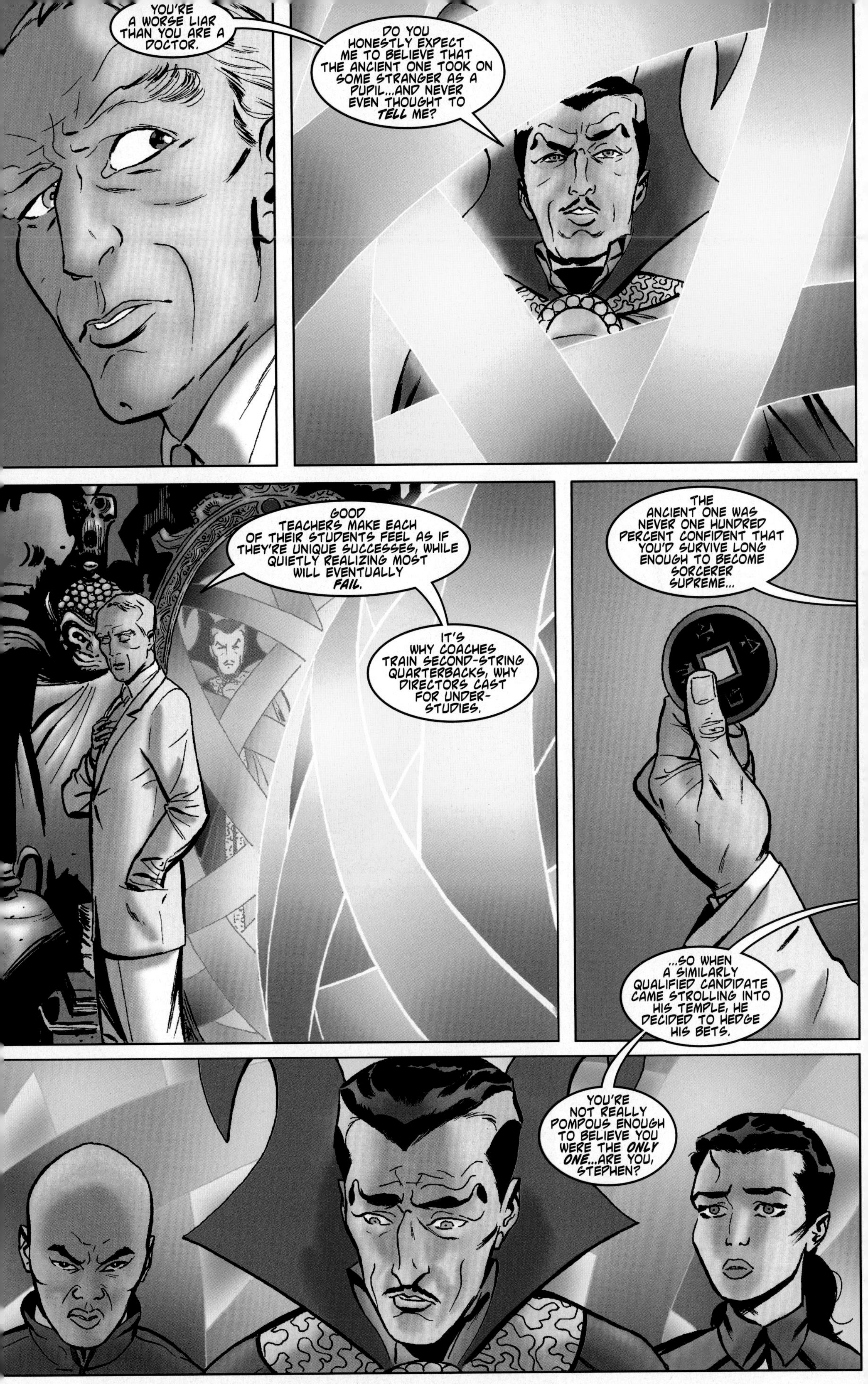
YOU'RE A WORSE LIAR THAN YOU ARE A DOCTOR.
DO YOU HONESTLY EXPECT ME TO BELIEVE THAT THE ANCIENT ONE TOOK ON SOME STRANGER AS A PUPIL...AND NEVER EVEN THOUGHT TO TELL ME?
GOOD TEACHERS MAKE EACH OF THEIR STUDENTS FEEL AS IF THEY'RE UNIQUE SUCCESSES, WHILE QUIETLY REALIZING MOST WILL EVENTUALLY FAIL.
IT'S WHY COACHES TRAIN SECOND-STRING QUARTERBACKS, WHY DIRECTORS CAST FOR UNDER-STUDIES.
THE ANCIENT ONE WAS NEVER ONE HUNDRED PERCENT CONFIDENT THAT YOU'D SURVIVE LONG ENOUGH TO BECOME SORCERER SUPREME...
...SO WHEN A SIMILARLY QUALIFIED CANDIDATE CAME STROLLING INTO HIS TEMPLE, HE DECIDED TO HEDGE HIS BETS.
YOU'RE NOT REALLY POMPOUS ENOUGH TO BELIEVE YOU WERE THE ONLY ONE...ARE YOU, STEPHEN?

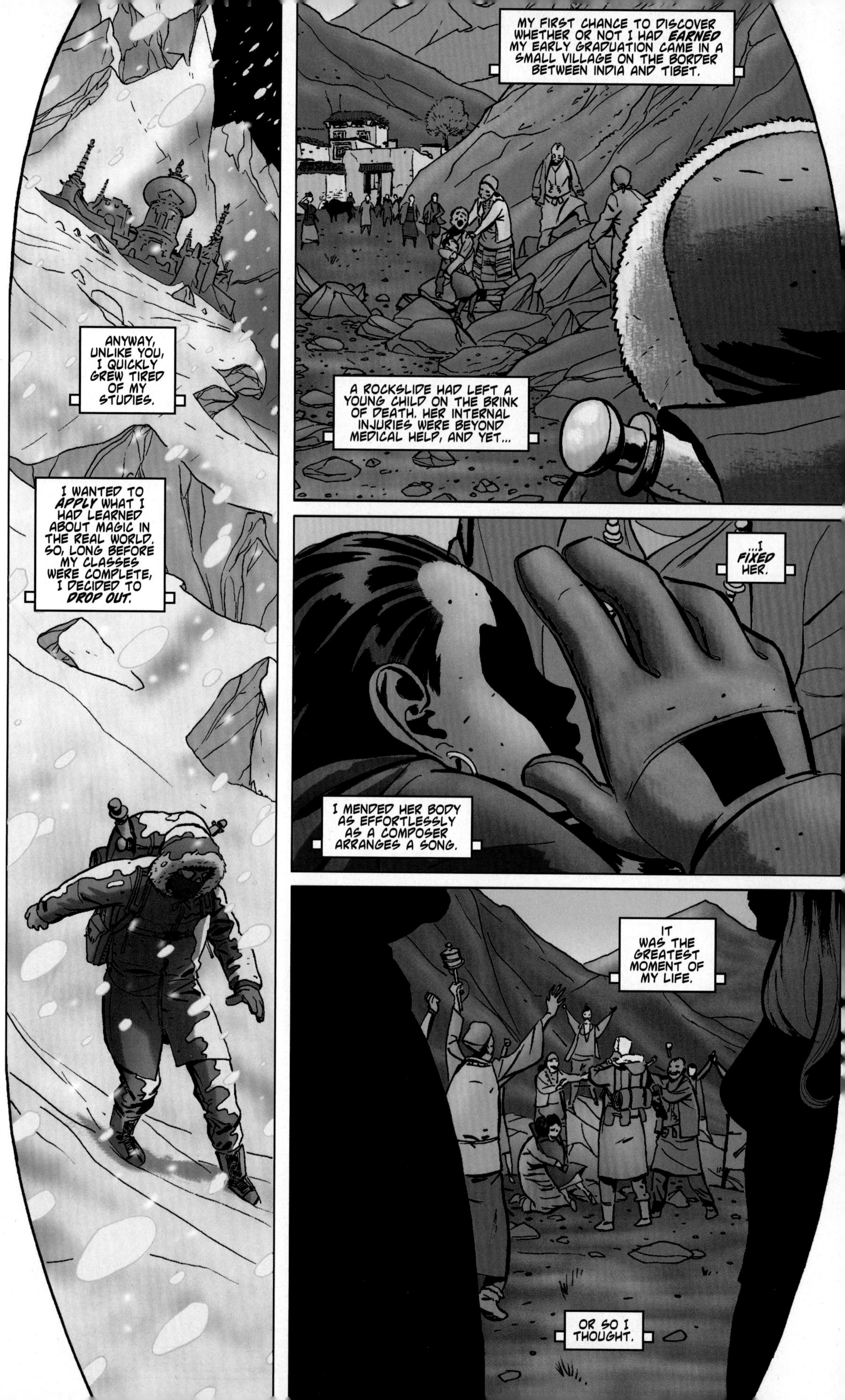
ANYWAY, UNLIKE YOU, I QUICKLY GREW TIRED OF MY STUDIES.
I WANTED TO *APPLY* WHAT I HAD LEARNED ABOUT MAGIC IN THE REAL WORLD. SO, LONG BEFORE MY CLASSES WERE COMPLETE, I DECIDED TO *DROP OUT*.
MY FIRST CHANCE TO DISCOVER WHETHER OR NOT I HAD *EARNED* MY EARLY GRADUATION CAME IN A SMALL VILLAGE ON THE BORDER BETWEEN INDIA AND TIBET.
A ROCKSLIDE HAD LEFT A YOUNG CHILD ON THE BRINK OF DEATH. HER INTERNAL INJURIES WERE BEYOND MEDICAL HELP, AND YET...
...I *FIXED* HER.
I MENDED HER BODY AS EFFORTLESSLY AS A COMPOSER ARRANGES A SONG.
IT WAS THE GREATEST MOMENT OF MY LIFE.
OR SO I THOUGHT.

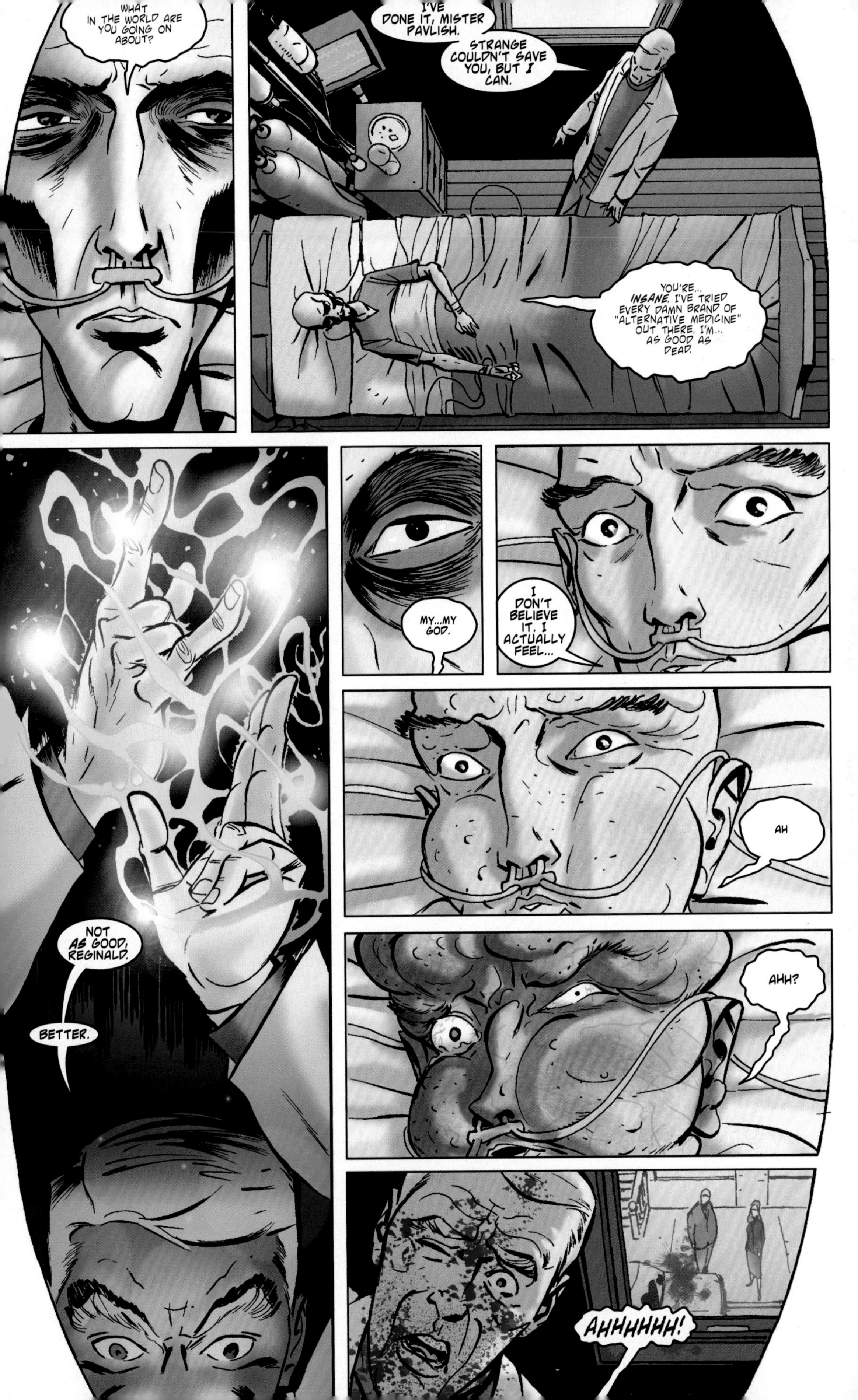
WHAT IN THE WORLD ARE YOU GOING ON ABOUT?
I'VE DONE IT, MISTER PAVLISH.
STRANGE COULDN'T SAVE YOU, BUT I CAN.
YOU'RE... INSANE. I'VE TRIED EVERY DAMN BRAND OF "ALTERNATIVE MEDICINE" OUT THERE. I'M... AS GOOD AS DEAD.
NOT AS GOOD, REGINALD.
BETTER.
MY...MY GOD.
I DON'T BELIEVE IT. I ACTUALLY FEEL...
AH
AHH?
AHHHHHH!

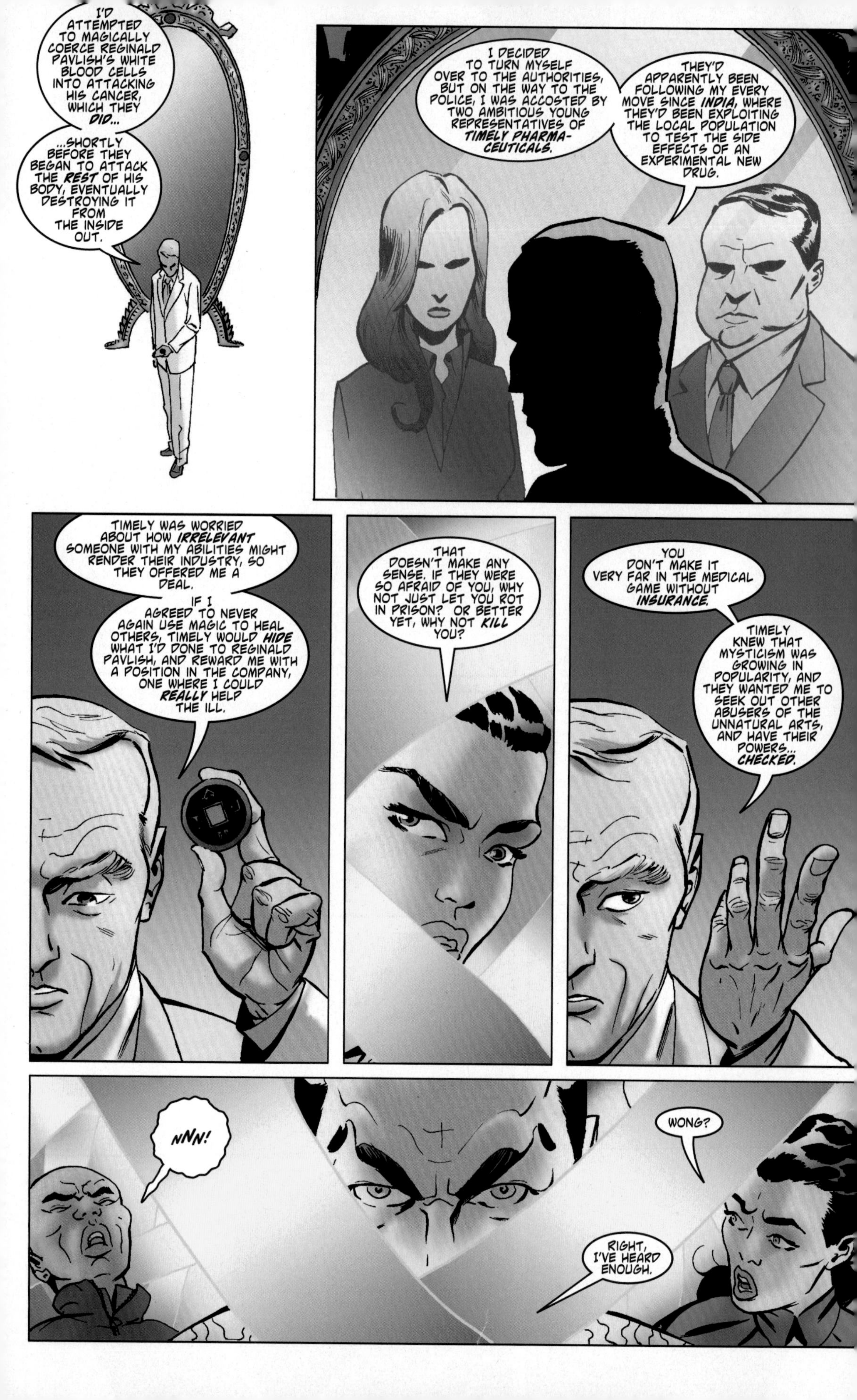
I'D ATTEMPTED TO MAGICALLY COERCE REGINALD PAVLISH'S WHITE BLOOD CELLS INTO ATTACKING HIS CANCER, WHICH THEY DID...
...SHORTLY BEFORE THEY BEGAN TO ATTACK THE REST OF HIS BODY, EVENTUALLY DESTROYING IT FROM THE INSIDE OUT.
I DECIDED TO TURN MYSELF OVER TO THE AUTHORITIES, BUT ON THE WAY TO THE POLICE, I WAS ACCOSTED BY TWO AMBITIOUS YOUNG REPRESENTATIVES OF TIMELY PHARMACEUTICALS.
THEY'D APPARENTLY BEEN FOLLOWING MY EVERY MOVE SINCE INDIA, WHERE THEY'D BEEN EXPLOITING THE LOCAL POPULATION TO TEST THE SIDE EFFECTS OF AN EXPERIMENTAL NEW DRUG.
TIMELY WAS WORRIED ABOUT HOW IRRELEVANT SOMEONE WITH MY ABILITIES MIGHT RENDER THEIR INDUSTRY, SO THEY OFFERED ME A DEAL.
IF I AGREED TO NEVER AGAIN USE MAGIC TO HEAL OTHERS, TIMELY WOULD HIDE WHAT I'D DONE TO REGINALD PAVLISH, AND REWARD ME WITH A POSITION IN THE COMPANY, ONE WHERE I COULD REALLY HELP THE ILL.
THAT DOESN'T MAKE ANY SENSE. IF THEY WERE SO AFRAID OF YOU, WHY NOT JUST LET YOU ROT IN PRISON? OR BETTER YET, WHY NOT KILL YOU?
YOU DON'T MAKE IT VERY FAR IN THE MEDICAL GAME WITHOUT INSURANCE.
TIMELY KNEW THAT MYSTICISM WAS GROWING IN POPULARITY, AND THEY WANTED ME TO SEEK OUT OTHER ABUSERS OF THE UNNATURAL ARTS, AND HAVE THEIR POWERS... CHECKED.
NNN!
WONG?
RIGHT, I'VE HEARD ENOUGH.

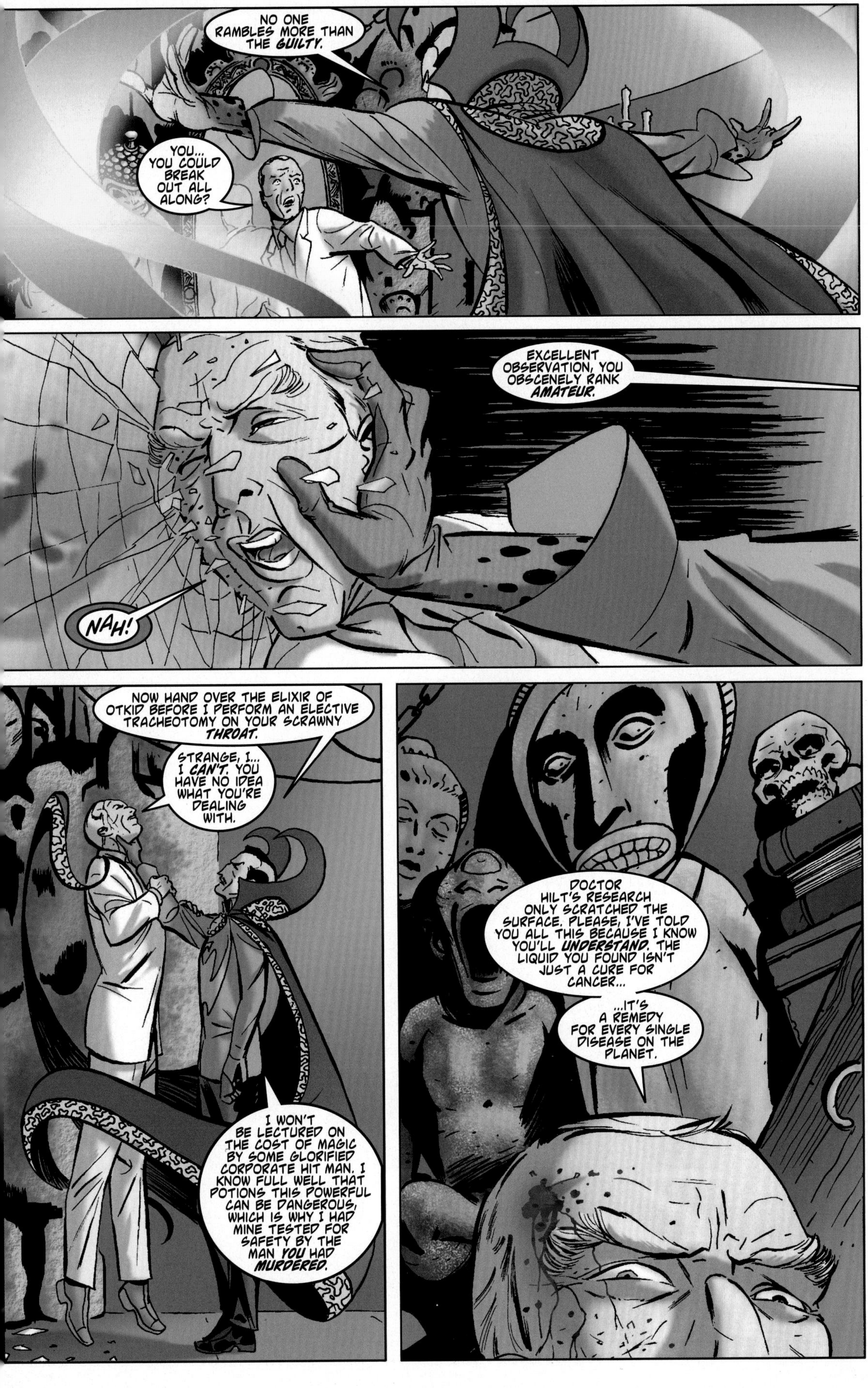
NO ONE RAMBLES MORE THAN THE GUILTY.
YOU... YOU COULD BREAK OUT ALL ALONG?
EXCELLENT OBSERVATION, YOU OBSCENELY RANK AMATEUR.
NAH!
NOW HAND OVER THE ELIXIR OF OTKID BEFORE I PERFORM AN ELECTIVE TRACHEOTOMY ON YOUR SCRAWNY THROAT.
STRANGE, I... I CAN'T. YOU HAVE NO IDEA WHAT YOU'RE DEALING WITH.
I WON'T BE LECTURED ON THE COST OF MAGIC BY SOME GLORIFIED CORPORATE HIT MAN. I KNOW FULL WELL THAT POTIONS THIS POWERFUL CAN BE DANGEROUS, WHICH IS WHY I HAD MINE TESTED FOR SAFETY BY THE MAN YOU HAD MURDERED.
DOCTOR HILT'S RESEARCH ONLY SCRATCHED THE SURFACE. PLEASE, I'VE TOLD YOU ALL THIS BECAUSE I KNOW YOU'LL UNDERSTAND. THE LIQUID YOU FOUND ISN'T JUST A CURE FOR CANCER...
...IT'S A REMEDY FOR EVERY SINGLE DISEASE ON THE PLANET.

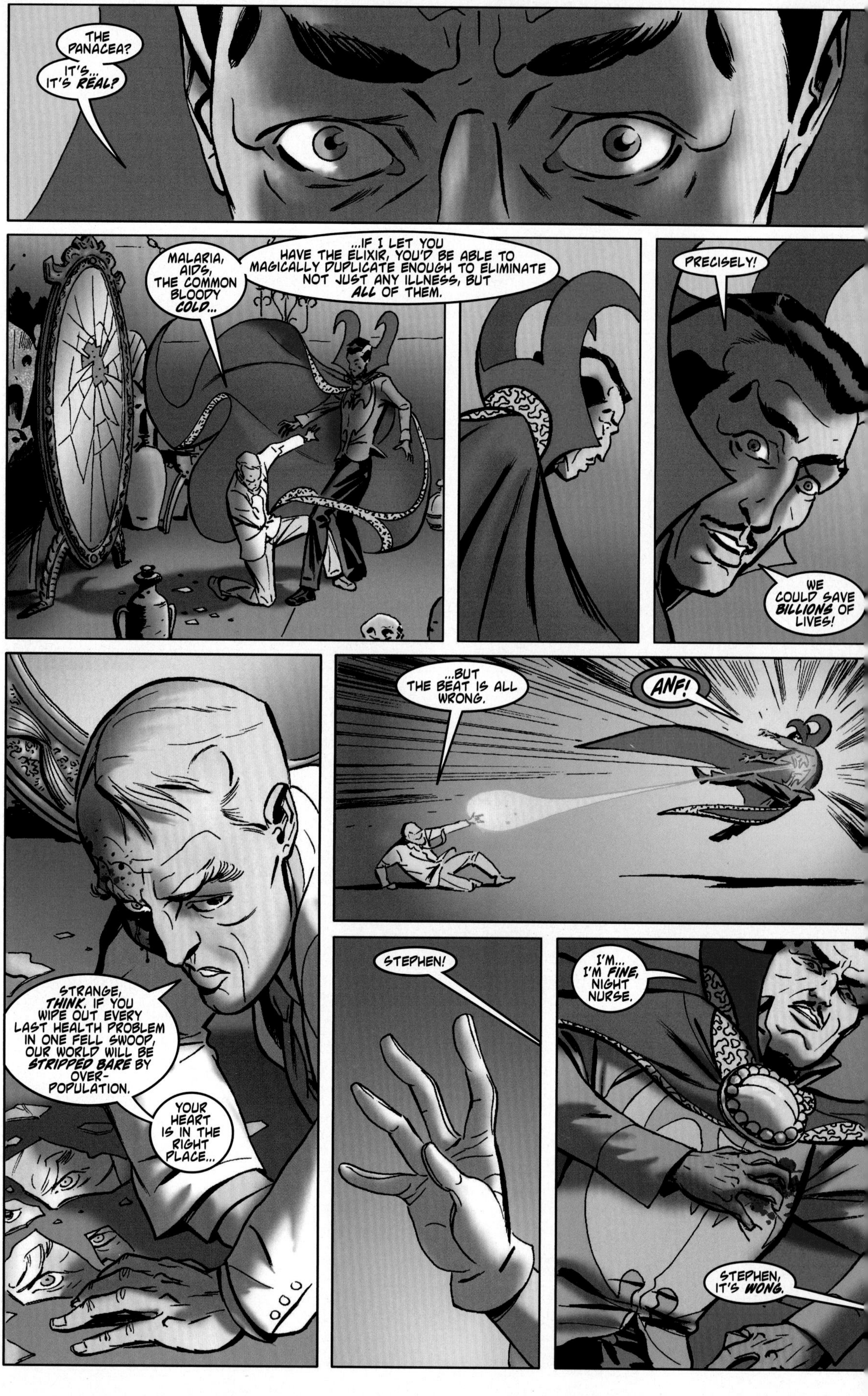
THE PANACEA?
IT'S... IT'S REAL?
MALARIA, AIDS, THE COMMON BLOODY COLD...
...IF I LET YOU HAVE THE ELIXIR, YOU'D BE ABLE TO MAGICALLY DUPLICATE ENOUGH TO ELIMINATE NOT JUST ANY ILLNESS, BUT ALL OF THEM.
PRECISELY!
WE COULD SAVE BILLIONS OF LIVES!
STRANGE, THINK. IF YOU WIPE OUT EVERY LAST HEALTH PROBLEM IN ONE FELL SWOOP, OUR WORLD WILL BE STRIPPED BARE BY OVER-POPULATION.
YOUR HEART IS IN THE RIGHT PLACE...
...BUT THE BEAT IS ALL WRONG.
ANF!
STEPHEN!
I'M... I'M FINE, NIGHT NURSE.
STEPHEN, IT'S WONG.

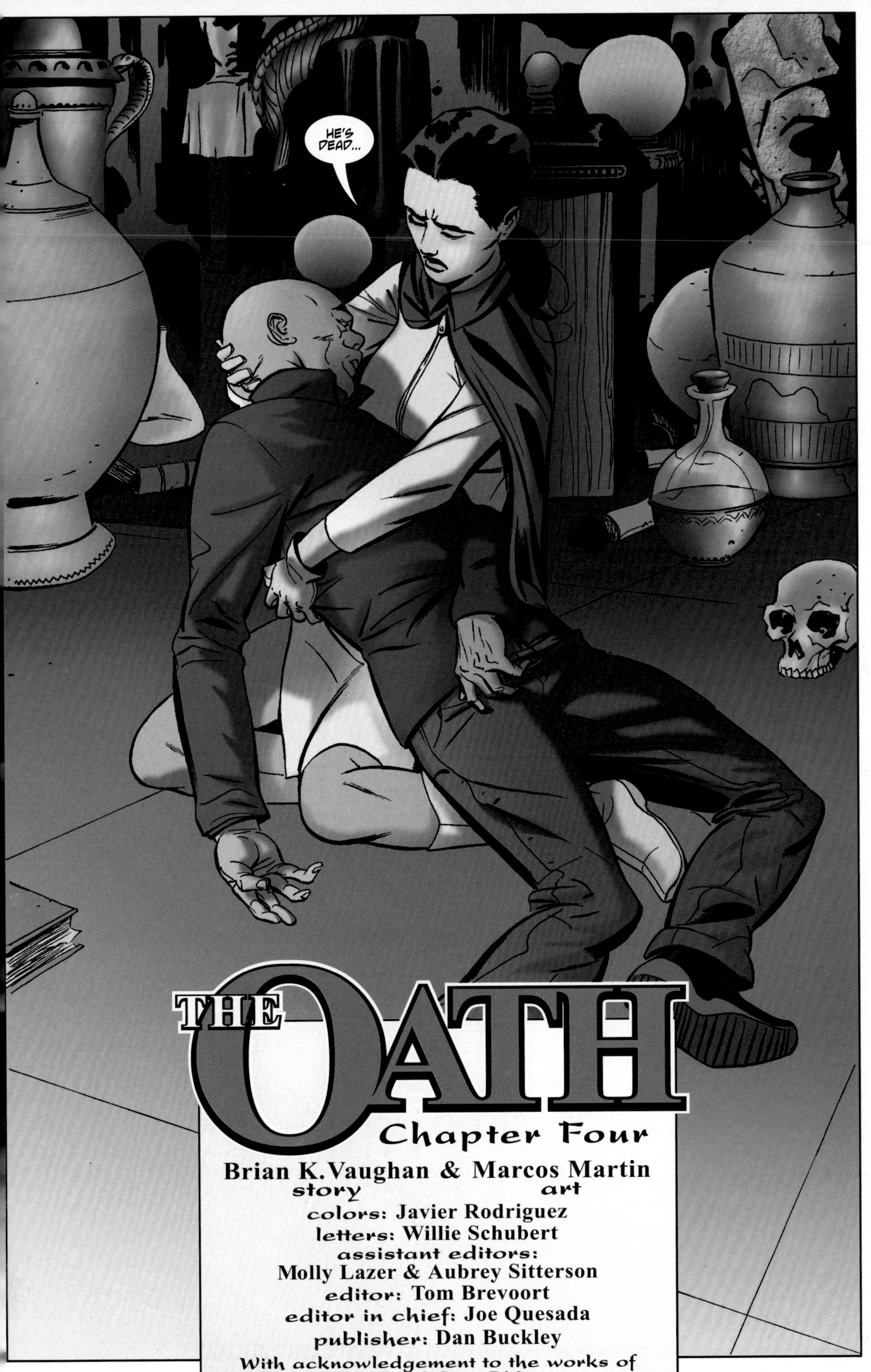

HE'S DEAD...

THE OATH

Chapter Four

Brian K. Vaughan & Marcos Martin
story art
colors: Javier Rodriguez
letters: Willie Schubert
assistant editors:
Molly Lazer & Aubrey Sitterson
editor: Tom Brevoort
editor in chief: Joe Quesada
publisher: Dan Buckley

With acknowledgement to the works of
Stan Lee & Steve Ditko

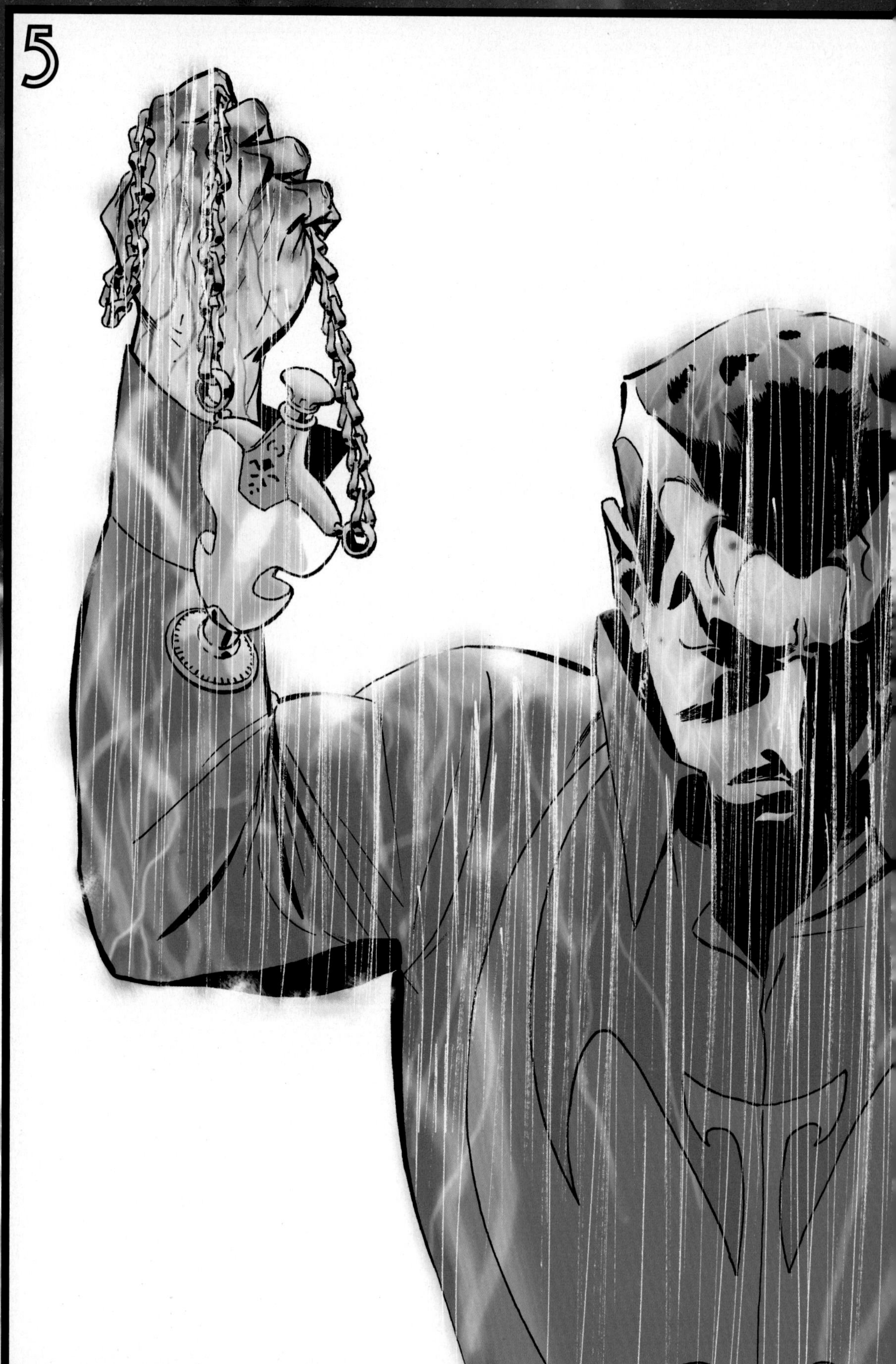
5

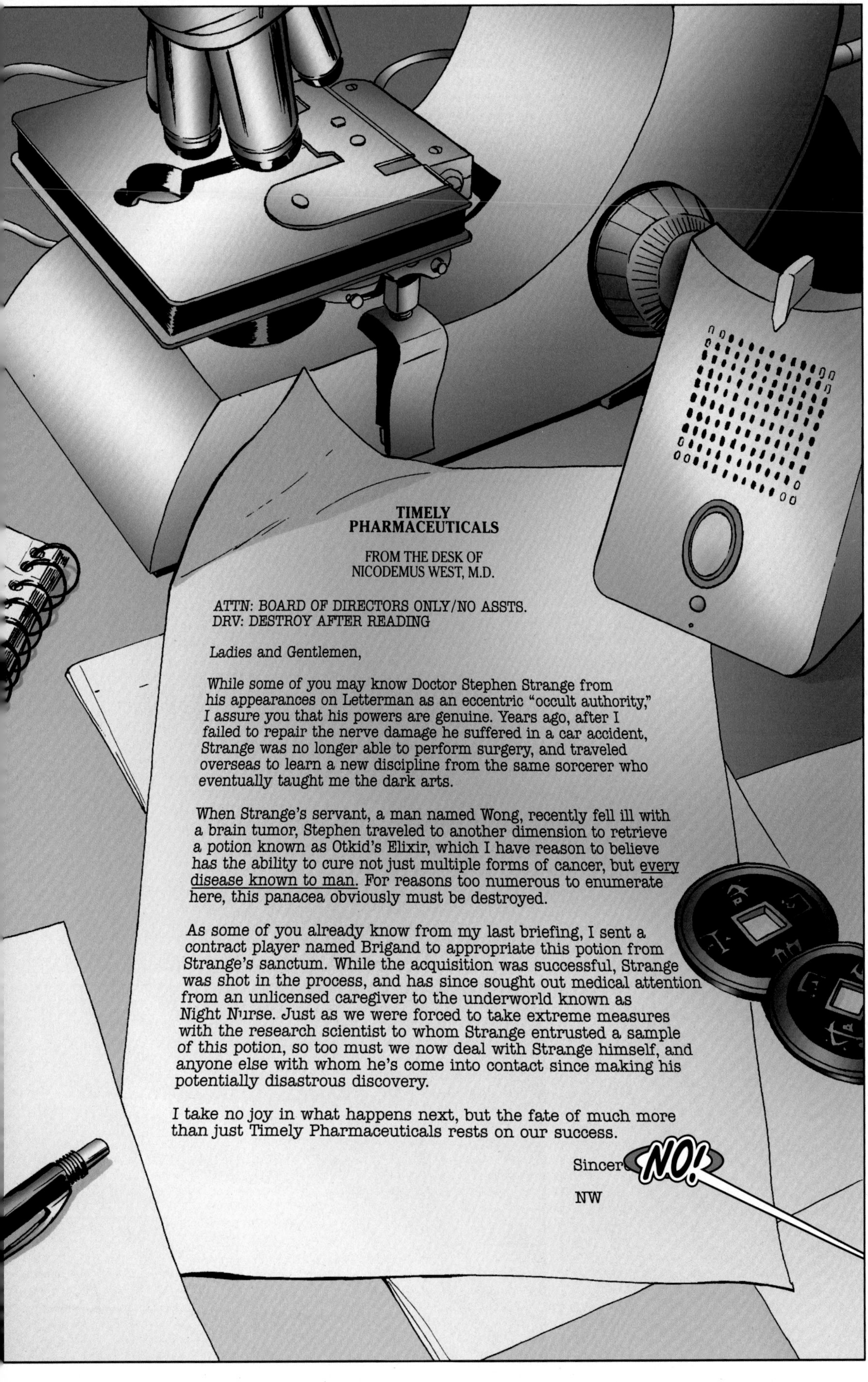
TIMELY
PHARMACEUTICALS
FROM THE DESK OF
NICODEMUS WEST, M.D.
ATTN: BOARD OF DIRECTORS ONLY/NO ASSTS.
DRV: DESTROY AFTER READING
Ladies and Gentlemen,
While some of you may know Doctor Stephen Strange from his appearances on Letterman as an eccentric "occult authority," I assure you that his powers are genuine. Years ago, after I failed to repair the nerve damage he suffered in a car accident, Strange was no longer able to perform surgery, and traveled overseas to learn a new discipline from the same sorcerer who eventually taught me the dark arts.
When Strange's servant, a man named Wong, recently fell ill with a brain tumor, Stephen traveled to another dimension to retrieve a potion known as Otkid's Elixir, which I have reason to believe has the ability to cure not just multiple forms of cancer, but every disease known to man. For reasons too numerous to enumerate here, this panacea obviously must be destroyed.
As some of you already know from my last briefing, I sent a contract player named Brigand to appropriate this potion from Strange's sanctum. While the acquisition was successful, Strange was shot in the process, and has since sought out medical attention from an unlicensed caregiver to the underworld known as Night Nurse. Just as we were forced to take extreme measures with the research scientist to whom Strange entrusted a sample of this potion, so too must we now deal with Strange himself, and anyone else with whom he's come into contact since making his potentially disastrous discovery.
I take no joy in what happens next, but the fate of much more than just Timely Pharmaceuticals rests on our success.
Sincer
NW
NO!

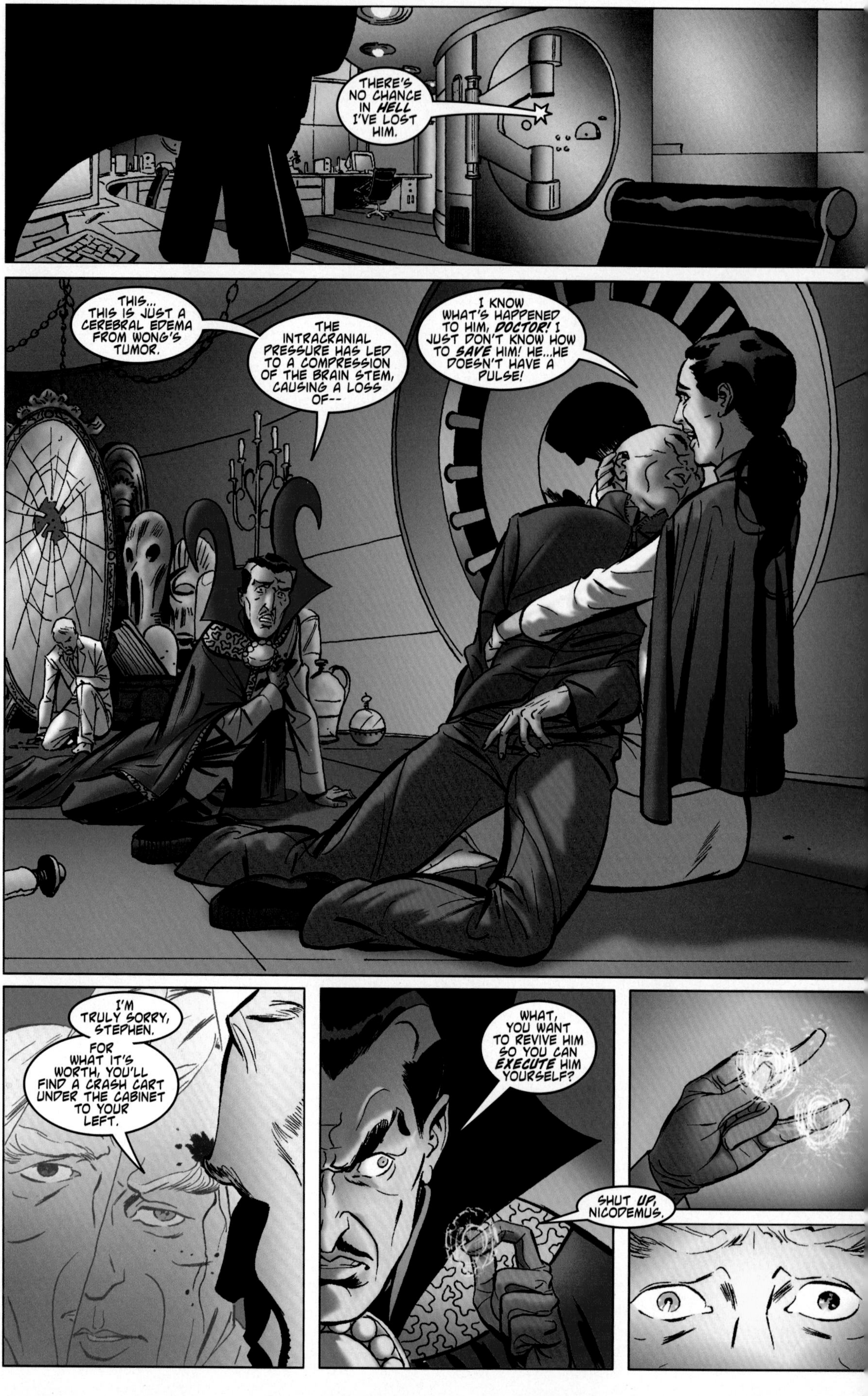
THERE'S NO CHANCE IN HELL I'VE LOST HIM.
THIS... THIS IS JUST A CEREBRAL EDEMA FROM WONG'S TUMOR.
THE INTRACRANIAL PRESSURE HAS LED TO A COMPRESSION OF THE BRAIN STEM, CAUSING A LOSS OF--
I KNOW WHAT'S HAPPENED TO HIM, DOCTOR! I JUST DON'T KNOW HOW TO SAVE HIM! HE...HE DOESN'T HAVE A PULSE!
I'M TRULY SORRY, STEPHEN.
FOR WHAT IT'S WORTH, YOU'LL FIND A CRASH CART UNDER THE CABINET TO YOUR LEFT.
WHAT, YOU WANT TO REVIVE HIM SO YOU CAN EXECUTE HIM YOURSELF?
SHUT UP, NICODEMUS.

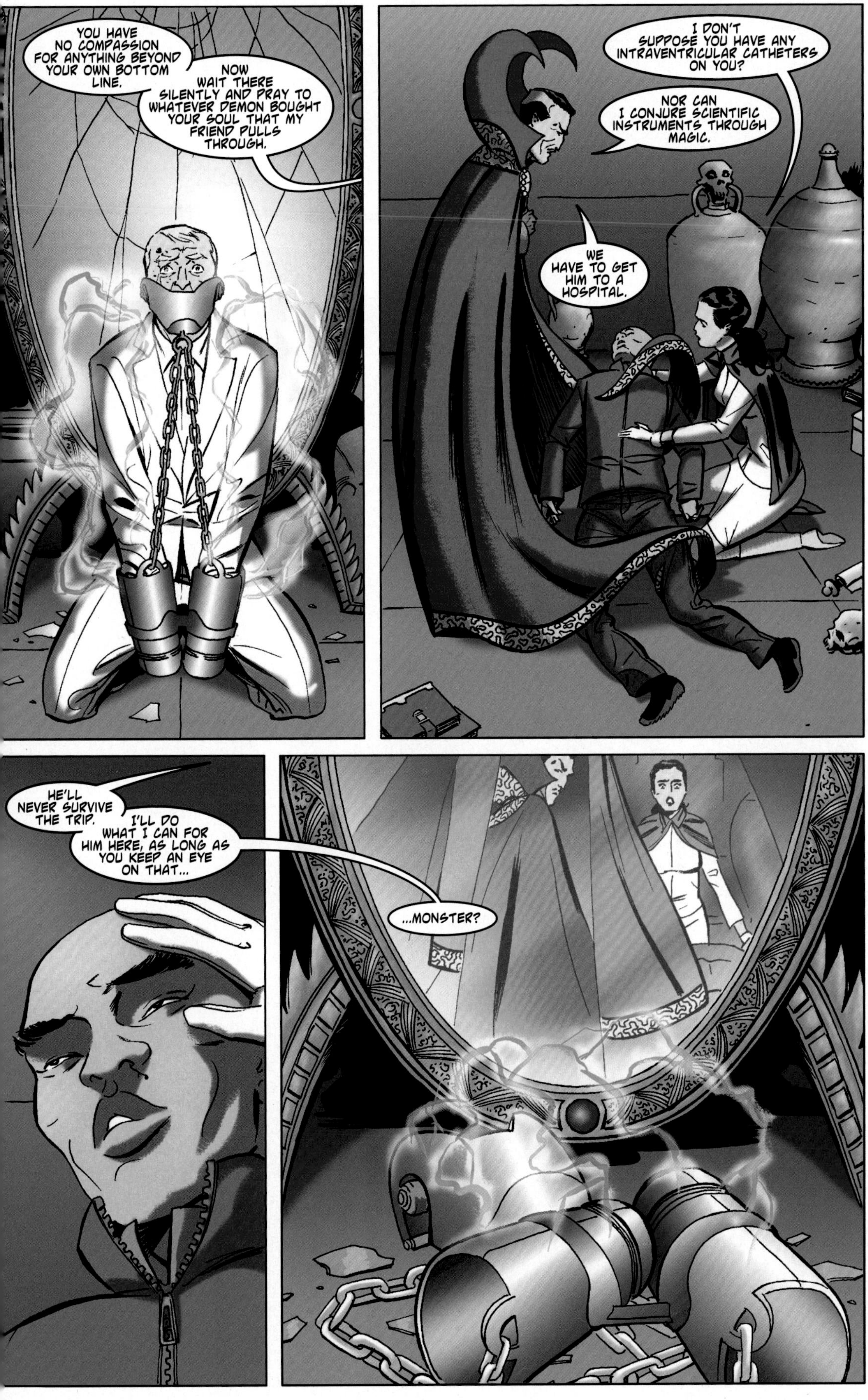
YOU HAVE NO COMPASSION FOR ANYTHING BEYOND YOUR OWN BOTTOM LINE.
NOW WAIT THERE SILENTLY AND PRAY TO WHATEVER DEMON BOUGHT YOUR SOUL THAT MY FRIEND PULLS THROUGH.
I DON'T SUPPOSE YOU HAVE ANY INTRAVENTRICULAR CATHETERS ON YOU?
NOR CAN I CONJURE SCIENTIFIC INSTRUMENTS THROUGH MAGIC.
WE HAVE TO GET HIM TO A HOSPITAL.
HE'LL NEVER SURVIVE THE TRIP.
I'LL DO WHAT I CAN FOR HIM HERE, AS LONG AS YOU KEEP AN EYE ON THAT...
...MONSTER?

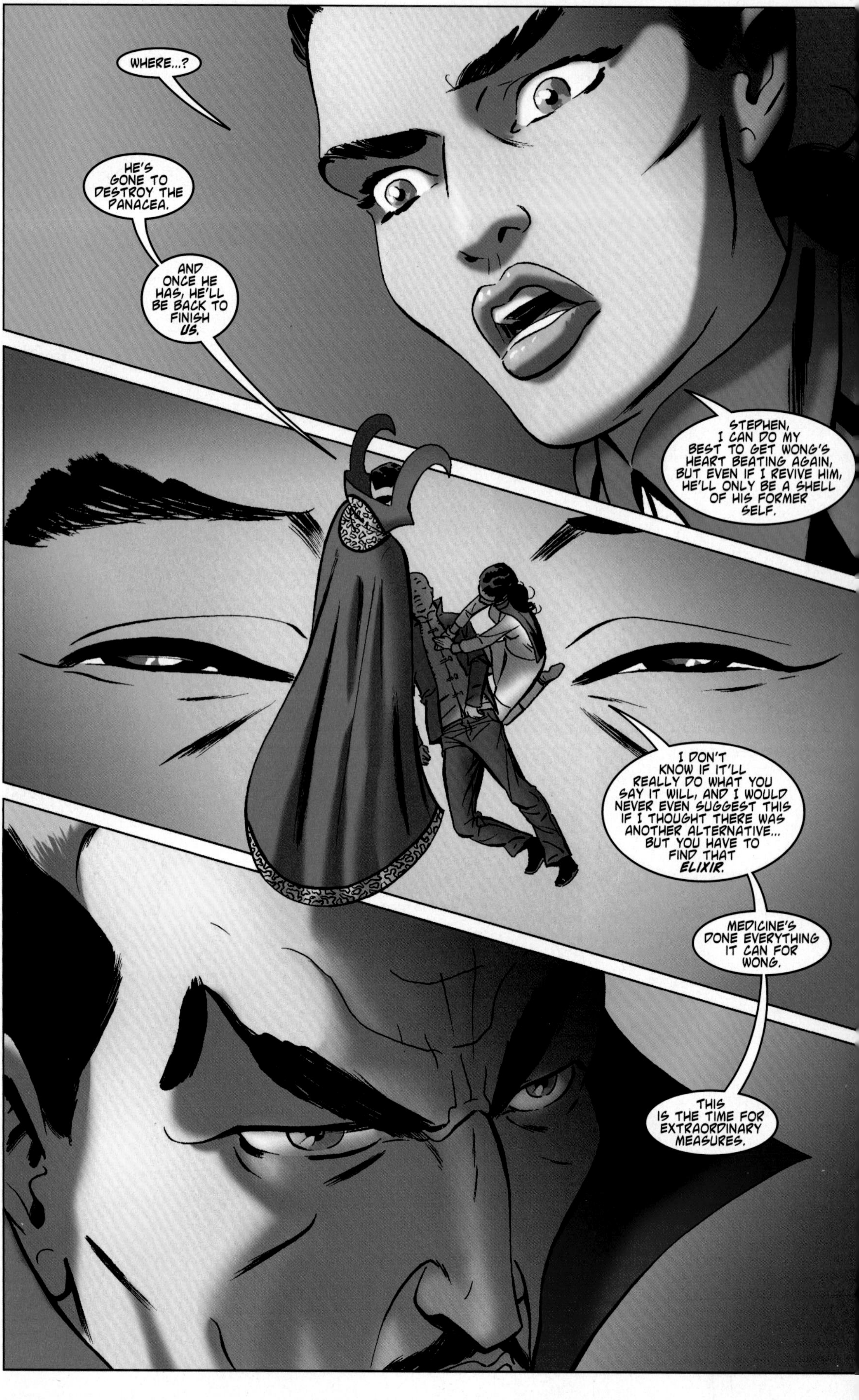
WHERE...?
HE'S GONE TO DESTROY THE PANACEA.
AND ONCE HE HAS, HE'LL BE BACK TO FINISH *US*.
STEPHEN, I CAN DO MY BEST TO GET WONG'S HEART BEATING AGAIN, BUT EVEN IF I REVIVE HIM, HE'LL ONLY BE A SHELL OF HIS FORMER SELF.
I DON'T KNOW IF IT'LL REALLY DO WHAT YOU SAY IT WILL, AND I WOULD NEVER EVEN SUGGEST THIS IF I THOUGHT THERE WAS ANOTHER ALTERNATIVE... BUT YOU HAVE TO FIND THAT *ELIXIR*.
MEDICINE'S DONE EVERYTHING IT CAN FOR WONG.
THIS IS THE TIME FOR EXTRAORDINARY MEASURES.

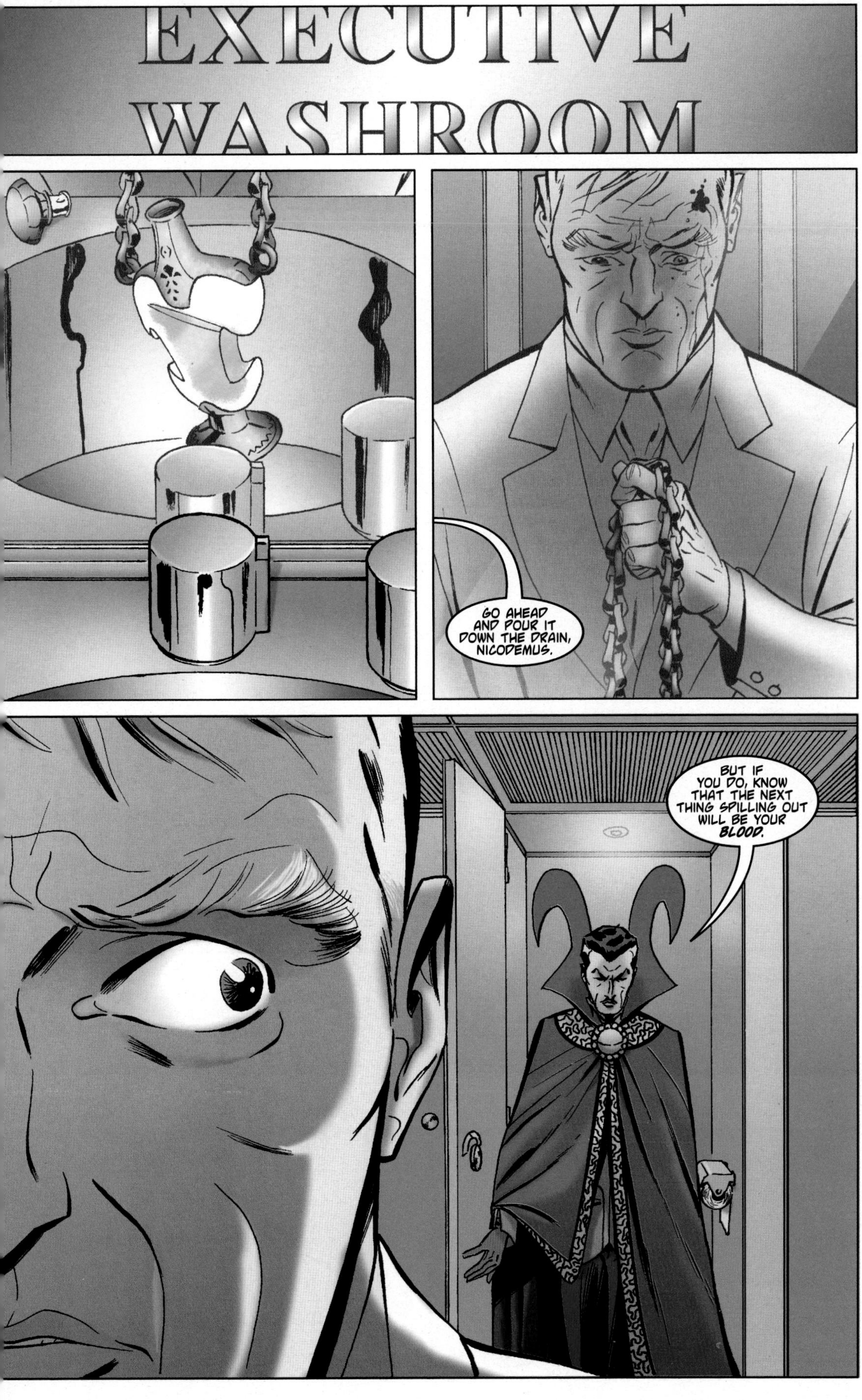
EXECUTIVE WASHROOM
GO AHEAD AND POUR IT DOWN THE DRAIN, NICODEMUS.
BUT IF YOU DO, KNOW THAT THE NEXT THING SPILLING OUT WILL BE YOUR *BLOOD*.

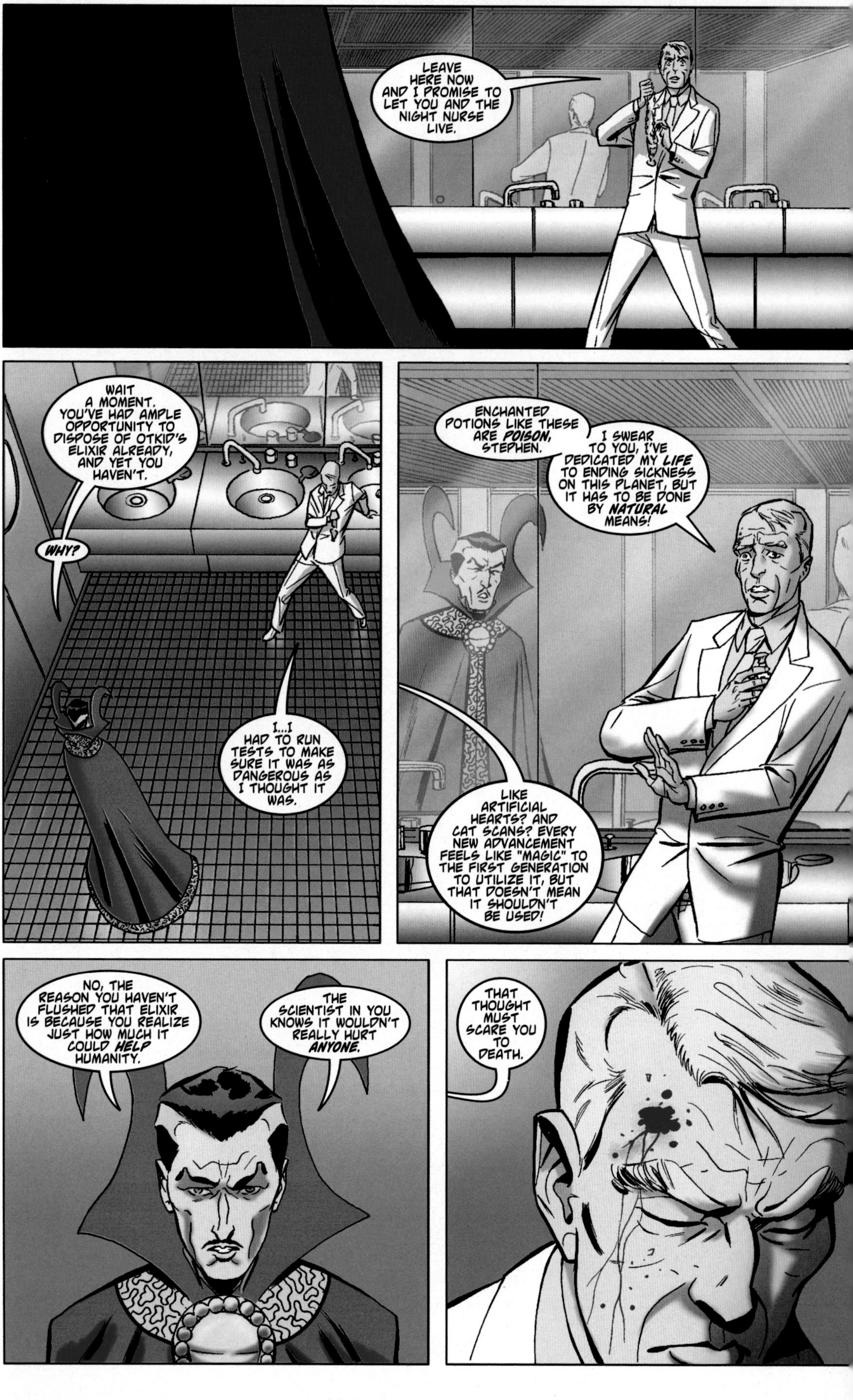
LEAVE HERE NOW AND I PROMISE TO LET YOU AND THE NIGHT NURSE LIVE.
WAIT A MOMENT. YOU'VE HAD AMPLE OPPORTUNITY TO DISPOSE OF OTKID'S ELIXIR ALREADY, AND YET YOU HAVEN'T.
WHY?
I...I HAD TO RUN TESTS TO MAKE SURE IT WAS AS DANGEROUS AS I THOUGHT IT WAS.
ENCHANTED POTIONS LIKE THESE ARE POISON, STEPHEN.
I SWEAR TO YOU, I'VE DEDICATED MY LIFE TO ENDING SICKNESS ON THIS PLANET, BUT IT HAS TO BE DONE BY NATURAL MEANS!
LIKE ARTIFICIAL HEARTS? AND CAT SCANS? EVERY NEW ADVANCEMENT FEELS LIKE "MAGIC" TO THE FIRST GENERATION TO UTILIZE IT, BUT THAT DOESN'T MEAN IT SHOULDN'T BE USED!
NO, THE REASON YOU HAVEN'T FLUSHED THAT ELIXIR IS BECAUSE YOU REALIZE JUST HOW MUCH IT COULD HELP HUMANITY.
THE SCIENTIST IN YOU KNOWS IT WOULDN'T REALLY HURT ANYONE.
THAT THOUGHT MUST SCARE YOU TO DEATH.

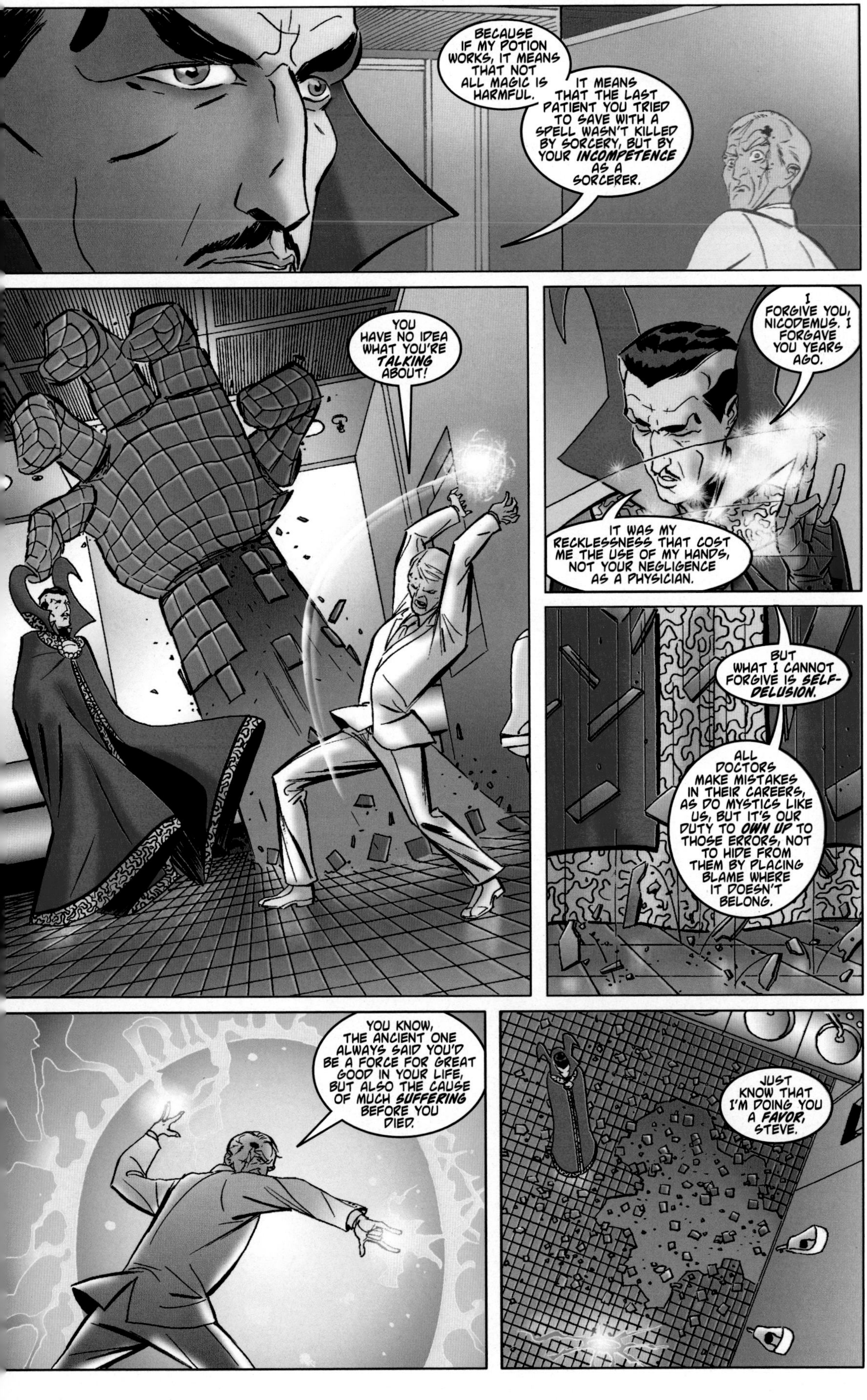
BECAUSE IF MY POTION WORKS, IT MEANS THAT NOT ALL MAGIC IS HARMFUL.
IT MEANS THAT THE LAST PATIENT YOU TRIED TO SAVE WITH A SPELL WASN'T KILLED BY SORCERY, BUT BY YOUR INCOMPETENCE AS A SORCERER.
YOU HAVE NO IDEA WHAT YOU'RE TALKING ABOUT!
I FORGIVE YOU, NICODEMUS. I FORGAVE YOU YEARS AGO.
IT WAS MY RECKLESSNESS THAT COST ME THE USE OF MY HANDS, NOT YOUR NEGLIGENCE AS A PHYSICIAN.
BUT WHAT I CANNOT FORGIVE IS SELF-DELUSION.
ALL DOCTORS MAKE MISTAKES IN THEIR CAREERS, AS DO MYSTICS LIKE US, BUT IT'S OUR DUTY TO OWN UP TO THOSE ERRORS, NOT TO HIDE FROM THEM BY PLACING BLAME WHERE IT DOESN'T BELONG.
YOU KNOW, THE ANCIENT ONE ALWAYS SAID YOU'D BE A FORCE FOR GREAT GOOD IN YOUR LIFE, BUT ALSO THE CAUSE OF MUCH SUFFERING BEFORE YOU DIED.
JUST KNOW THAT I'M DOING YOU A FAVOR, STEVE.

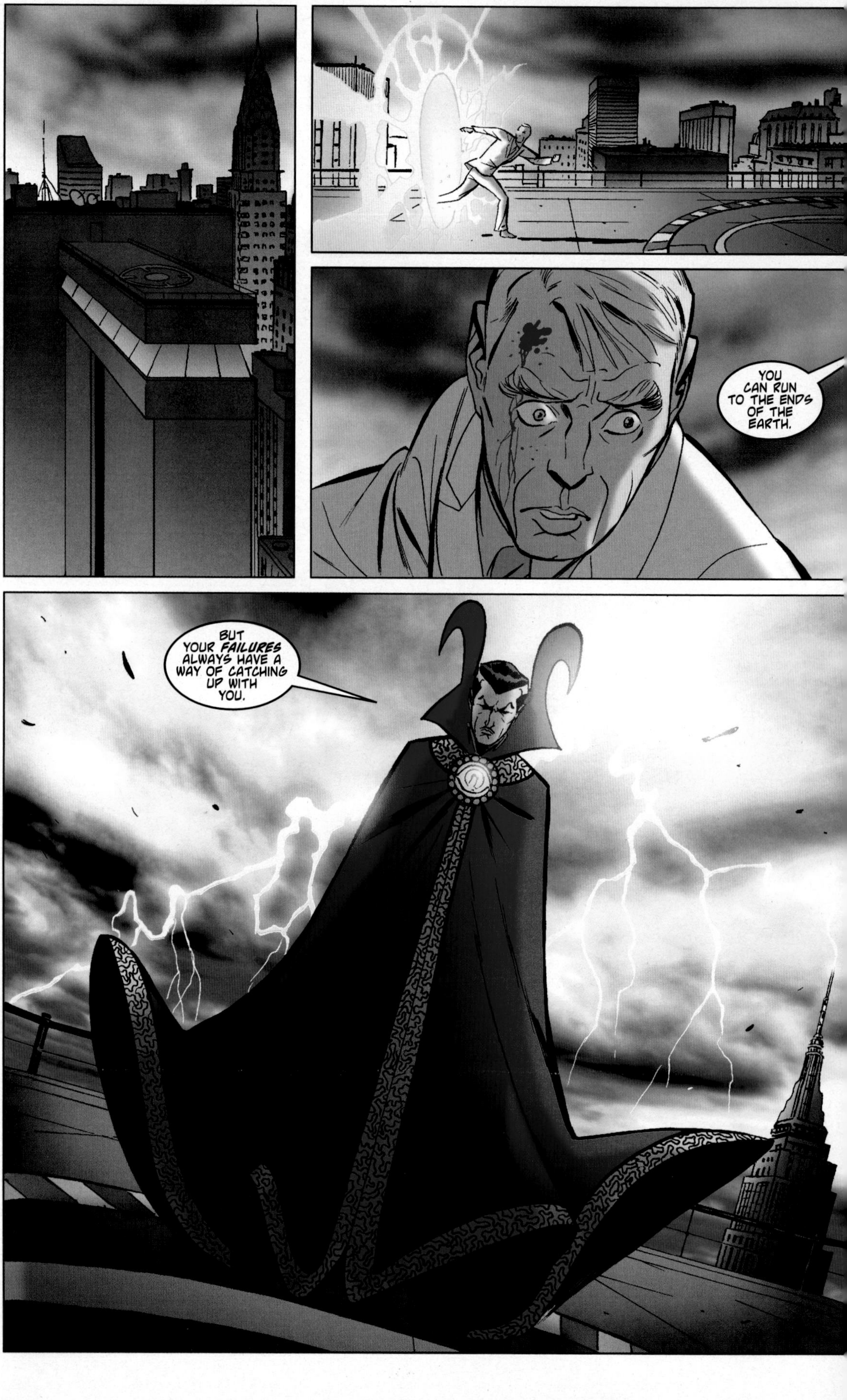
YOU CAN RUN TO THE ENDS OF THE EARTH.
BUT YOUR FAILURES ALWAYS HAVE A WAY OF CATCHING UP WITH YOU.

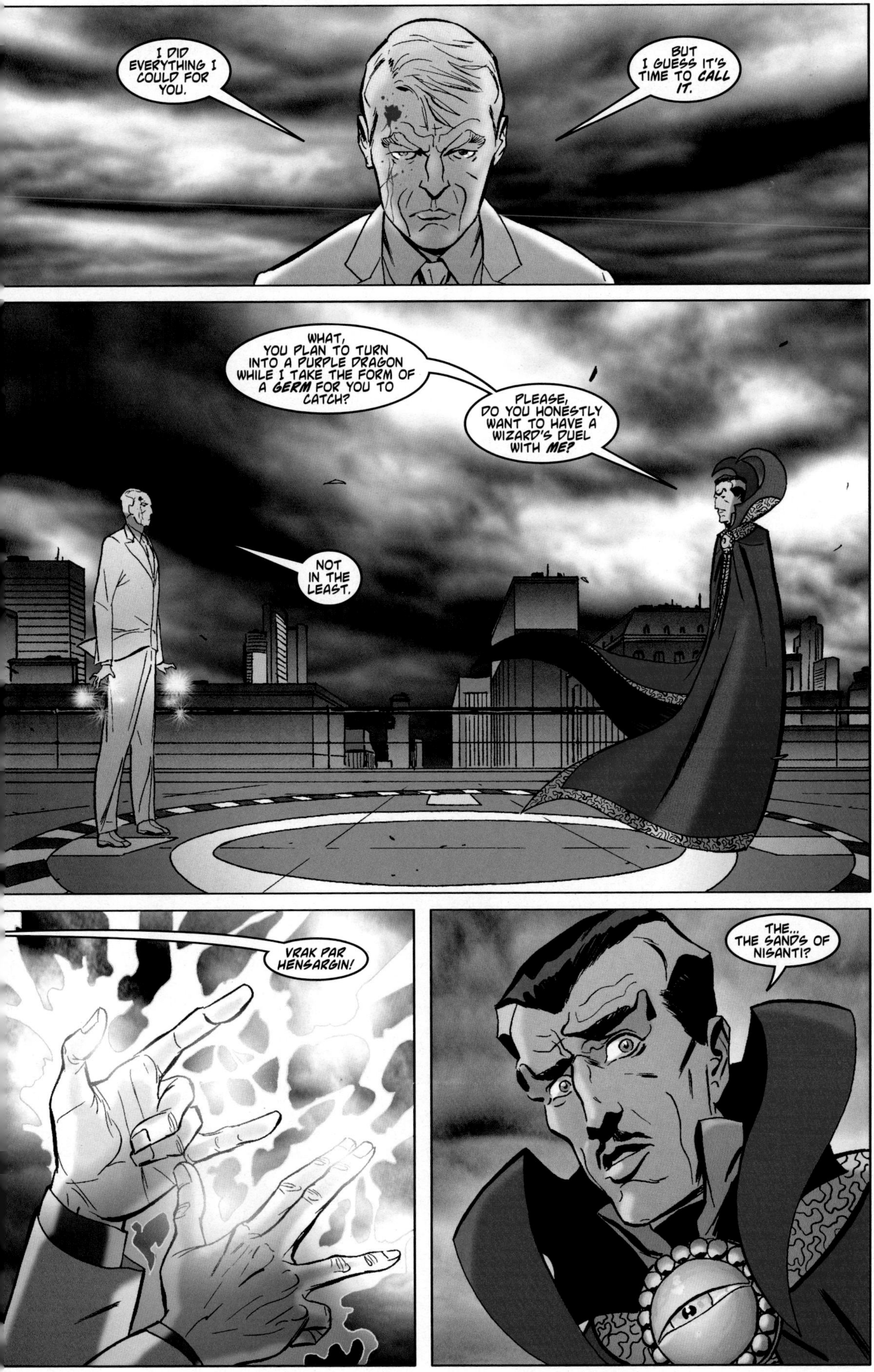
I DID EVERYTHING I COULD FOR YOU.
BUT I GUESS IT'S TIME TO CALL IT.
WHAT, YOU PLAN TO TURN INTO A PURPLE DRAGON WHILE I TAKE THE FORM OF A GERM FOR YOU TO CATCH?
PLEASE, DO YOU HONESTLY WANT TO HAVE A WIZARD'S DUEL WITH ME?
NOT IN THE LEAST.
VRAK PAR HENSARGIN!
THE... THE SANDS OF NISANTI?

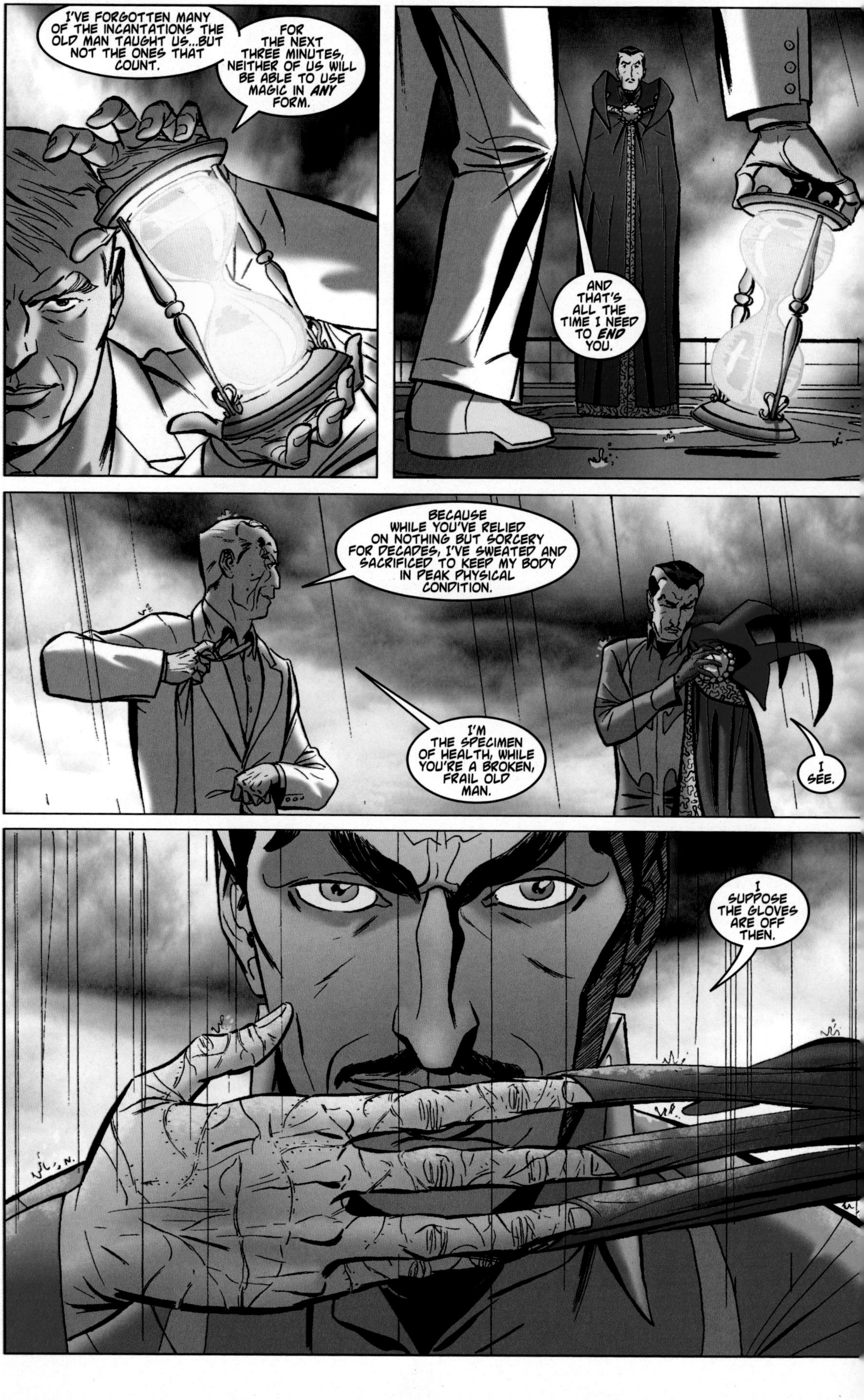
I'VE FORGOTTEN MANY OF THE INCANTATIONS THE OLD MAN TAUGHT US...BUT NOT THE ONES THAT COUNT.
FOR THE NEXT THREE MINUTES, NEITHER OF US WILL BE ABLE TO USE MAGIC IN ANY FORM.
AND THAT'S ALL THE TIME I NEED TO END YOU.
BECAUSE WHILE YOU'VE RELIED ON NOTHING BUT SORCERY FOR DECADES, I'VE SWEATED AND SACRIFICED TO KEEP MY BODY IN PEAK PHYSICAL CONDITION.
I'M THE SPECIMEN OF HEALTH, WHILE YOU'RE A BROKEN, FRAIL OLD MAN.
I SEE.
I SUPPOSE THE GLOVES ARE OFF THEN.

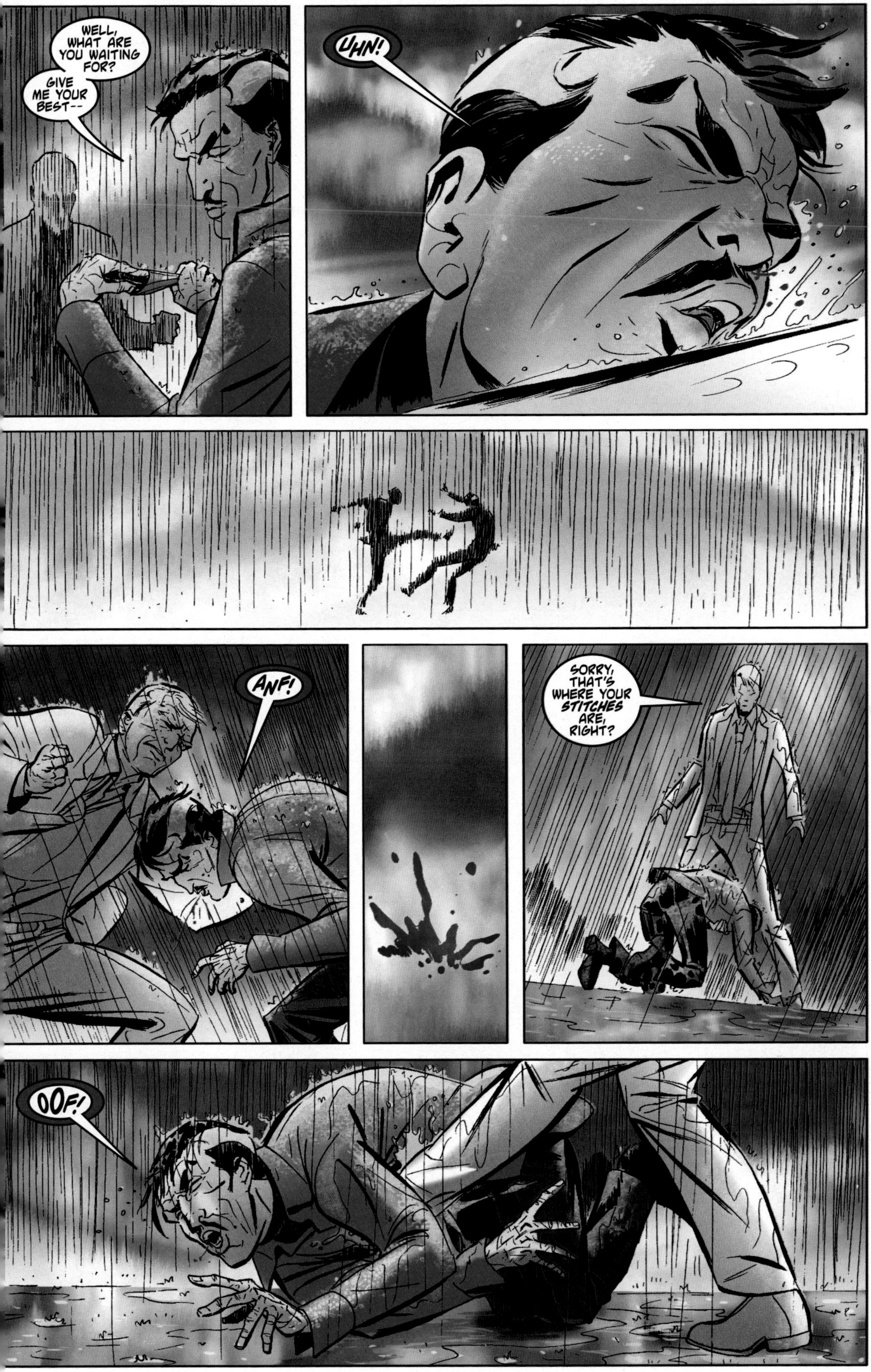
WELL, WHAT ARE YOU WAITING FOR?
GIVE ME YOUR BEST--
UHN!
ANF!
SORRY, THAT'S WHERE YOUR STITCHES ARE, RIGHT?
OOF!

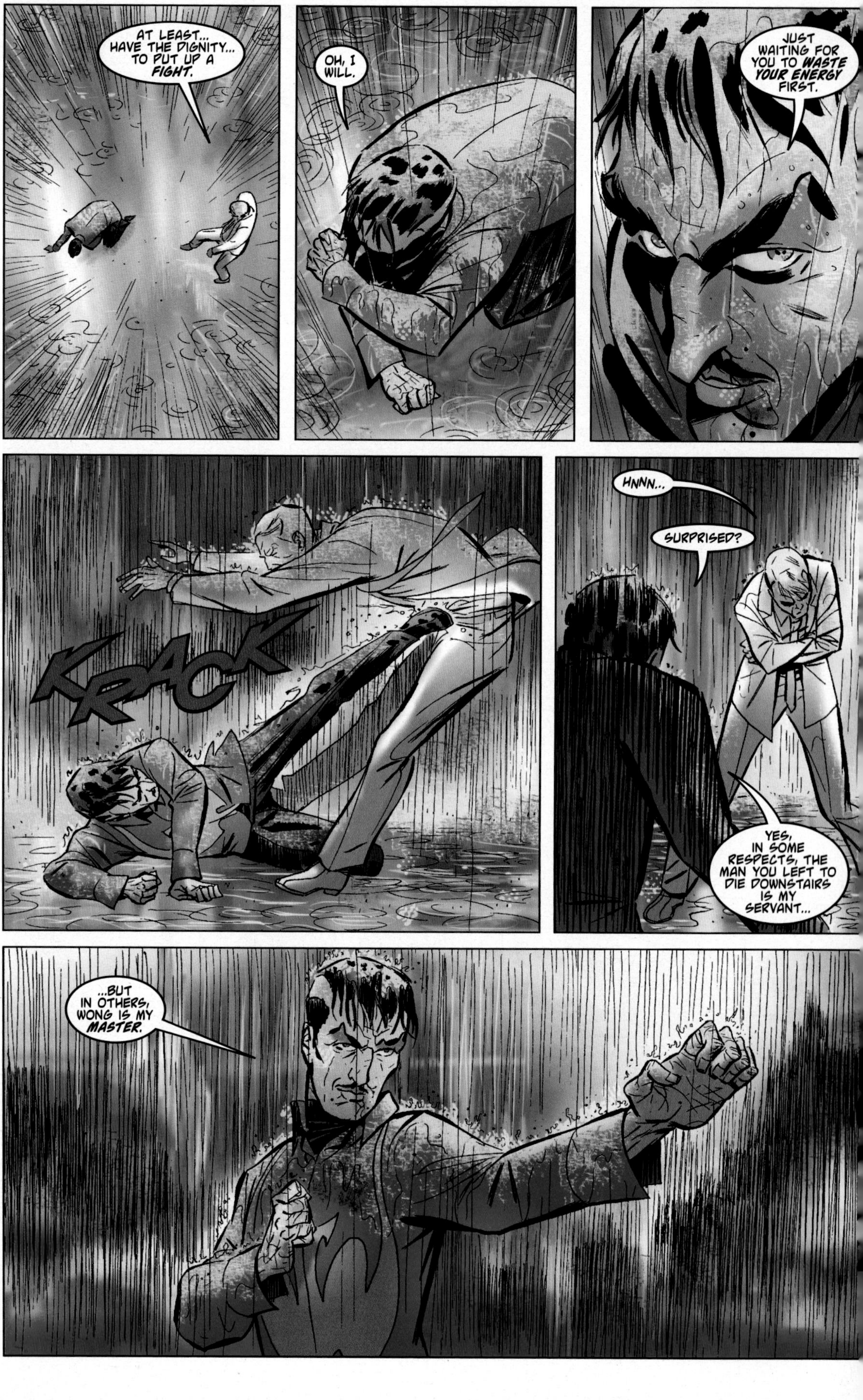
AT LEAST... HAVE THE DIGNITY... TO PUT UP A *FIGHT*.
OH, I WILL.
JUST WAITING FOR YOU TO *WASTE YOUR ENERGY* FIRST.
KRACK
HNNN...
SURPRISED?
YES, IN SOME RESPECTS, THE MAN YOU LEFT TO DIE DOWNSTAIRS IS MY SERVANT...
...BUT IN OTHERS, WONG IS MY *MASTER*.

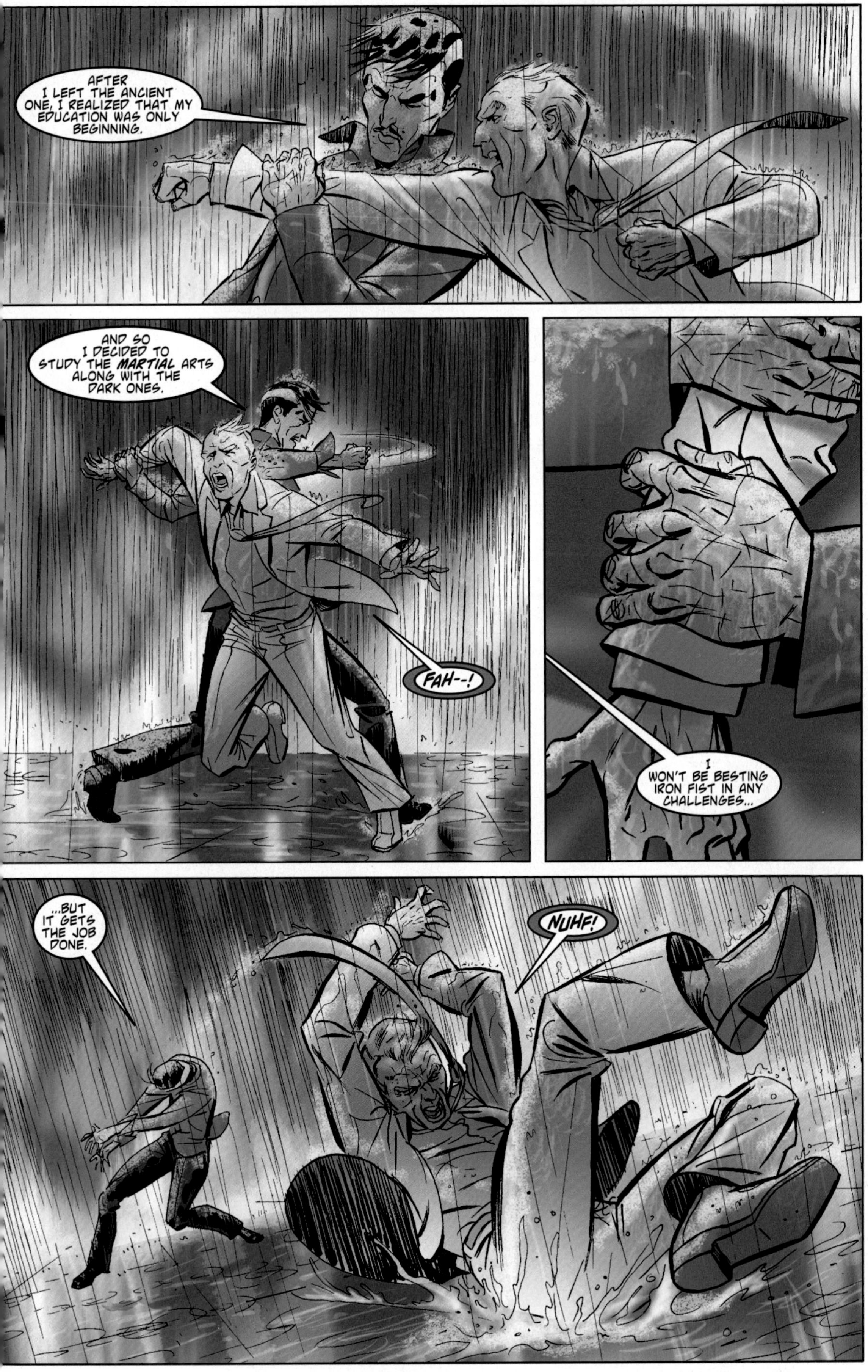
AFTER I LEFT THE ANCIENT ONE, I REALIZED THAT MY EDUCATION WAS ONLY BEGINNING.
AND SO I DECIDED TO STUDY THE *MARTIAL* ARTS ALONG WITH THE DARK ONES.
FAH--!
I WON'T BE BESTING IRON FIST IN ANY CHALLENGES...
...BUT IT GETS THE JOB DONE.
NUHF!

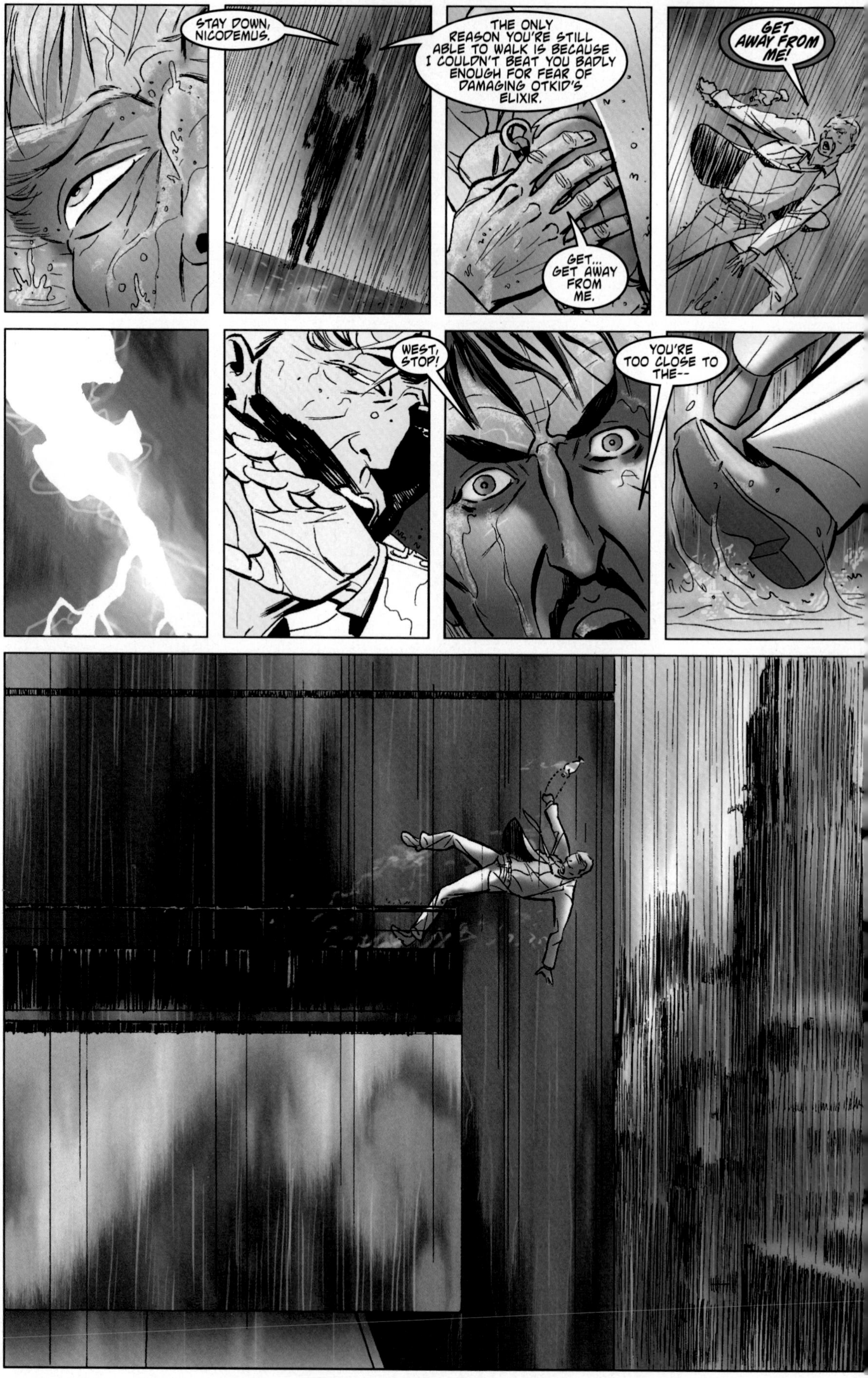
STAY DOWN, NICODEMUS.
THE ONLY REASON YOU'RE STILL ABLE TO WALK IS BECAUSE I COULDN'T BEAT YOU BADLY ENOUGH FOR FEAR OF DAMAGING OTKID'S ELIXIR.
GET... GET AWAY FROM ME.
GET AWAY FROM ME!
WEST, STOP!
YOU'RE TOO CLOSE TO THE--

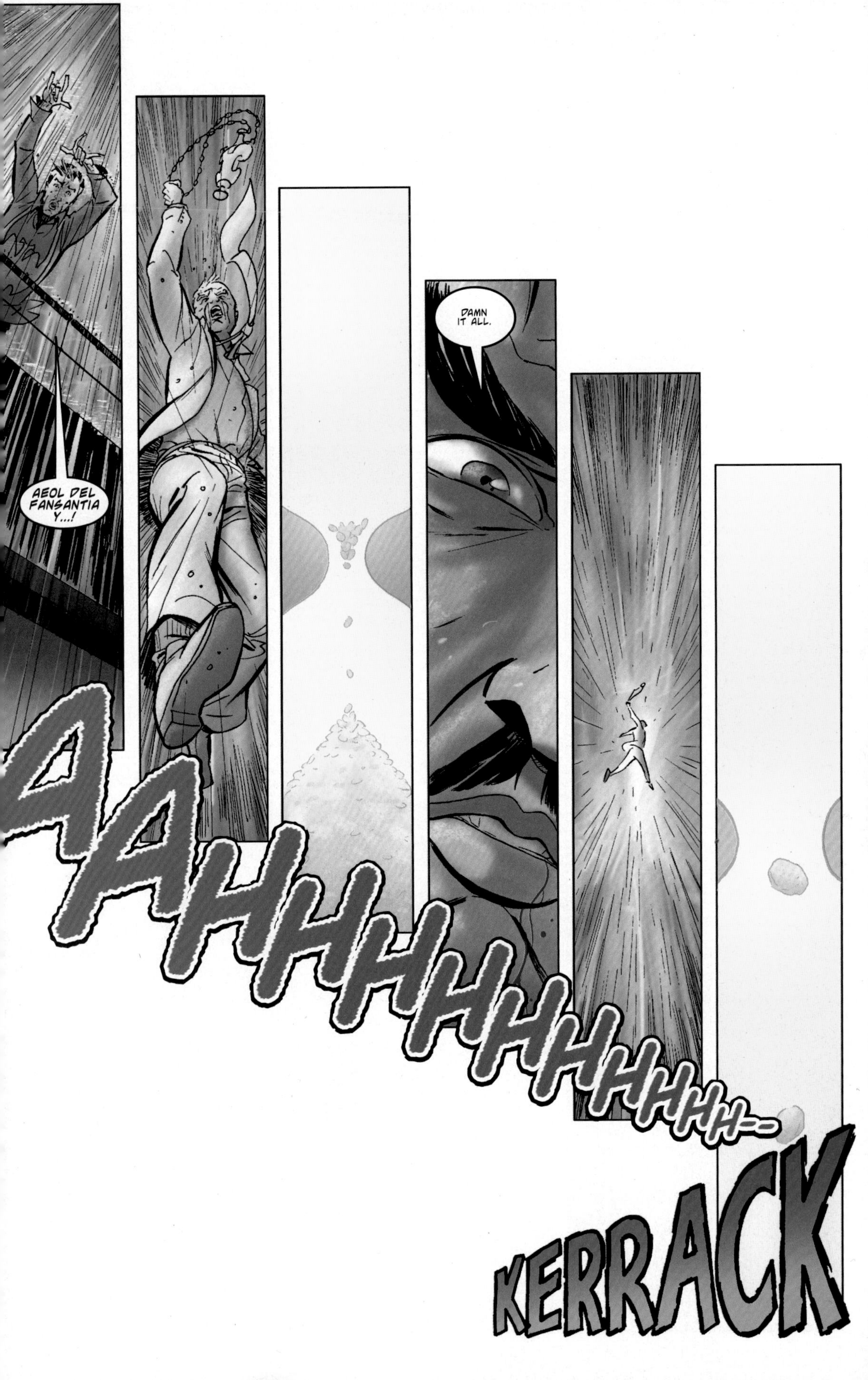
AEOL DEL FANSANTIA Y...!
DAMN IT ALL.
AAHHHHHHHHHHHHH--
KERRACK

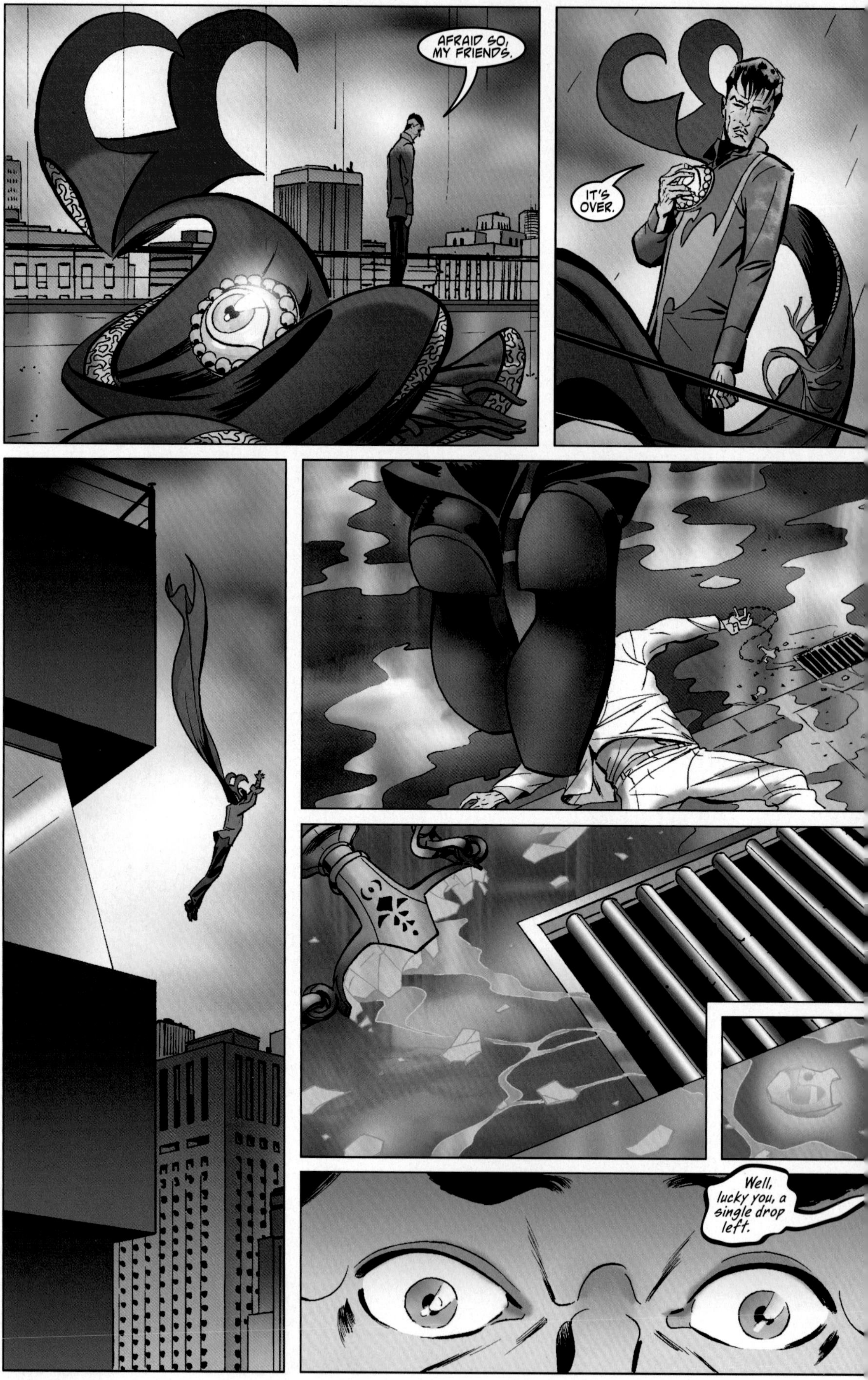
AFRAID SO, MY FRIENDS.
IT'S OVER.
Well, lucky you, a single drop left.

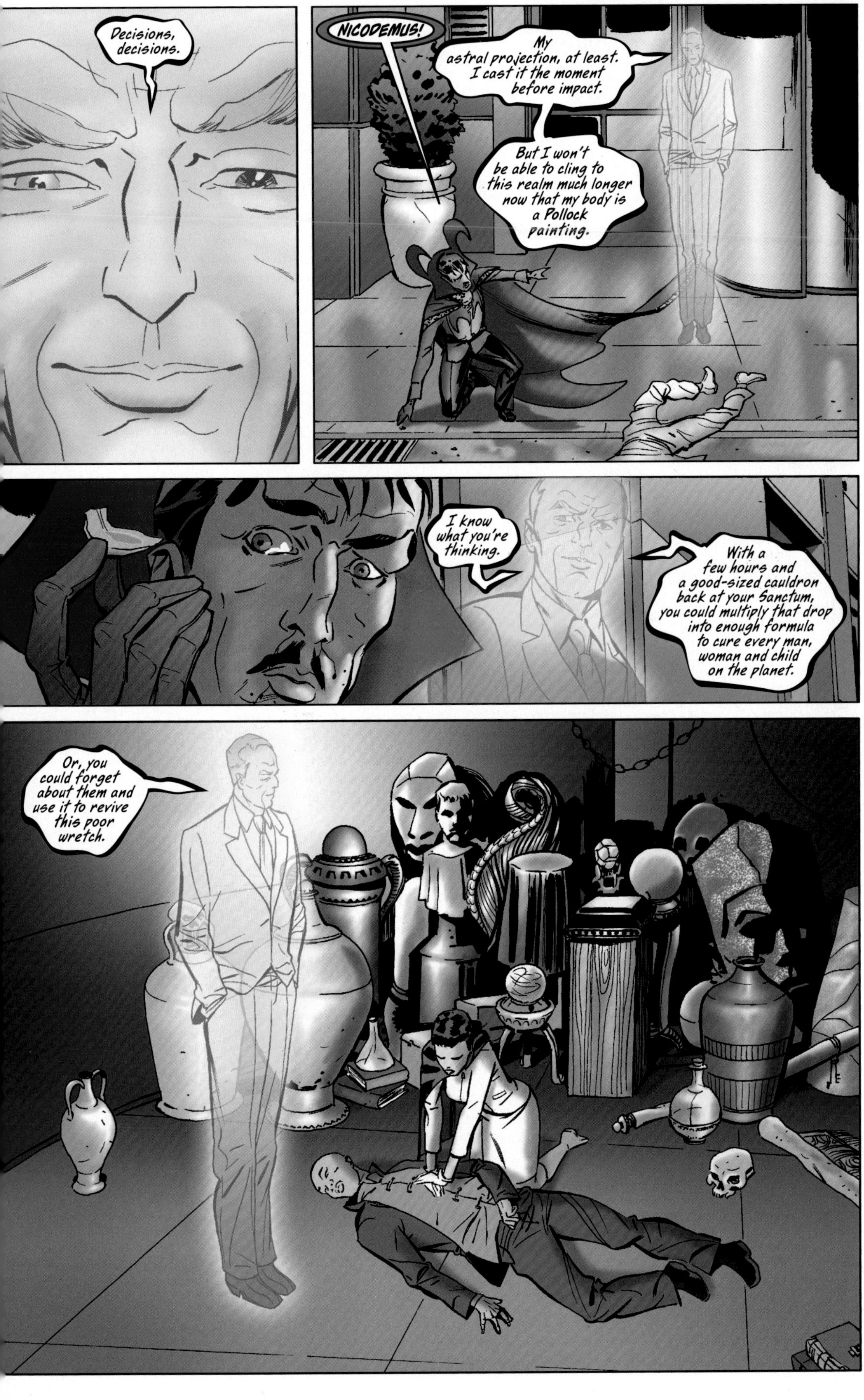
Decisions, decisions.
NICODEMUS!
My astral projection, at least. I cast it the moment before impact.
But I won't be able to cling to this realm much longer now that my body is a Pollock painting.
I know what you're thinking.
With a few hours and a good-sized cauldron back at your Sanctum, you could multiply that drop into enough formula to cure every man, woman and child on the planet.
Or, you could forget about them and use it to revive this poor wretch.

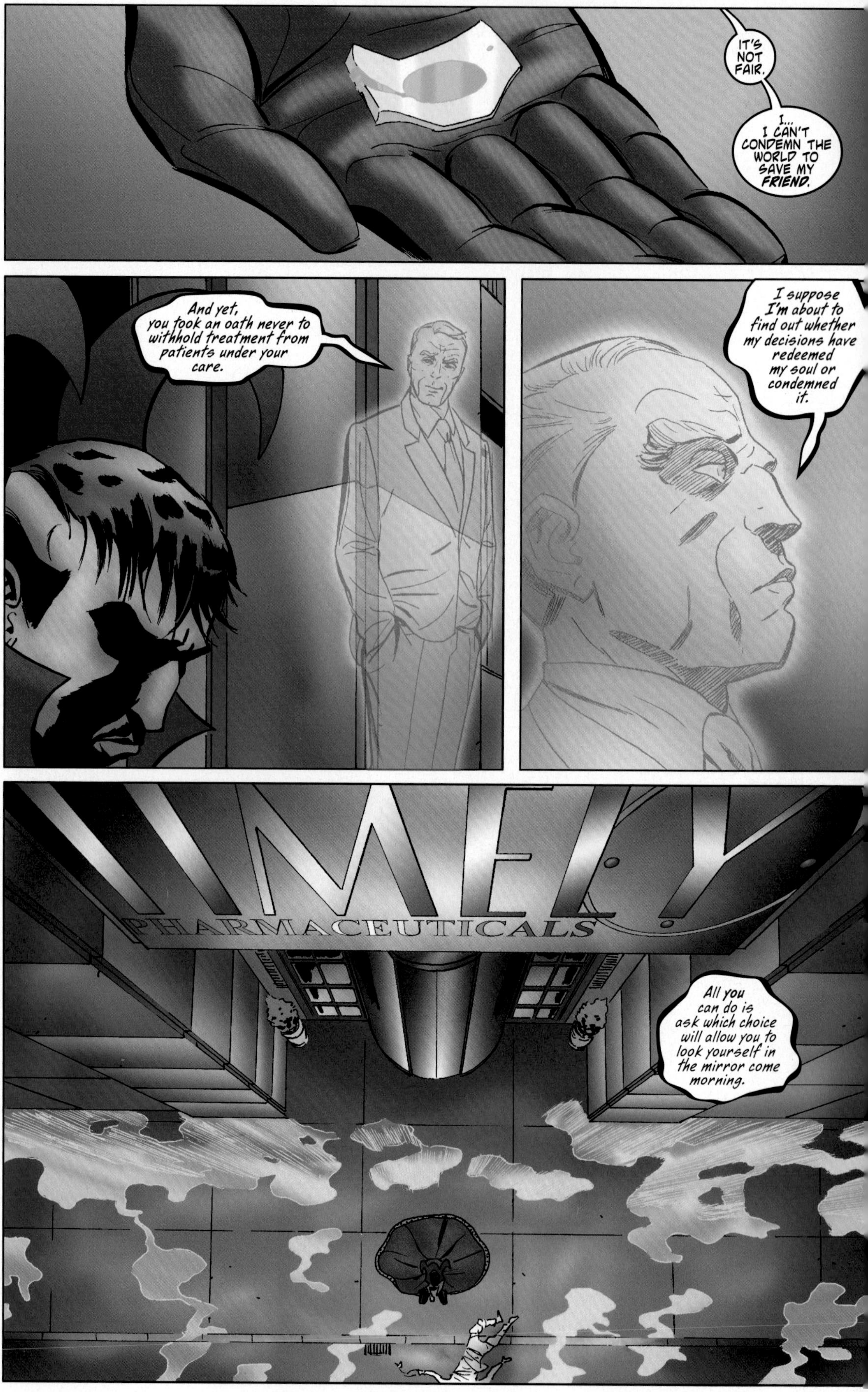
IT'S NOT FAIR.
I... I CAN'T CONDEMN THE WORLD TO SAVE MY **FRIEND**.
And yet, you took an oath never to withhold treatment from patients under your care.
I suppose I'm about to find out whether my decisions have redeemed my soul or condemned it.
PHARMACEUTICALS
All **you** can do is ask which choice will allow you to look yourself in the mirror come morning.

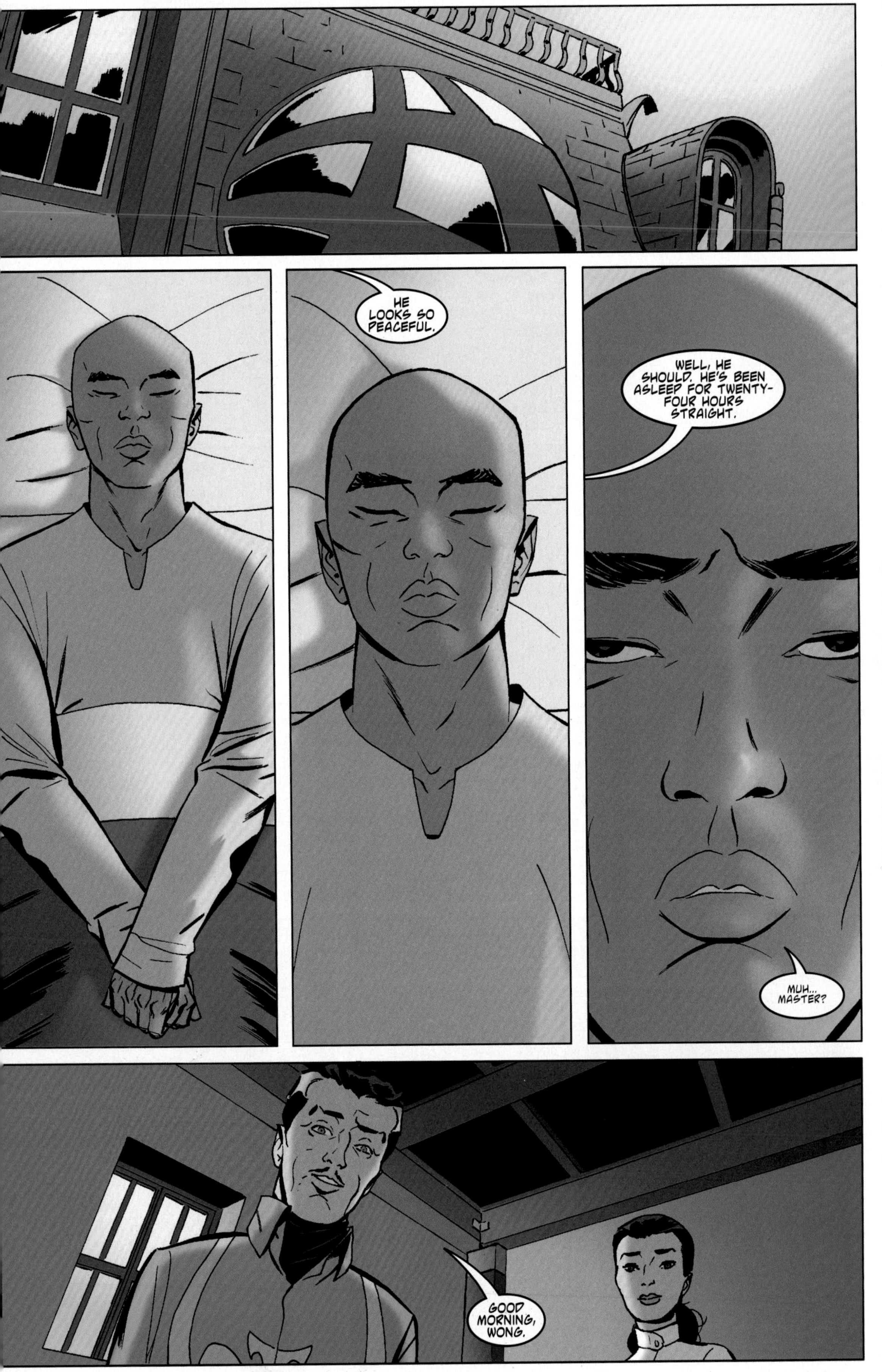
HE LOOKS SO PEACEFUL.
WELL, HE SHOULD. HE'S BEEN ASLEEP FOR TWENTY-FOUR HOURS STRAIGHT.
MUH... MASTER?
GOOD MORNING, WONG.

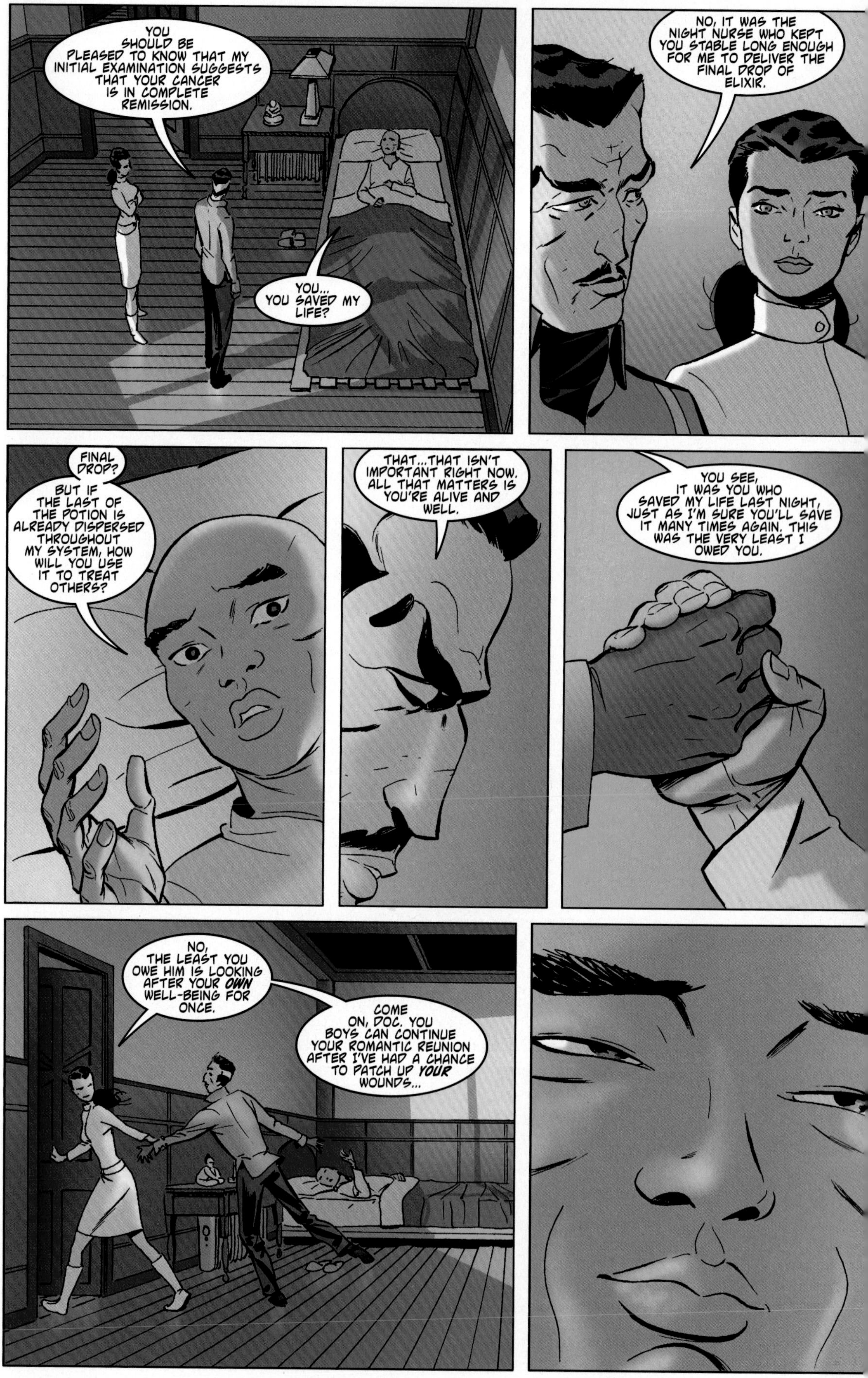
YOU SHOULD BE PLEASED TO KNOW THAT MY INITIAL EXAMINATION SUGGESTS THAT YOUR CANCER IS IN COMPLETE REMISSION.
YOU... YOU SAVED MY LIFE?
NO, IT WAS THE NIGHT NURSE WHO KEPT YOU STABLE LONG ENOUGH FOR ME TO DELIVER THE FINAL DROP OF ELIXIR.
FINAL DROP?
BUT IF THE LAST OF THE POTION IS ALREADY DISPERSED THROUGHOUT MY SYSTEM, HOW WILL YOU USE IT TO TREAT OTHERS?
THAT...THAT ISN'T IMPORTANT RIGHT NOW. ALL THAT MATTERS IS YOU'RE ALIVE AND WELL.
YOU SEE, IT WAS YOU WHO SAVED MY LIFE LAST NIGHT, JUST AS I'M SURE YOU'LL SAVE IT MANY TIMES AGAIN. THIS WAS THE VERY LEAST I OWED YOU.
NO, THE LEAST YOU OWE HIM IS LOOKING AFTER YOUR OWN WELL-BEING FOR ONCE.
COME ON, DOC. YOU BOYS CAN CONTINUE YOUR ROMANTIC REUNION AFTER I'VE HAD A CHANCE TO PATCH UP YOUR WOUNDS...

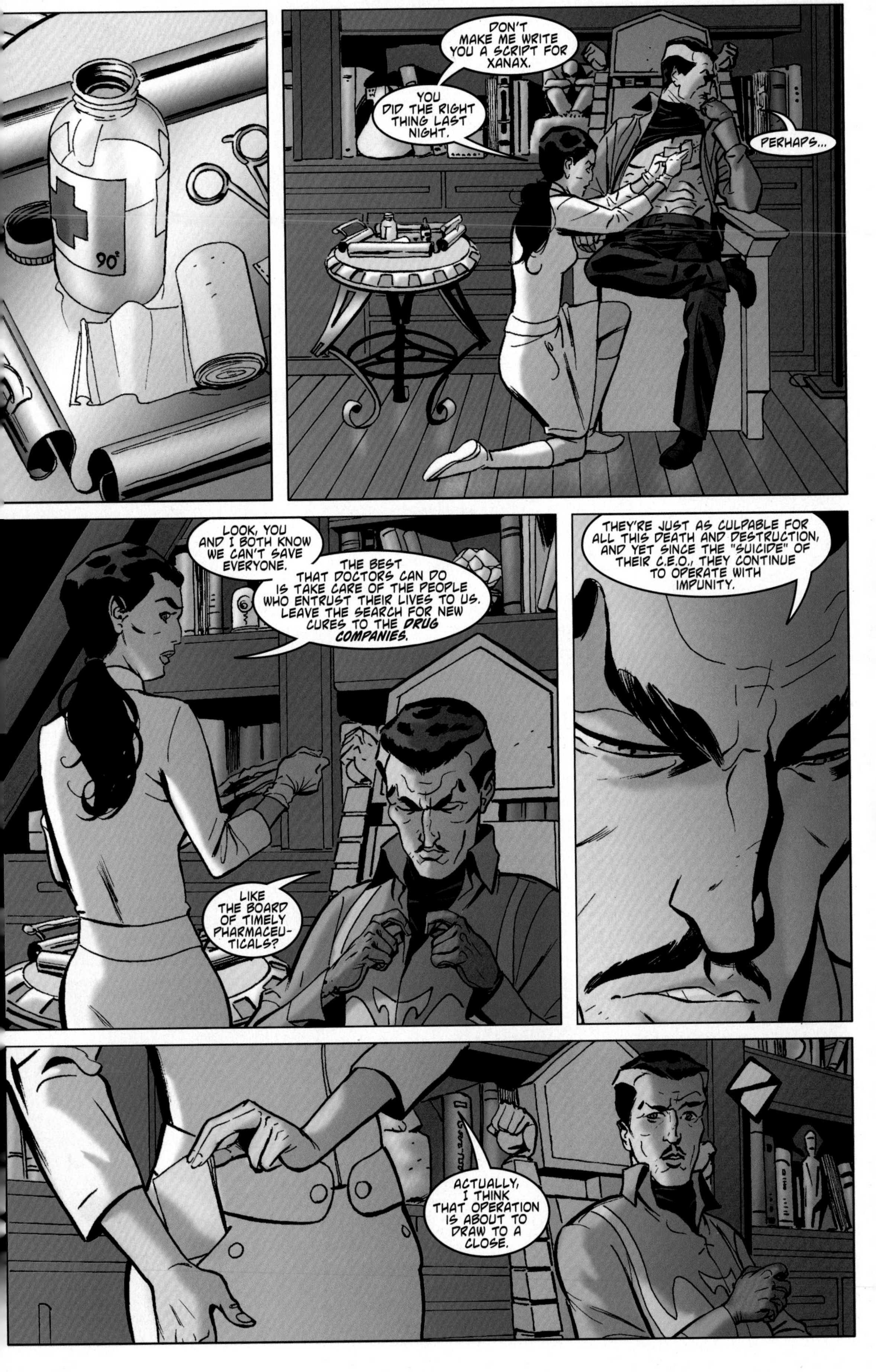
DON'T MAKE ME WRITE YOU A SCRIPT FOR XANAX.
YOU DID THE RIGHT THING LAST NIGHT.
PERHAPS...
LOOK, YOU AND I BOTH KNOW WE CAN'T SAVE EVERYONE.
THE BEST THAT DOCTORS CAN DO IS TAKE CARE OF THE PEOPLE WHO ENTRUST THEIR LIVES TO US. LEAVE THE SEARCH FOR NEW CURES TO THE DRUG COMPANIES.
LIKE THE BOARD OF TIMELY PHARMACEU-TICALS?
THEY'RE JUST AS CULPABLE FOR ALL THIS DEATH AND DESTRUCTION, AND YET SINCE THE "SUICIDE" OF THEIR C.E.O., THEY CONTINUE TO OPERATE WITH IMPUNITY.
ACTUALLY, I THINK THAT OPERATION IS ABOUT TO DRAW TO A CLOSE.
90°

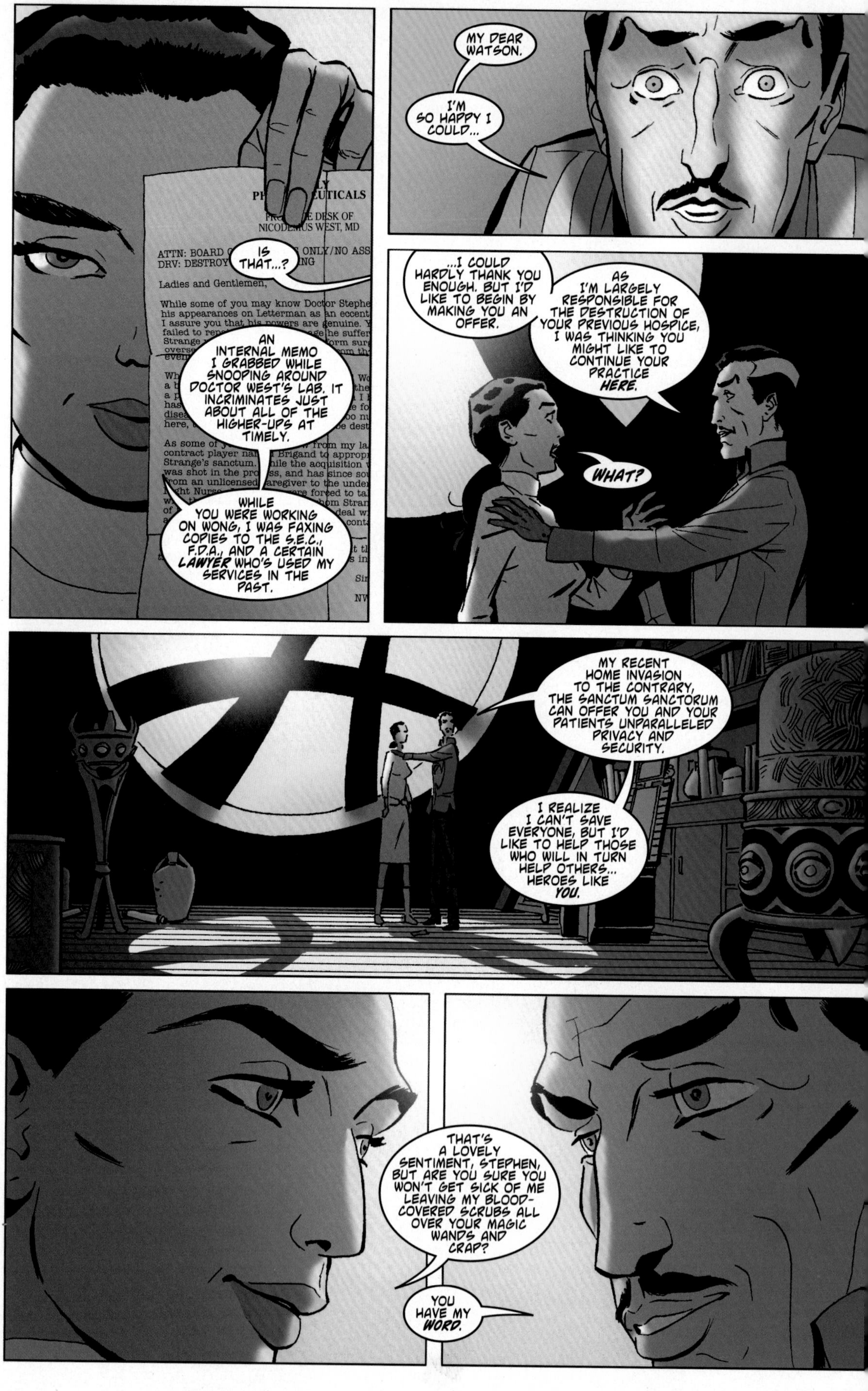
Ladies and Gentlemen,
IS THAT...?
AN INTERNAL MEMO I GRABBED WHILE SNOOPING AROUND DOCTOR WEST'S LAB. IT INCRIMINATES JUST ABOUT ALL OF THE HIGHER-UPS AT TIMELY.
WHILE YOU WERE WORKING ON WONG, I WAS FAXING COPIES TO THE S.E.C., F.D.A., AND A CERTAIN LAWYER WHO'S USED MY SERVICES IN THE PAST.
MY DEAR WATSON.
I'M SO HAPPY I COULD...
...I COULD HARDLY THANK YOU ENOUGH. BUT I'D LIKE TO BEGIN BY MAKING YOU AN OFFER.
AS I'M LARGELY RESPONSIBLE FOR THE DESTRUCTION OF YOUR PREVIOUS HOSPICE, I WAS THINKING YOU MIGHT LIKE TO CONTINUE YOUR PRACTICE HERE.
WHAT?
MY RECENT HOME INVASION TO THE CONTRARY, THE SANCTUM SANCTORUM CAN OFFER YOU AND YOUR PATIENTS UNPARALLELED PRIVACY AND SECURITY.
I REALIZE I CAN'T SAVE EVERYONE, BUT I'D LIKE TO HELP THOSE WHO WILL IN TURN HELP OTHERS... HEROES LIKE YOU.
THAT'S A LOVELY SENTIMENT, STEPHEN, BUT ARE YOU SURE YOU WON'T GET SICK OF ME LEAVING MY BLOOD-COVERED SCRUBS ALL OVER YOUR MAGIC WANDS AND CRAP?
YOU HAVE MY WORD.

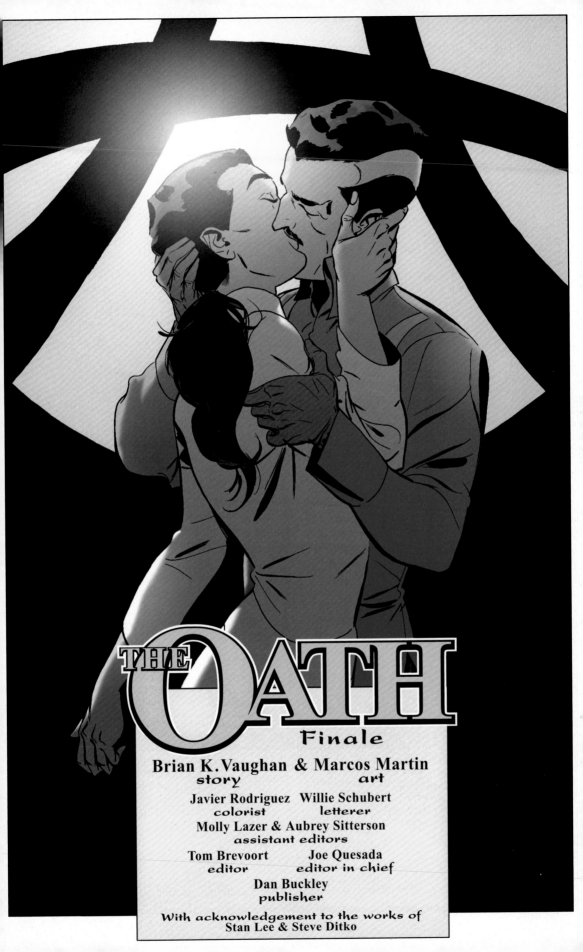

THE OATH

Finale

Brian K. Vaughan & Marcos Martin
story   art

Javier Rodriguez   Willie Schubert
colorist   letterer

Molly Lazer & Aubrey Sitterson
assistant editors

Tom Brevoort   Joe Quesada
editor   editor-in-chief

Dan Buckley
publisher

With acknowledgement to the works of
Stan Lee & Steve Ditko

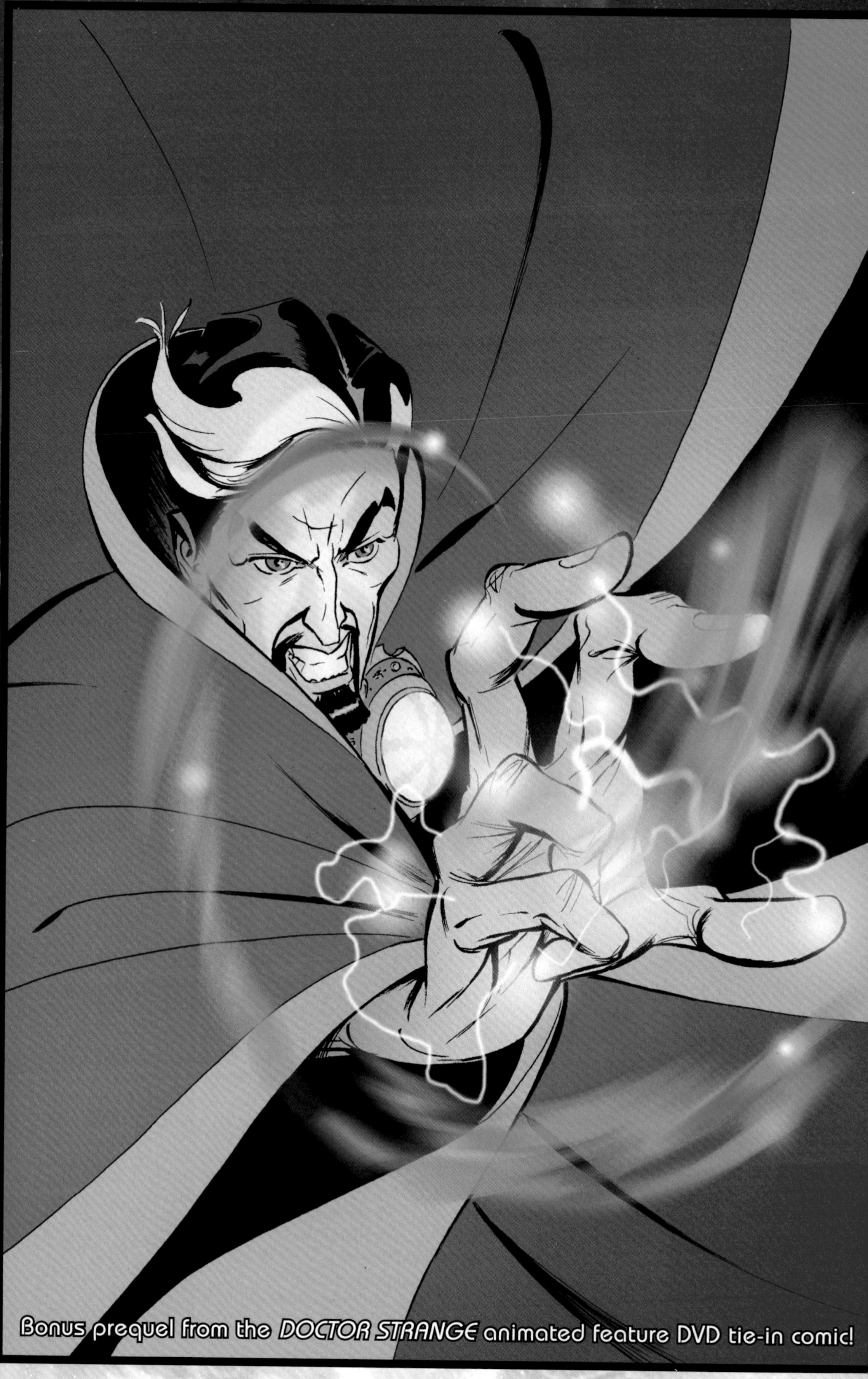
Bonus prequel from the DOCTOR STRANGE animated feature DVD tie-in comic!

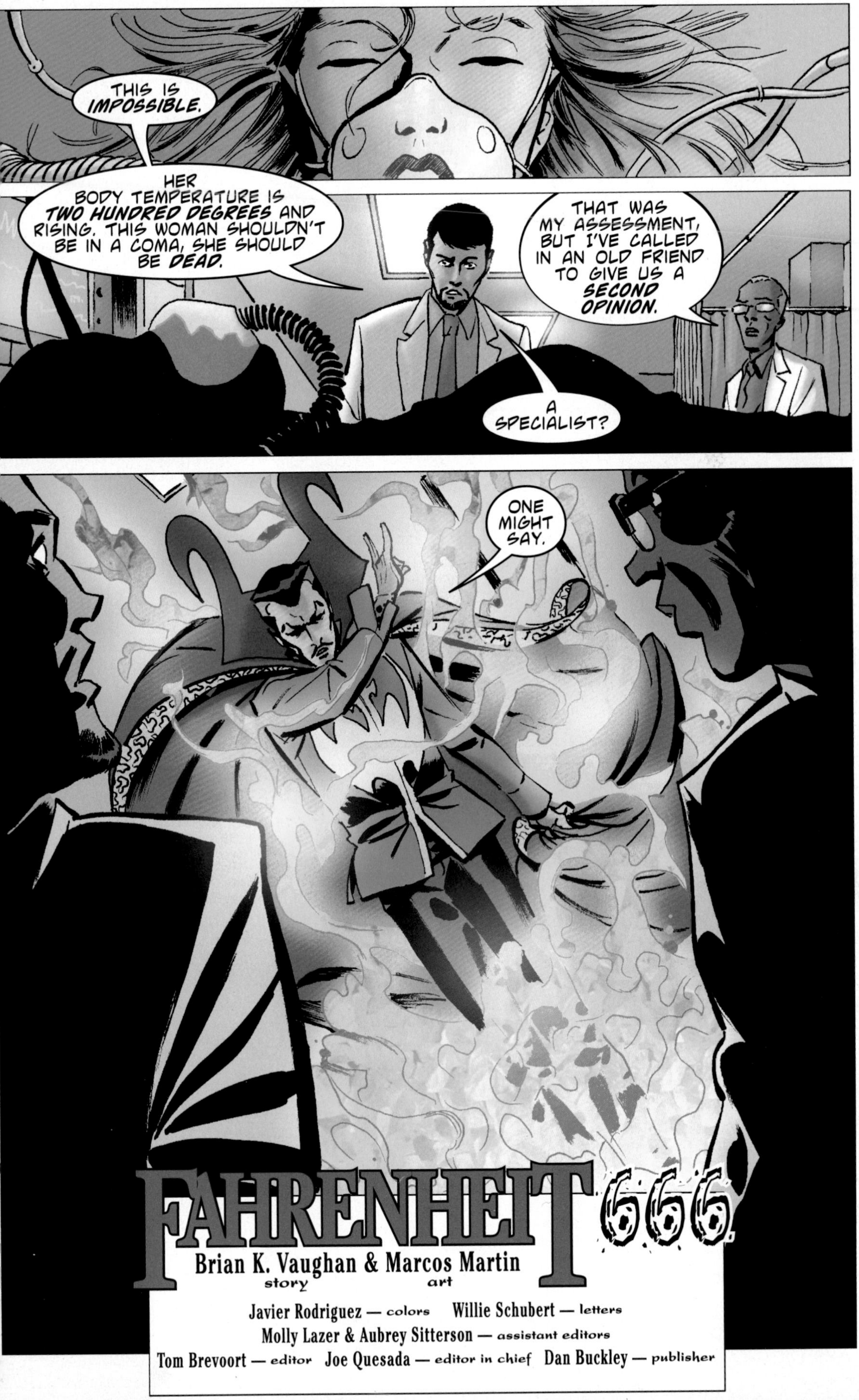
THIS IS IMPOSSIBLE.
HER BODY TEMPERATURE IS TWO HUNDRED DEGREES AND RISING. THIS WOMAN SHOULDN'T BE IN A COMA, SHE SHOULD BE DEAD.
THAT WAS MY ASSESSMENT, BUT I'VE CALLED IN AN OLD FRIEND TO GIVE US A SECOND OPINION.
A SPECIALIST?
ONE MIGHT SAY.
FAHRENHEIT 666
Brian K. Vaughan & Marcos Martin
story art
Javier Rodriguez — colors Willie Schubert — letters
Molly Lazer & Aubrey Sitterson — assistant editors
Tom Brevoort — editor Joe Quesada — editor in chief Dan Buckley — publisher

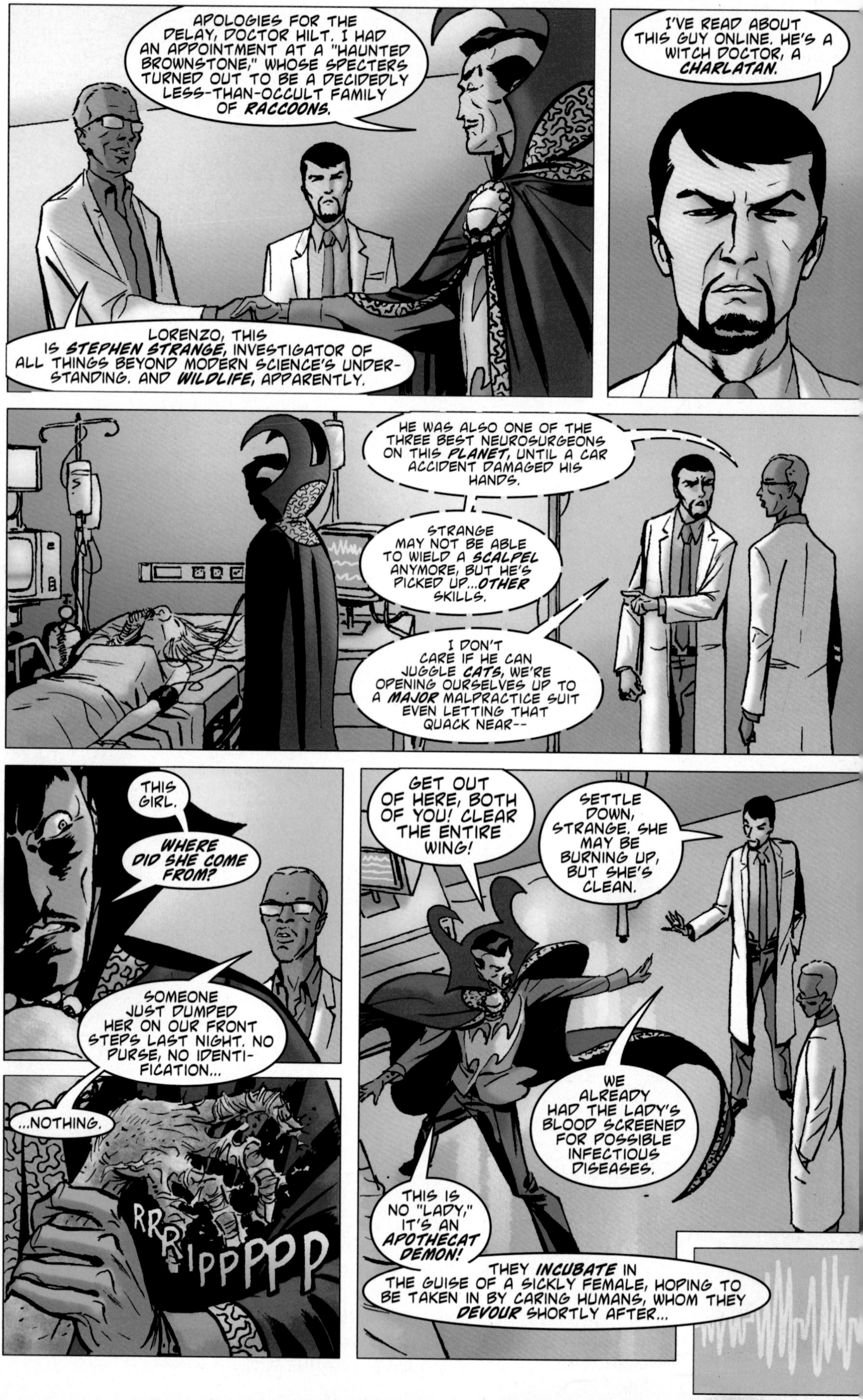
APOLOGIES FOR THE DELAY, DOCTOR HILT. I HAD AN APPOINTMENT AT A "HAUNTED BROWNSTONE," WHOSE SPECTERS TURNED OUT TO BE A DECIDEDLY LESS-THAN-OCCULT FAMILY OF RACCOONS.
LORENZO, THIS IS STEPHEN STRANGE, INVESTIGATOR OF ALL THINGS BEYOND MODERN SCIENCE'S UNDERSTANDING. AND WILDLIFE, APPARENTLY.
I'VE READ ABOUT THIS GUY ONLINE. HE'S A WITCH DOCTOR, A CHARLATAN.
HE WAS ALSO ONE OF THE THREE BEST NEUROSURGEONS ON THIS PLANET, UNTIL A CAR ACCIDENT DAMAGED HIS HANDS.
STRANGE MAY NOT BE ABLE TO WIELD A SCALPEL ANYMORE, BUT HE'S PICKED UP...OTHER SKILLS.
I DON'T CARE IF HE CAN JUGGLE CATS, WE'RE OPENING OURSELVES UP TO A MAJOR MALPRACTICE SUIT EVEN LETTING THAT QUACK NEAR--
THIS GIRL.
WHERE DID SHE COME FROM?
SOMEONE JUST DUMPED HER ON OUR FRONT STEPS LAST NIGHT. NO PURSE, NO IDENTIFICATION...
...NOTHING.
RRRIPPPPPP
GET OUT OF HERE, BOTH OF YOU! CLEAR THE ENTIRE WING!
SETTLE DOWN, STRANGE. SHE MAY BE BURNING UP, BUT SHE'S CLEAN.
WE ALREADY HAD THE LADY'S BLOOD SCREENED FOR POSSIBLE INFECTIOUS DISEASES.
THIS IS NO "LADY," IT'S AN APOTHECAT DEMON!
THEY INCUBATE IN THE GUISE OF A SICKLY FEMALE, HOPING TO BE TAKEN IN BY CARING HUMANS, WHOM THEY DEVOUR SHORTLY AFTER...

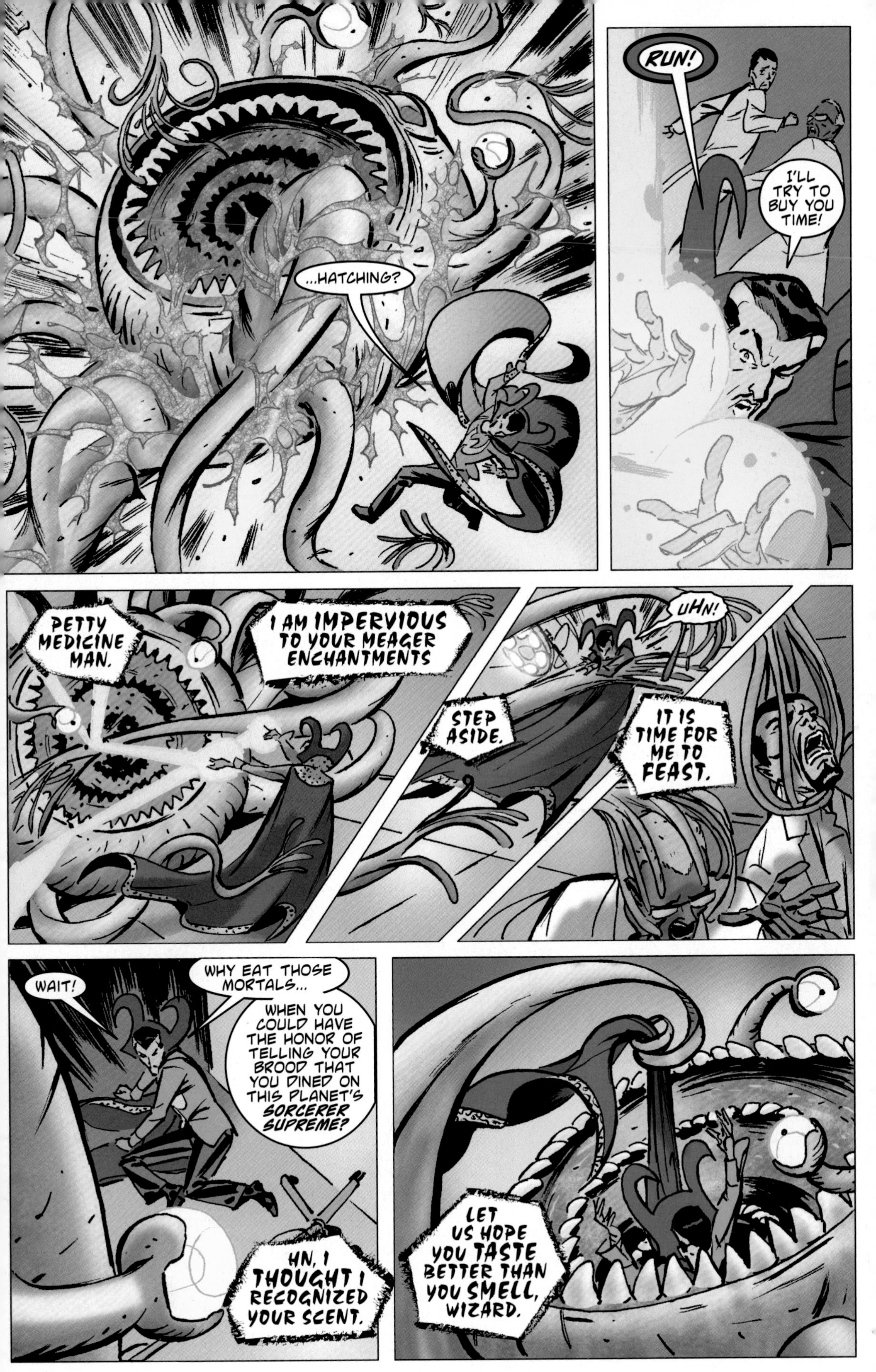
...HATCHING?
RUN!
I'LL TRY TO BUY YOU TIME!
PETTY MEDICINE MAN.
I AM IMPERVIOUS TO YOUR MEAGER ENCHANTMENTS
uHn!
STEP ASIDE.
IT IS TIME FOR ME TO FEAST.
WAIT!
WHY EAT THOSE MORTALS...
WHEN YOU COULD HAVE THE HONOR OF TELLING YOUR BROOD THAT YOU DINED ON THIS PLANET'S SORCERER SUPREME?
HN, I THOUGHT I RECOGNIZED YOUR SCENT.
LET US HOPE YOU TASTE BETTER THAN YOU SMELL, WIZARD.

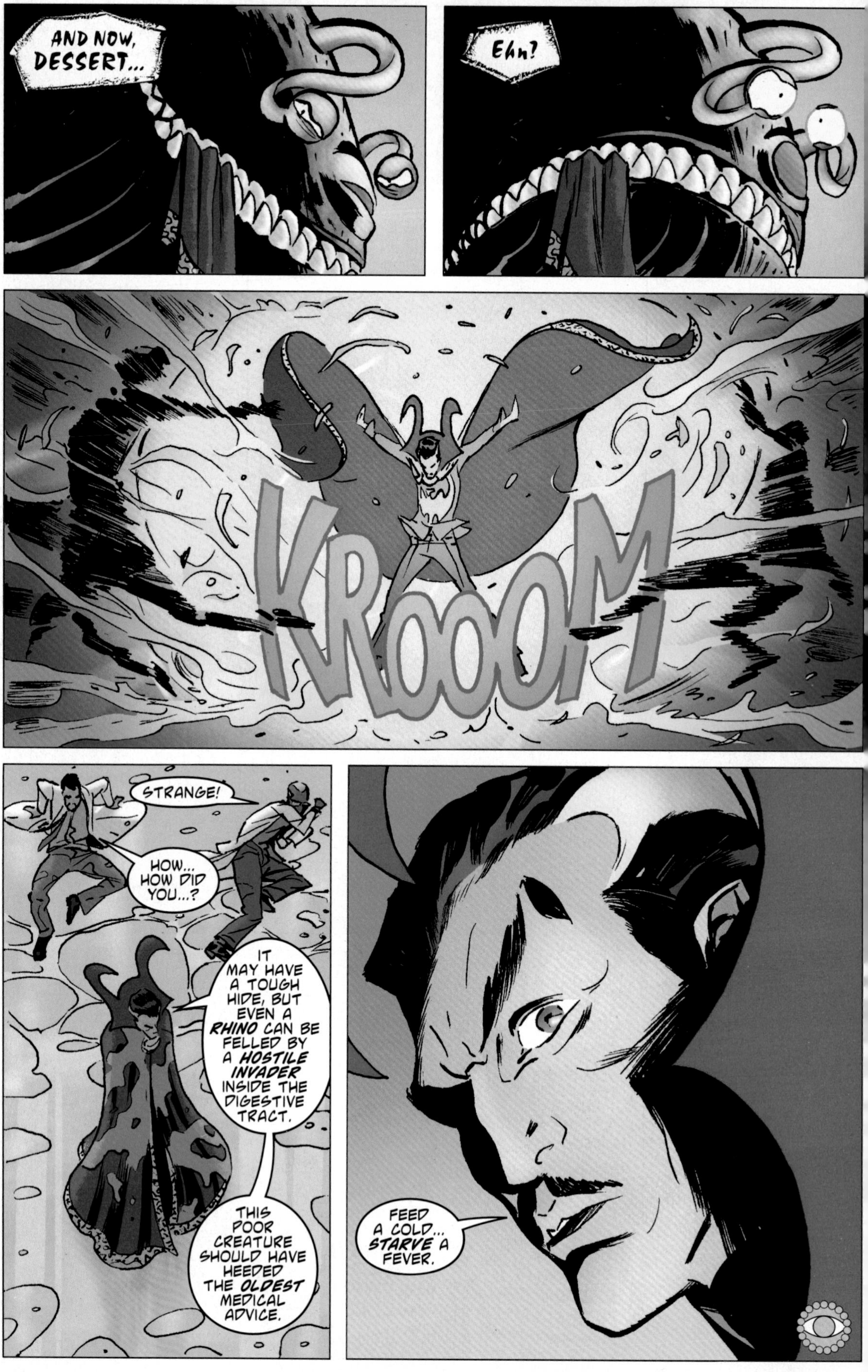

AND NOW, DESSERT...
Ehn?
KROOOM
STRANGE!
HOW... HOW DID YOU...?
IT MAY HAVE A TOUGH HIDE, BUT EVEN A RHINO CAN BE FELLED BY A HOSTILE INVADER INSIDE THE DIGESTIVE TRACT.
THIS POOR CREATURE SHOULD HAVE HEEDED THE OLDEST MEDICAL ADVICE.
FEED A COLD... STARVE A FEVER.

DOCTOR STRANGE SKETCHBOOK
BY MARCOS MARTIN

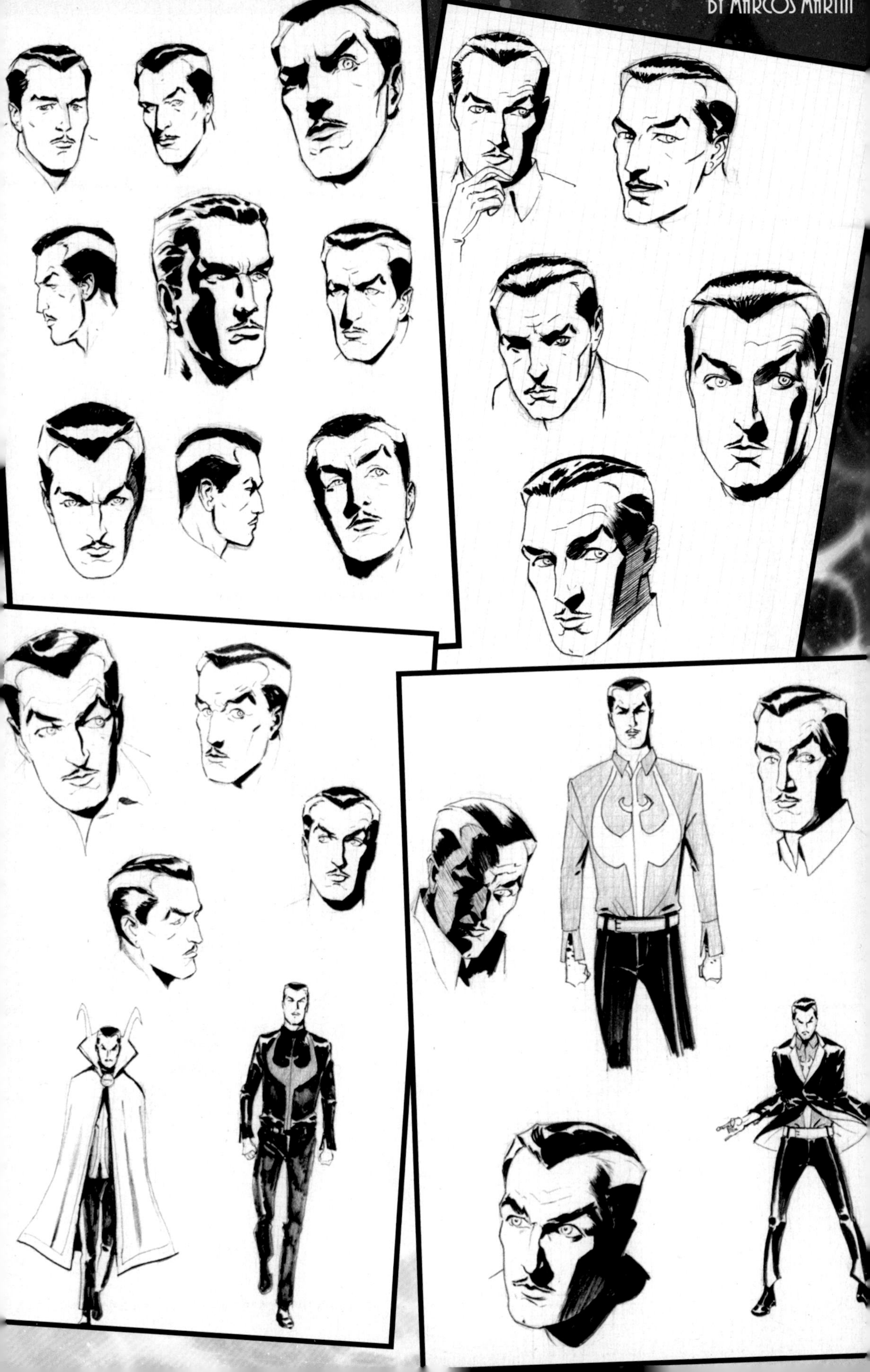

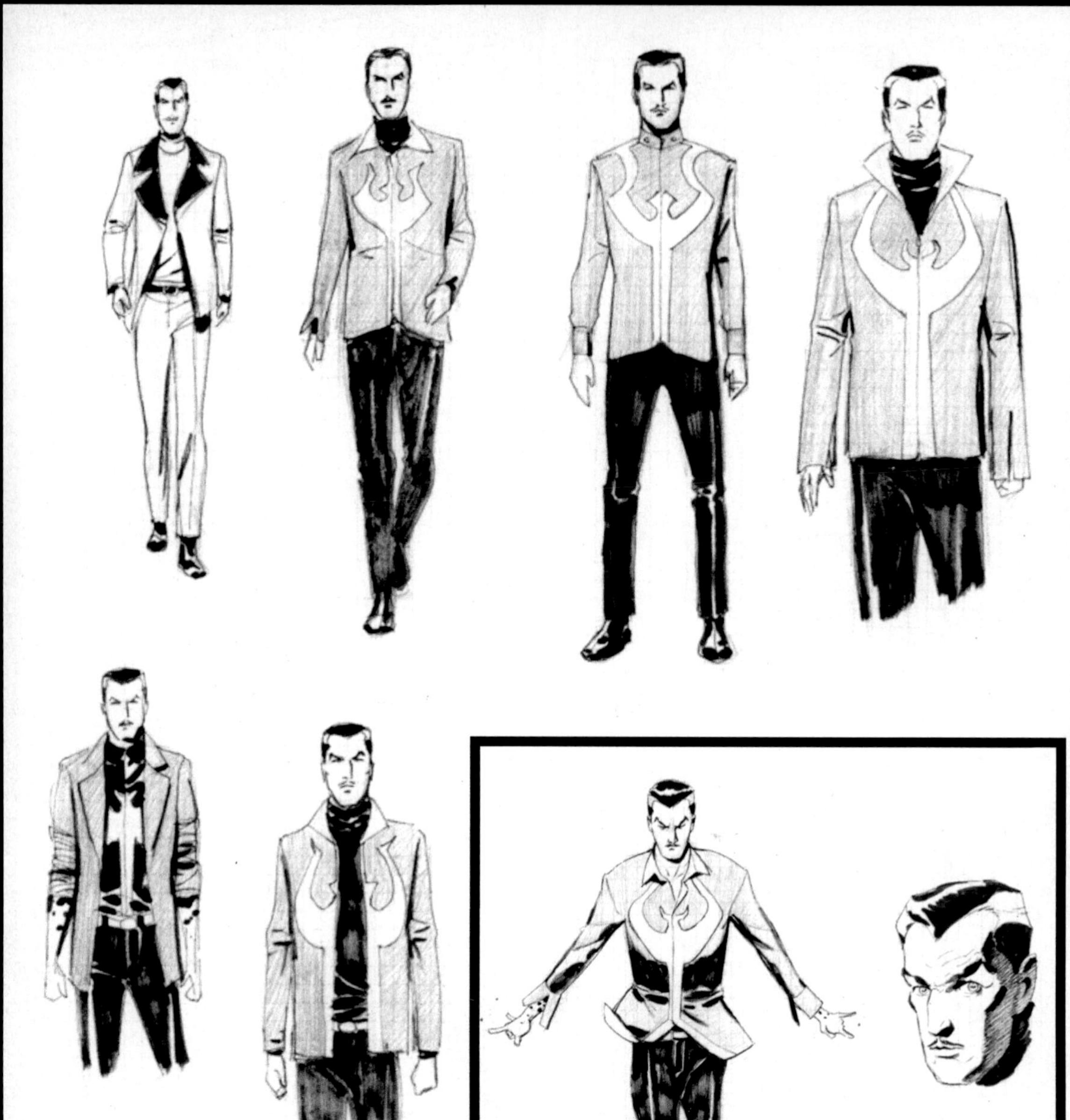
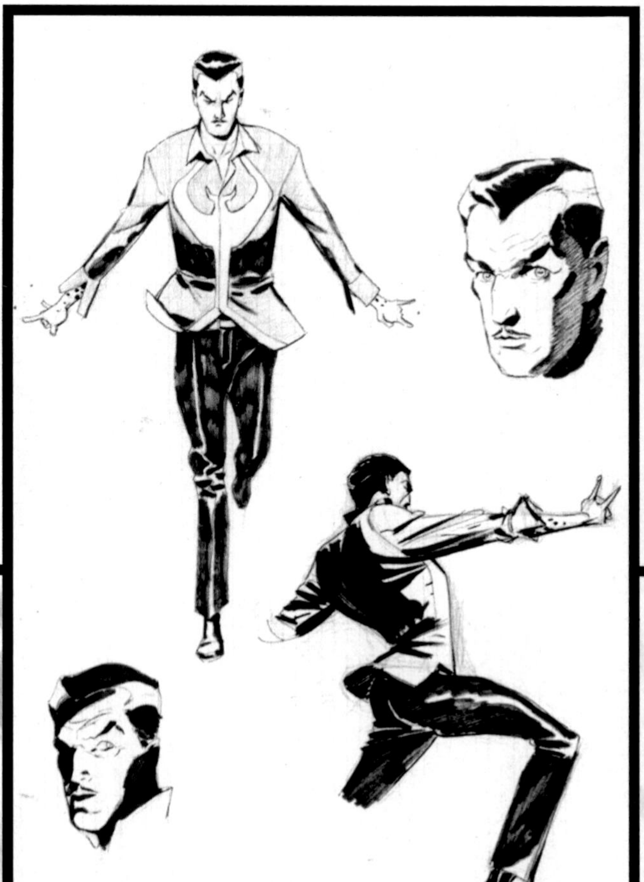

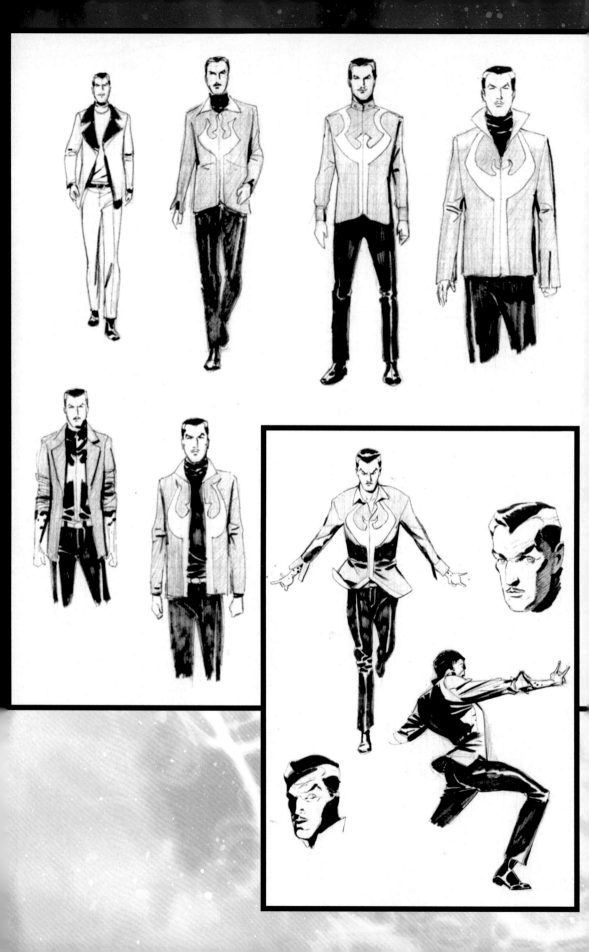

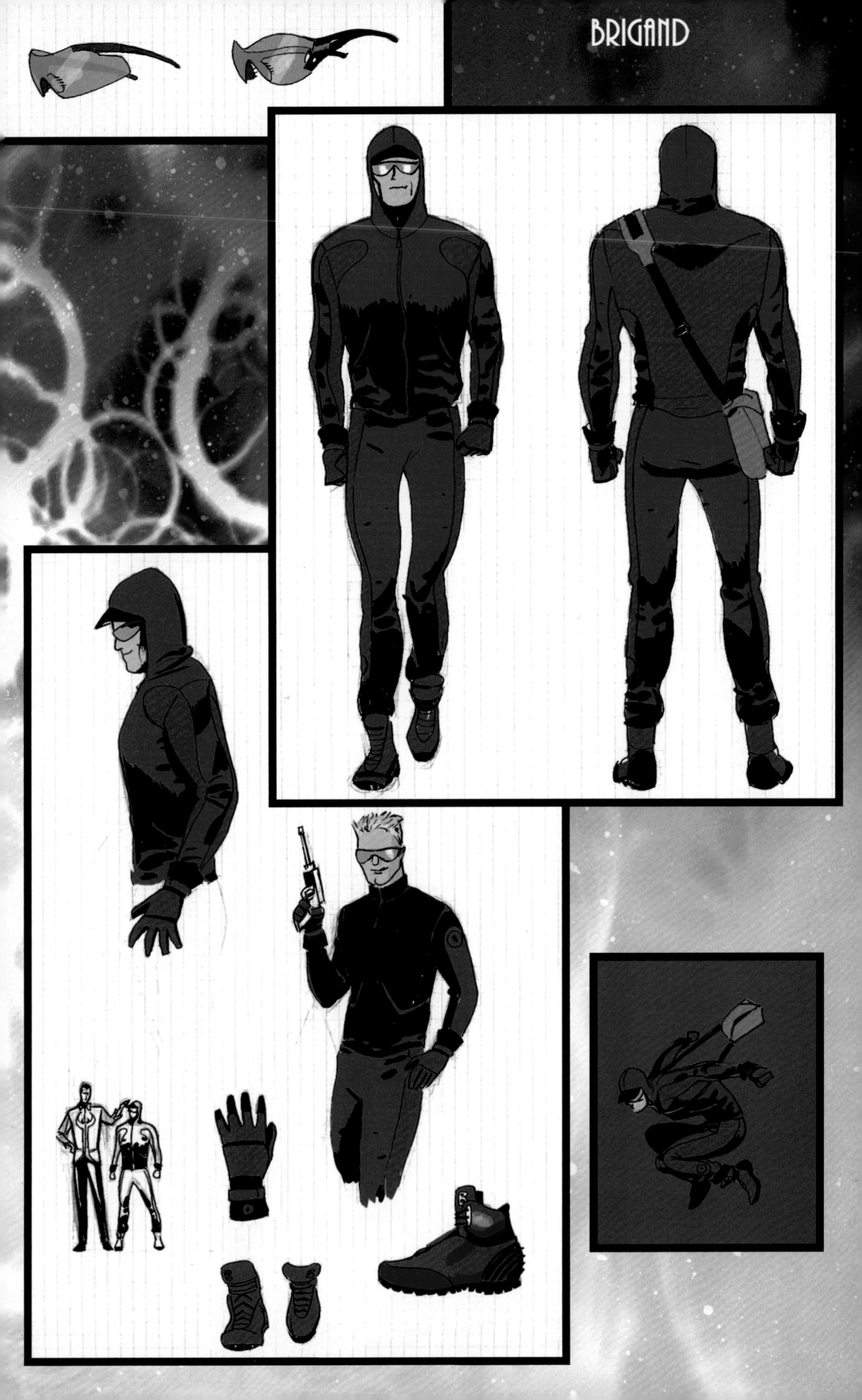
BRIGAND

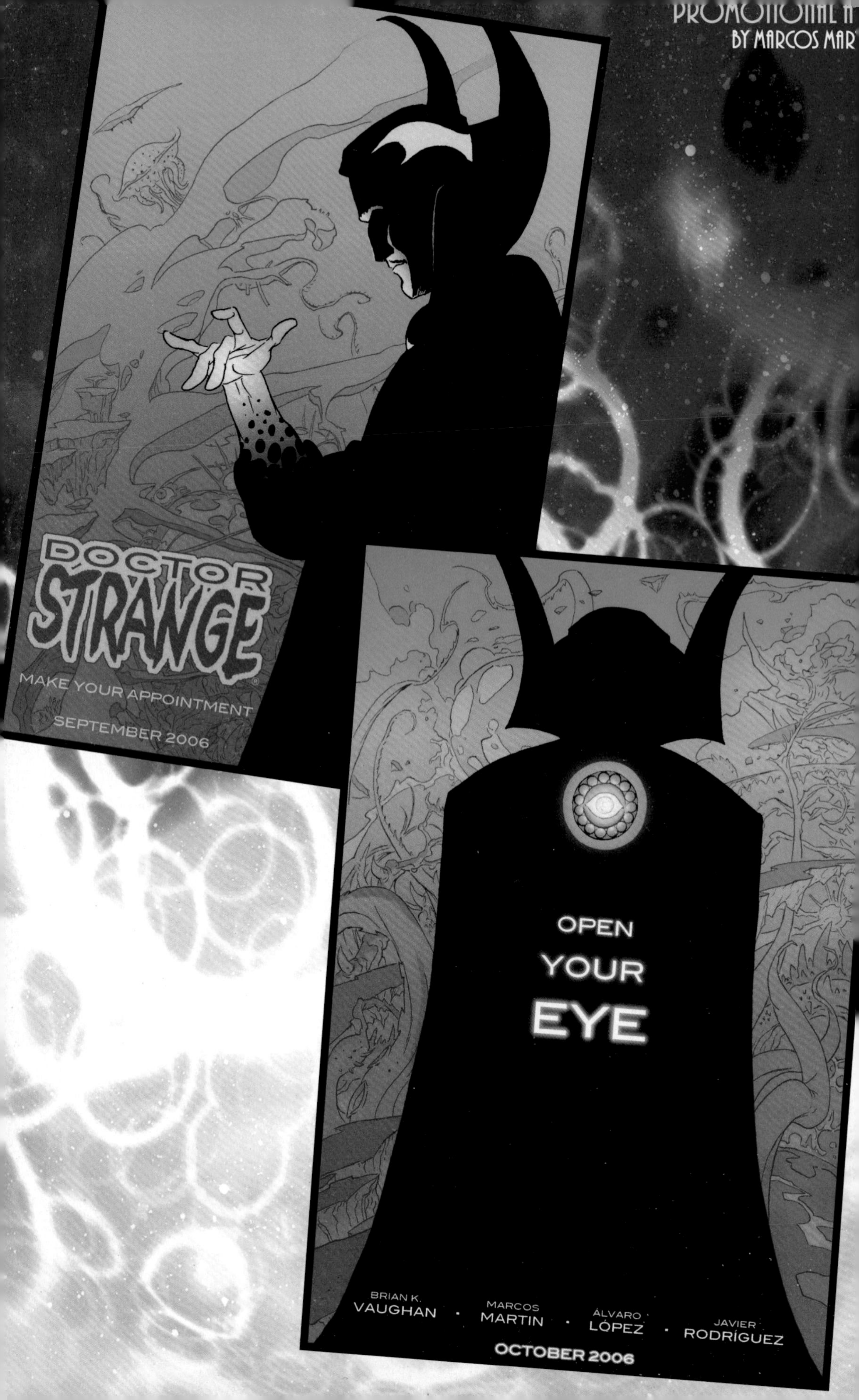
PROMOTIONAL
BY MARCOS MAR
DOCTOR STRANGE
MAKE YOUR APPOINTMENT
SEPTEMBER 2006
OPEN YOUR EYE
BRIAN K. VAUGHAN · MARCOS MARTIN · ÁLVARO LÓPEZ · JAVIER RODRÍGUEZ
OCTOBER 2006